Management of Organizational Culture as a Stabilizer of Changes

Management of Organizational Culture as a Stabilizer of Changes

Organizational Culture Management Dilemmas

Ibrahiem M. M. El Emary
Anna Brzozowska
Dagmara Bubel

CRC Press
Taylor & Francis Group
Boca Raton London New York

CRC Press is an imprint of the
Taylor & Francis Group, an **informa** business

First edition published 2020
by CRC Press
6000 Broken Sound Parkway NW, Suite 300, Boca Raton, FL 33487-2742

and by CRC Press
2 Park Square, Milton Park, Abingdon, Oxon, OX14 4RN

© 2020 Taylor & Francis Group, LLC

CRC Press is an imprint of Taylor & Francis Group, LLC

ISBN: 978-0-367-46059-4 (hbk)
ISBN: 978-1-003-02894-9 (ebk)

Typeset in Times
by codeMantra

Contents

Authors

Ibrahiem M. M. El Emary received the Dr. Eng. degree in 1998 from the Electronic and Communication Department, Faculty of Engineering, Ain Shams University, Egypt. From 1998 to 2002, he was an assistant professor of computer sciences in different faculties and institutes in Egypt. From 2002 to 2010, he worked as a visiting professor of computer science and systems in two universities in Jordan. Currently, he is a visiting professor at King Abdulaziz University, Jeddah, Kingdom of Saudi Arabia. His research interests cover various analytic and discrete event simulation techniques, performance evaluation of communication networks, application of intelligent techniques in managing computer communication network and performing a comparative study between various policies and strategies of routing, congestion control and sub-netting of computer communication networks. He has published more than 200 articles in various refereed international journals and conferences covering computer networks, artificial intelligence, expert systems, software agents, information retrieval, e-learning, case-based reasoning, image processing and pattern recognition, and robotic engineering. Currently, he is interested in conducting scientific research in wireless sensor networks in the viewpoint of enhancing its algorithms of congestion control and routing protocols. He has published two books with Taylor & Francis (*Wireless Sensor Networks: From Theory to Applications* and *Shaping the Future of ICT: Trends in Information Technology, Communications Engineering, and Management*) and participated in publishing a book with John Wiley. Also, he has participated in publishing five book chapters in two international books (published by IGI: *Optimizing and Managing Digital Telecommunication Systems Using Data Mining and Knowledge Discovery Approaches*); he is a co-editor of two books edited by two international publishers (Springer Verlag: *Emergent Evaluation Criteria for Collaborative Learning Environment* and LAP Lampert: *Computational Techniques and Algorithms for Image Processing* and *LAP LAMBERT Academic Publishing*). He acts as Membership of the International Organizing Committee of ICCMIT, and has participated in organizing six international conferences in Europe from 2015 to 2020. Finally, he joined Who's Who for five successive years from 2014 until 2019.

Anna Brzozowska is an associate professor in economics in the discipline of management studies. Currently, she works in the Department of Business Informatics and Ecosystems, Faculty of Management, at Częstochowa University of Technology, Poland. She is the author or co-author of about 90 scientific publications. She has actively participated in more than 30 conferences, mainly international, as well as in a few research projects. She is the editor of the journal *Eureka: Social and Humanities,* and the editor of selected editions of the Research Bulletin of the Technical University of Częstochowa. She is also a scientific committee member of the *Economics, Management and Sustainability* Scientific Journal. Anna Brzozowska is a member of the scientific discipline of management and quality science at the Faculty of Management. She is also a member of the habilitation committees established by the Central Commission for degrees and titles. Her research activities are focused on enterprise management processes and the integration chain, its logistics aspects and institutional environment, influencing management in light of integration activities that oscillate around the use and management of EU projects. These issues develop systematically by conducting research, participating in thematic groups and research and development teams as well as through cooperation with business and local and regional authorities. Her main research and study is the broadly defined concept of management in agribusiness and the European Union integration processes; IT in business; managing projects; and organization of management, logistics, and transport processes. Her scientific interests are also focused on the management of organizational culture in the international aspect. She presents this subject matter from the perspective of knowledge and intellectual capital management. She is a reviewer of scientific papers and a promoter of doctoral theses.

Dagmara Bubel obtained her PhD in humanities. She is a professor of sciences in economics and the director of the Main Library of Częstochowa University of Technology. She is an academic teacher teaching courses in science studies.

Her interests, in terms of theoretical, empirical and application areas, are concentrated around the issues of intellectual capital management in organizations. As the concept of intellectual capital management regards people as the most valuable potential of an enterprise, directly related to its strategy, in this respect, she conducted an analysis of the selected aspects of the functioning of small- and medium-sized enterprises.

Initially, her scientific studies addressed the problems of the following issues: management in organizations and management of knowledge, information and communication, etc. Additionally, the subject of her scientific studies oscillated around logistics management and management in agribusiness. It should be stressed that the active engagement of an organization is one of the most important characteristics of the democratic society, an element that ties and activates the local community. Her research interests were connected with broadly understood restructuring of enterprises, which undergo changes in the aspect of not only material resources, but also intangible ones, i.e., organizational culture. When designing an organization, it is necessary to take into account elements of the structure and the ties that connect them. Decision-making powers and responsibilities are assigned, and then executory processes are formalized. She presented exploitive concepts, such as diagnostic approaches to designing an organization.

Introduction

Increasing globalization processes in many aspects force today's enterprises to make organizational changes. A special part is played in this regard by organizational culture, as along with change, it constitutes an inseparable cause-and-effect relationship. This means that it can facilitate changes, and then the process of adapting to desirable changes runs more smoothly, or hinder the implementation of changes, which may make it more difficult to survive in a highly competitive market. Thus, it is vital to show the importance of change in the life of every organization and how organizational culture impacts its perception.

"No enterprise is proud today of being unchanged or the same as ten years ago. Stability is understood more as a sign of stagnation than reliability, and enterprises that do not change and do not evolve are commonly regarded as fossilized." This quotation and the fact that most scholars that are concerned with organizations admit that an enterprise's culture has a huge impact on its operation encourage a closer examination of this issue.

An organization equated with organizational culture is established and rests on "acts of faith," as people identify it as a real construct and act in accordance with the interpretations they create. Organizational actors play their roles, thereby creating identity and reacting to the social order, i.e., reinforcing it through activities that facilitate consensus building or questioning it. A dialogue with others and creation of narratives are the social actions through which the identity is constructed. In reading the organizational reality, people tend to adopt simple solutions based on "interpretation keys," which are implicitly adopted and often shared by organizational members such as a metaphor, stereotypes, archetypes, paradoxes and antinomy. This is a pragmatic approach, in which the reliability of adopted solutions is more important than their precision.

According to the authors of this publication, people who manage organizations—guided by interpretations, goals and narratives—implicitly or explicitly create the concepts of the development of their organizations. Significant, often new, meanings that the leaders try to pass to employees and other organizational actors are the key element of such concepts. This process of management is connected with creating a vision of the organizational reality through narratives and is a complex interaction, as it has a character of the process of communication. Apart from the vision of the organizational reality promoted by the leader, there are counter-visions created by oppositional subcultures.

Therefore, according to the authors of this publication, it is also important to present the nature of organizational culture in terms of dichotomous views on it. The authors indicate contradictory stances of the representatives of the cultural approach and antinomian views in the following areas:

- Diagnosing organizational culture with regard to its explicit versus implicit components
- Shaping and changing culture through evolution versus revolution
- Typology of cultures in terms of strength versus weakness

Organizational culture is an integral part of organizations, at each stage of their functioning. This is connected with the necessity of making the right choices, which today have always uncertain outcomes. The paradoxical character of management is nothing new. Contradictions are inscribed in the development of this scientific discipline. A paradox means that there are two or more elements, expressed in the form of principles or values, that seem to be contradictory, but despite this contradiction, none of them can be excluded. In other words, both ways have to be chosen at the same time. According to the authors of this publication, paradoxical is the situation when fast-changing markets require almost immediate reaction and response, while the elements of an organization, as the foundation of continuance and development, have to be stable and transparent. Paradoxes do not seek simple compromises, but provide an opportunity to take advantage of the potential of two extreme possibilities. They result from dichotomous divisions, which exclude each other, but also complement each other to form a whole. Thus, today's organizations face a challenge of using logic and intuition at the same time, creating hybrids of a strong and weak organizational culture, taking opposing stances depending on the situation, maintaining standard procedures when it is necessary to be flexible or solving the dilemmas connected with building strong relations with other organizations.

Paradoxes are particularly clearly inscribed in those areas of management that are imprecise, soft and have blurred boundaries. Organizational culture is certainly one of them. Even defining this concept is difficult. Organization is said to have a culture (as its element, resource, intraorganizational variable) but also to be culture (as a root metaphor for an organization). Another debatable issue is, in the opinion of the authors of this publication, the process of shaping organizational culture. On the one hand, there are views that organizational culture can be shaped, and ready-made tools that can be used in this process are offered. On the other hand, organizational culture, as an independent variable, determined by the national culture, cannot be shaped and any attempts to manage this area may be counterproductive.

The contradictions of the efforts to analyze and research organizational culture lead to unorganized, seemingly antinomian, yet frustrating views on the possibility of its identification, diagnosis and change. As far as the diagnosis of organizational culture is concerned, the authors of this publication indicate the problem of its multilevel structure, especially the visible and hidden levels. In the situation of changes to organizational culture, either evolutionary or revolutionary path is offered. The question arises: Is it better to make thorough, but more painful changes, or to gradually introduce small improvements? Confusion is also caused by the issue of the strength and weakness of organizational culture.

Although the topic of organizational culture is widely addressed in scientific studies, the authors notice that there is an insufficient number of publications that present its essence in a comprehensive way. Therefore, this publication is their attempt to explain this phenomenon through the prism of the contradictions it generates. The views of the representatives of the cultural approach are only apparently antinomian; in reality, they constitute complementary dichotomous views. The authors concentrate their considerations around the paradoxical nature of organizational culture. The starting point is a discussion about the contradictions of the efforts to analyze and research organizational culture, which provides a context for further divagation about the dichotomous nature of organizational culture, especially the issue of its shaping and changing, and perceiving the strength and weakness of culture.

The literature review conducted to answer the question about the relationship between organizational culture and the process of organizational change highlights the multitude of perspectives in the analysis of this area. It seems reasonable to treat these perspectives as complementary and enabling the achievement of the synergistic effect in research studies. Building sharp oppositions between the different paradigms does not lead to the achievement of added value, but rather causes the different research communities to shut themselves off to the potential of other communities. At the same time, the results of the literature review show the impossibility of providing a clear answer to the question regarding the description and explanation of the relationship between organizational culture and organizational change. On the one hand, this phenomenon is desirable, because it results in enriching the research literature and provides tools and research material for analyses fulfilling the requirement of theoretical triangulation. On the other hand, it is hard to resist the impression that apart from diversity, the studies in the area concerned are subject to high fragmentation. Naturally, this can be regarded as a characteristic feature of the development stage of the field. Undoubtedly, there is potential, but also a need to conduct comprehensive research projects that will contribute to better description, explanation and prediction of social processes occurring during organizational changes. It seems, however, that an obstacle to such projects is not weakness of the theory underlying them, but rather the realities of conducting empirical studies, which are often characterized by researchers' limited access to closed social systems, which formal organizations mostly are. It seems that in this context, it is especially important to develop cooperation between organizational management practitioners and representatives of the academia.

Paradoxes are a natural part of human life and every form of human activity. Therefore, we see dilemmas in the area of organizational culture, which, after all, is human creation. As is shown, most of the contradictions mentioned herein—whether in the cultural approach or in the nature of organizational culture—are apparent alternatives between stability or development, tradition or innovation. In reality however, it is balancing between dichotomous perspectives. Indeed, "it is necessary to confront chaos with the traditional order and as a result balance on the verge of chaos…" At this point, the authors of this publication want to stress that balancing in a dichotomous space requires deliberate and conscious acting. We should, however, bear in mind that organizational cultures exist as a product of human activity; therefore, how they develop and change depends on a human being. Dichotomies are inscribed in the nature of organizational culture. We should not avoid or be afraid of them, bearing in mind that their coexistence may bring benefits. Paradoxes are not necessary evil, but are a natural element of the life of an organization and in an organization.

Knowledge and Success of an Organization

1

It is worth starting the discussion about the relationship between organizational culture and the process of organizational change by outlining the meanings of these two notions. The publication will present dominant directions in thinking about organizational culture and organizational change as well as their studies. The aim of these preliminary reflections is to provide a broader perspective for the research studies in the field of interest analyzed further in greater detail.

1.1 KNOWLEDGE AS A STRATEGIC RESOURCE OF AN ORGANIZATION

When analyzing knowledge as an organization's strategic resource, the first step is to determine the usefulness of possessed knowledge in terms of the implementation of the organization's strategy (strategic value of knowledge). When an organization has excess knowledge relative to the knowledge necessary for sustaining competitive advantage, the problem is not so much about acquiring new knowledge as about proper use of the knowledge in possession. An organization that is better at using its knowledge than its competitors gains advantage over them. Better use of knowledge means better access to it, possibility of creating different combinations of knowledge and using it in a way that leads to identifiable progress in products, services and processes. This means that it is necessary to search for the most beneficial ways of using knowledge within an organization and in many competitive niches. Yee, Tan and Thurasamy (2019, pp. 1–3) claim that all organizations grow when they skillfully coordinate their activities and ensure consistency in everything they do. This is a very important problem also with respect to the field of knowledge. Various knowledge resources need to be allocated in different parts of an organization in a way that allows them to effectively support those responsible for operational and strategic decisions. The right knowledge should be at the right place and at the right time so that it can be used by a decision-maker in the decision-making process. For that to happen, it is necessary to develop the capacity for transferring knowledge so that it becomes common to the whole organization.

This is the second level of the evolution of knowledge management (the first one is "capturing" knowledge, while the third one is generating new knowledge). In an organization, there must exist a constant flow of knowledge between organizational units, people, and significant activities and events.

An organization's knowledge resources, supplemented by the knowledge acquired from the environment and generated in the organization, play a significant part in decision-making processes. New knowledge is also created in organizations as a result of learning processes, which generate new ideas, concepts or innovations. Learning is a sequence of constant experimenting and thinking by humans that goes beyond the existing limitations in problem-solving. It is supplemented by adaptive learning, which involves incremental enriching of knowledge as a response to problems arising in the environment. When organizational members interact with the environment within the organization and with the environment of the whole organization, they continuously perceive changes as they occur; they absorb new information and reject old one. The sum of new information may be relatively small, the changes may be slight, but the organization can learn to adapt to these changes. Adaptive learning at the level of an entire organization is about adaptation to the environment. Organizational members are able to identify problems in the organization's environment, develop an appropriate strategy, or modify it, and implement it in a way that ensures that the problems are solved. If the learning process is continued, the results achieved by the organization become the basis for learning and drawing conclusions about the need to correct how things are done. In this way, an organization tries to adapt to the changes and difficulties that exist or will emerge in its environment. These adaptation processes are undertaken within the organization's mental model (Burke 2017, pp. 217–221), which comprises the elements of individual models that are common to the key managers who have an impact on the entire organization. This occurs in the domain of the dominant system of values, individual and group interests and organizational subcultures in the organization.

The learning process is determined by the norms and values regarded as rational in an organization. This means that on the one hand, an organization notices the factors in its environment that can represent potential opportunities or threats to it, but on the other hand, it does not question the existing norms and values through which the reality is assessed. Thus, adaptive learning is a process of assessing the effectiveness of achieving certain objectives by reacting to changes in the environment (Truong 2016, pp. 1185–1193).

Adaptive learning should be an integral part of a system. The knowledge possessed by an organization can be a result of experiences gained during important activities. It can be learning that precedes actions, learning during actions or post-factum learning. There is a view in the literature that this type of learning is very important for an organization. It is, however, a result of subjective assessment. When designing systems for learning based on significant events, a checklist of actions and events can be created. Of importance is also learning before action, as it anticipates probable events. It concentrates on concrete problems that can bring success. It consists of three stages, which are presented in Figure 1.1.

With learning during actions, executors of actions, who are best positioned to observe what is happening and how "things are going," can immediately take appropriate measures. It is important to preserve the knowledge so that it can be used to achieve future successes, using the four-question procedure shown in Figure 1.2.

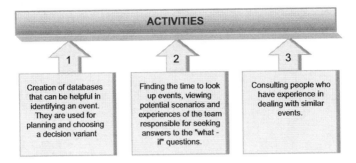

FIGURE 1.1 Learning stages influencing the success of an organization. (Own work based on: Nikodemus P., Integration von Wissensmanagement und kooperativem Lernen, [in:] *Lernprozessorientiertes Wissensmanagement und kooperatives Lernen*, Springer, Wiesbaden, 2017, pp. 155–238.)

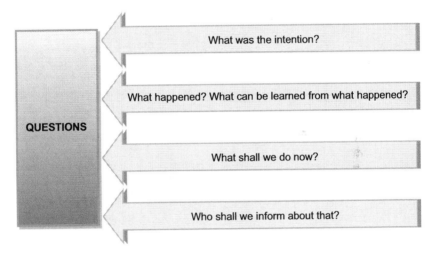

FIGURE 1.2 Key aspects of knowledge that drive the achievement of success in an organization. (Own work based on: Pawlowsky P., *Wissensmanagement*, Walter de Gruyter GmbH & Co KG, 2019, pp. 201–205.)

These or other similar approaches facilitate ordered reflection during the event. In post-factum learning, all the participants of the action have to be engaged in defining what was a success and what can be done differently in the future, which can be achieved through the steps shown in Figure 1.3.

In terms of knowledge management, it is necessary to consider how to use the reflections that are a result of the day-to-day intellectual work of knowledge workers as well as their actions that increase the knowledge resources of the organization. It is especially important to create an atmosphere in which people feel that their ideas are treated seriously. Moreover, there are various systems that encourage people to be more active (e.g., communities of practice). Knowledge is stored by various means as shown in Figure 1.4.

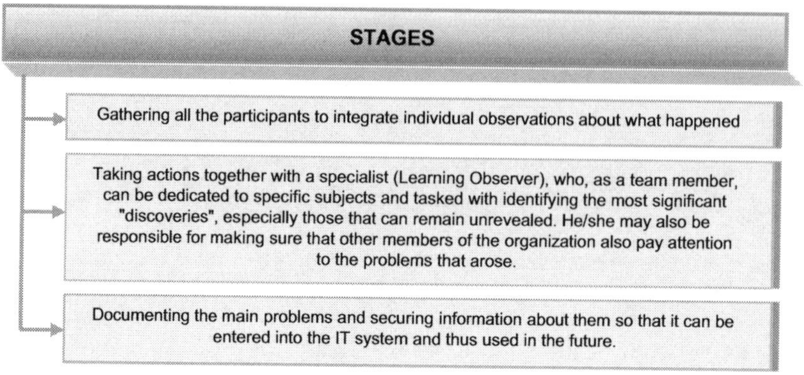

STAGES

Gathering all the participants to integrate individual observations about what happened

Taking actions together with a specialist (Learning Observer), who, as a team member, can be dedicated to specific subjects and tasked with identifying the most significant "discoveries", especially those that can remain unrevealed. He/she may also be responsible for making sure that other members of the organization also pay attention to the problems that arose.

Documenting the main problems and securing information about them so that it can be entered into the IT system and thus used in the future.

FIGURE 1.3   Learning stages. (Own work based on: Winkler K., Heinz T., Wagner B., Gut zu wissen: Herausforderung New Work–Wissen managen und Lernen fördern, [in:] *Zukunft der Arbeit–Perspektive Mensch*, Springer Gabler, Wiesbaden, 2018, pp. 193–203.)

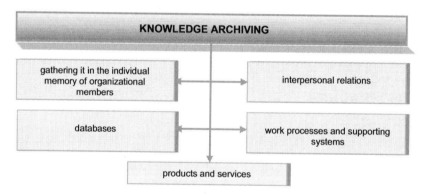

KNOWLEDGE ARCHIVING

gathering it in the individual memory of organizational members

interpersonal relations

databases

work processes and supporting systems

products and services

FIGURE 1.4   Elements of knowledge archiving. (Own work based on: Klein L., Business excellence execution, [in:] *Business Excellence*, Springer Gabler, Wiesbaden, 2018, pp. 11–24.)

People preserve both implicit and explicit knowledge, which is generated as a result of their day-to-day experiences as they produce and deliver products and services and participate in processes that create the conditions enabling the organization to function. It is their individual knowledge. At the beginning, it has the character of tacit knowledge, which is only used by those who possess it. This knowledge is enriched not only when more and more experience is gained during day-to-day work and there are appropriate conditions for using it. This knowledge, combined with the organization's knowledge available to an individual employee, especially a decision-maker, creates a new quality (value) of his/her individual knowledge. Individual people are in various relations with others, forming different types of formal and informal groups. Within them, there is a flow of tacit and explicit knowledge and a group memory is created in which important knowledge is stored. Knowledge is also preserved through interpersonal relations. Work processes characterized by cooperation between people create conditions for preserving common knowledge.

Databases are sets of explicit knowledge. Work processes and supporting systems are essentially a result of designing processes and systems by means of explicit knowledge of an organization. Knowledge is rooted in this case in operational activities. It can be characterized as knowledge about how to meet consumer needs, perform control processes and coordinate contractors' activities. Knowledge also resides in behavior patterns during past decisions. Most of these processes are standardized, codified and transferred to the different parts of the organization. Products and services contain knowledge that is necessary for meeting consumer needs.

Creating appropriate conditions for the flow of knowledge requires standardization of the interface and practices, technological support necessary for coordinating knowledge resources, a culture of trust and openness that facilitates knowledge sharing, and finally a coherent group of people responsible for managing activities aimed at implementing knowledge-related objectives (the so-called practices). Standardization is crucial, as organizations have numerous internal boundaries and networks (functional, structural, cultural, national). For knowledge to flow across such boundaries, a mechanism is needed to enable such boundaries to be overcome. This mechanism is knowledge standardization, which can facilitate the coordination of the flow of knowledge. Technologies are often used to create tools and techniques for structuring, communicating and effectively using knowledge resources. Applied technologies mainly enable the sharing of explicit knowledge. However, this issue will not be discussed here in more detail. Instead, we will move on to another factor impacting knowledge flow—organizational culture.

1.2 CREATION OF KNOWLEDGE IN AN ORGANIZATION IN THE CONTEXT OF DECISION-MAKING

Organizational culture plays an essential part in forming behaviors that lead to knowledge creation, sharing and use, as it shapes assumptions as to what knowledge is and what knowledge should be managed; it impacts the relations between individual knowledge and organizational knowledge; it creates a context for social interactions, which determine how knowledge should be used in specific situations (who should exercise control, who is responsible for knowledge sharing); and it impacts the shaping of the processes of knowledge creation, verification and distribution.

Organizational culture also creates the causes of people's aversion to knowledge sharing or using the knowledge of others (Figure 1.5).

The factors of organizational culture that play an important role in organizations that have best practices in terms of effective use of knowledge are described in Figure 1.6. These practices include engaging people in what makes them interested in using knowledge and motivating them to share their knowledge and come up with ideas together with others. The conclusions from the above practices are as follows (Figure 1.6).

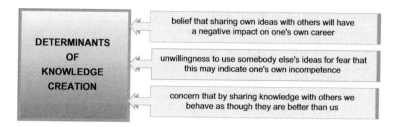

FIGURE 1.5 Knowledge-determining factors. (Own work based on: Asrar-Ul-Haq M., Anwar S., A systematic review of knowledge management and knowledge sharing: Trends, issues, and challenges. *Cogent Business & Management*, 2016, 3.1: 1127744.)

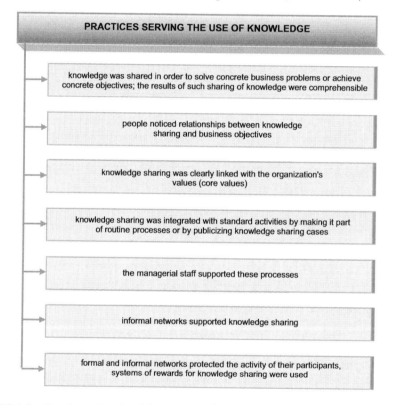

FIGURE 1.6 Good practices implying the use of knowledge. (Own work based on: Hislop D., Bosua R., Helms R., *Knowledge Management in Organizations: A Critical Introduction*, Oxford University Press, 2018, pp. 78–82.)

Knowledge-sharing processes, even the informal ones, should be controlled by management, which is a symptom of strategic management that aims to maintain an organization in a state of controlled changes. However, the problem here is people managing knowledge to achieve expected results.

New knowledge underlies innovative processes, which determine the future of an organization, while the existing knowledge is essential for improving products and services, creating a basis for achieving the expected current results. Therefore, it is necessary to both create or obtain new knowledge and effectively use the existing knowledge. These two sides of the process of knowledge management cause tensions that can turn into contradictions. First, people may have concerns because of the fear of the "unknown." It results from the fact that they are losing their previous status, have to learn new things and have less power or lose it altogether, and their previous posts are becoming irrelevant. Recognition of the role of new knowledge does not always come with structural changes that support its acquisition.

Another area of tensions is more difficult to identify. This is because knowledge that is deeply embedded in an organization impacts the way of perceiving, creating and using new knowledge. In order to understand this problem, we should reflect on the consequences of exploiting the possessed knowledge. Successes are achieved when appropriate incentives exist for the exchange of tacit and explicit knowledge of people and their groups. Specialization is an important factor in this exchange. High specialization is conducive to emergence of new ideas that are converted into innovations. But at the same time, it hinders the flow of knowledge, and as a result, decisions are often made intuitively.

Another problem is that an organization may try to use various interesting novelties in the area of knowledge, while failing to make a "full" use of the knowledge it possesses. This may take the form of criticizing what "we know" without examining the actual causes of failures. Therefore, the following principle is recommended: Successes achieved thanks to possessed knowledge require constant monitoring and structural support. As a rule, the bigger the number of successes achieved based on the existing knowledge, the greater the pressure to invest in it (because it is more likely to be useful), the more difficult it is for new knowledge to "break through," and as a consequence, the organization is losing the flexibility necessary for competing. Tensions may also arise in the environment and the so-called timescale (Al Saifi 2019, pp. 55–80). An environment that facilitates exploration and exploitation of knowledge is characterized by a limited discipline of requirements for employees, and vice versa. The problem of time relates to the value obtained from the existing knowledge versus the value from new knowledge in the future.

Tensions may also arise in connection with the necessity of "rejecting" the existing, now useless knowledge. Knowledge is sometimes deeply rooted in the existing practices, shaping behaviors and limiting activity in new areas. What is more, this rooting exists in people's mental models and in the so-called dominant logic of groups of people, impacting the perception of the reality and the organization's place in it. This affects decisions and activities. All this has an effect on organizational members' attitude to radical changes, and consequently on the organization's attitude to the future.

The ability and opportunity to create and use knowledge is a source of creation and sustenance of competitive advantage. This requires converting and transferring knowledge between three types of knowledge sources, which are as follows (Wutti and Hayden 2019, pp. 130–133):

- Competencies of organizational members
- Experience in organizing and coordinating activities aimed at delivering products and providing services
- Relations with the external world

Knowledge can positively impact the development of an organization when it enables it to find new ways of achieving its objectives, and at the same time use it for what has so far been done well. Creation of new knowledge requires the elements as shown in Figure 1.7.

Using the possessed knowledge requires the following (Hislop, Bosua and Helms 2018, pp. 291–297):

a. Creating a database
b. Learning before, during and after tasks
c. Supporting activities connected with the creation of data warehouses, socializing activities
d. Propagating and maintaining various forms of an organization's memory
e. Developing knowledge flow across all levels and parts of an organization
f. Standardization of the interface and good practices, creation of appropriate solutions in the area of technology
g. Coordinating works on the flow of knowledge
h. Creating own culture of trust and openness, which facilitates knowledge sharing
i. Encouraging people to use good practices and share knowledge

Proper creation and use of knowledge are difficult, as these two sides of an organization's activity do not support each other. Quite the opposite, they may cause tensions and contradictions. Knowledge that is deeply rooted in an organization can create

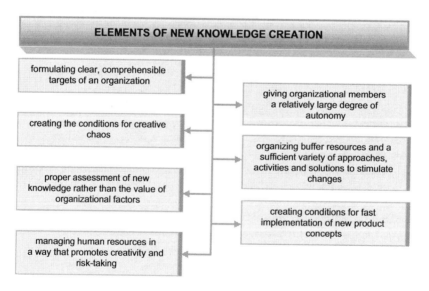

FIGURE 1.7   Determinants of new knowledge creation. (Own work based on: Nonaka I., Toyama R., The knowledge-creating theory revisited: knowledge creation as a synthesizing process, [in:] *The Essentials of Knowledge Management*, Palgrave Macmillan, London, 2015, pp. 95–110.)

barriers to changes. Optimizing the use of possessed knowledge and creation of new one requires the best possible transformation of individual knowledge into structures, processes, products and systems that enable the use of values that can be achieved thanks to new knowledge. Therefore, it is necessary to inspire, create the principles of participation, increase the flexibility of organizational structures and create new posts in order to cause changes in organizational culture.

The decision-making process considered in terms of knowledge management should be analyzed bearing in mind that decisions are rational only to a limited extent. Their limitations of rationality increase, because knowledge creators and users are not only decision-makers but also knowledge workers (Figure 1.8).

Taking into account these conditions enables a good compatibility between the operation of groups and the entire organization in the sphere of value creation and

KNOWLEDGE CONNECTED WITH DECISION-MAKING IS DEFINED AS:

Possibility of justifying the validity of beliefs ("know-what" and "know-that"), which provides a "raw material" for decision-making ("what to do") and contains facts and assumptions based on the values espoused by decision-makers.

Ability to act ("know-how"), which stems from mental and physical abilities of decision-makers, procedures and principles. This is the basic knowledge that guides us when we take actions.

Know-what", when it is shared by the majority of the decision-makers, causes relatively consistent (similar in a given situation and in a given time) decisions to be made despite a huge diversity of people and situations within an organization. However, when we start to examine the evolution of the assumptions underlying decisions, this consistency of decisions becomes dubious. This is because in decision-making an important role is played by subjectively felt experiences (own, somebody else's). A decision-maker relies on them to a large extent when seeking the ways to solve the problem he/she faces.

Appropriate organizational support. If the expectations of a group's members are met, the roles they fulfill are the factor that holds the group together. However they also need appropriate organizational support, integration with other elements of the businesses, as well as technological support of integration processes and cooperation.

The culture of trust and openness. It can be either an external factor or developed by the team itself

Permission from an organization. It can be active or passive. The minimum requirement is the organization's willingness to tolerate this form of work and provide its members with the right amount of time and necessary resources. Convergence of stances and creation of values both for the organization and its members facilitates the identification of various ways of forming and maintaining this type of groups.

FIGURE 1.8 Conditions of knowledge use in terms of decision-making. (Own work based on: Welge M.K., Al-Laham A., Eulerich M., Die empirische strategy-process-Forschung im Überblick, [in:] *Strategisches Management*, Springer Gabler, Wiesbaden, 2017, pp. 167–190.)

strengthening of identity. However, context is important here—what is desirable and accepted in one organization can be unaccepted in another. Many organizations see a potential benefit offered by such groups in terms of "connecting" people from different areas of the organization, which, in the formal structure, are separated by established barriers. This is supported by IT technologies (intranet). Their use resulted in electronic communication being probably more popular than direct "face-to-face" communication. This, however, does not facilitate the sharing of tacit knowledge, which is better expressed through direct human contacts.

As stresses, apart from unquestionable advantages, communities of practice are a useful tool for combining individual and organizational learning. They contribute to increased work satisfaction among knowledge workers. Employees become aware of their value in the area of knowledge management, realize that they are responsible for their own careers and have to be focused on the future of their organization and their role. They perceive the value of opportunities that can be exploited. They find more attractive those organizations that can create chances for knowledge workers to participate in running a community of practice in the area of their professional knowledge. Participation in such groups enables individuals to notice opportunities on the map of their own "knowledge landscape" within their organization. The individual, group and organizational landscapes dynamically co-create the "knowledge landscape," causing knowledge to flow between them and new knowledge peaks to emerge (Winkel 2019, pp. 128–138).

It is important to mention the concept of increasing return (Marques et al. 2019, pp. 489–507), which is based on the assumption that an increase in value occurs not only in products and services, but also in invisible benefits gained in a long span of time. This is the so-called network effect. Knowledge is a special resource due to the effect of increasing return. This concept is based on the assumption that contrary to physical and financial resources, knowledge resources do not diminish as a result of their use but increase.

This phenomenon results from the accumulation of knowledge over long spans of time and from the so-called network effects. Over long spans of time, knowledge is used multiple times by a growing number of its users, which enables flow of information and knowledge within global organizations as well as among people in global space also beyond global organizations. Here, the metaphor of knowledge distribution as a snowball effect is applied. One knowledge user usually attracts many others.

In practice, the application of the concept of increasing return usually takes place in four stages, which are as follows (Jedynak 2011, pp. 237–252):

1. Defining objectives and selecting underdeveloped markets, in particular rising markets
2. Achieving the leverage effect through an increase in the value of knowledge by creating a wide and cheap access to it
3. Connecting the so-called autonomous agents with one another, who include knowledge users, consumers and other stakeholders, who not only use but also expand knowledge; feedback loops enabling learning are strengthened
4. Creating a situation when using knowledge becomes a standard

The snowball effect occurs when an organization increases the intensity and scope of learning. The greater the knowledge diffusion in an organization, the bigger values it can create. The organization "receives" more knowledge than it "gives to others." It applies not only to values objictified in products, but also invisible benefits obtained over long spans of time. They are a network effect created as a result of an organization's learning through feedback loops with its partners in the network. The above-presented points have the following implications for organizations (Punt et al. 2016, pp. 1960–1973):

1. The more an organization bases management on knowledge, the more effective it can be.
2. A pioneer in knowledge use can gain competitive advantage when it makes it available to its partners and if it "traps" them in its operational systems; in this way, competitive advantage can be sustained over long spans of time.
3. Competitive advantage gained as a result of strong operational links with other organizations can be strengthened through continuous implementation of innovations in the form of incremental changes.

The concept of increasing return also has implications at the strategic level (Figure 1.9).

A learning organization treats knowledge as a priority strategic resource. Such an organization invests in people and people allow it to make increasing return on investing in them in the form of economic values they create. It attracts ambitious individuals who want to learn. A double learning feedback loop is created (Serrat 2017, pp. 57–67), and it causes an increase in value added in an organization and the networks it creates through cross-organizational ties.

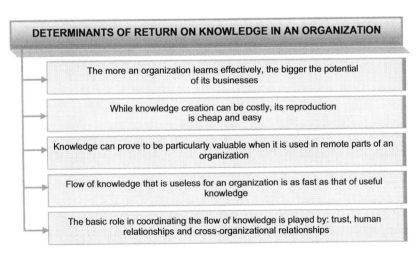

FIGURE 1.9 Elements of the concept of increasing return on knowledge at the strategic level. (Own work based on: Dicle M.F., Increasing return response to changes in risk. *Review of Financial Economics*, 2019, 37.1: 197–215.)

1.3 KNOWLEDGE INTEGRATION AS A KEY SUCCESS FACTOR OF AN ORGANIZATION

Another problem is knowledge creation, which can be costly, while its replication is relatively easy and cheap. If products of knowledge (e.g., software) are used by more and more people, then the return on investment into these products increases—the snowball effect is created. If products of knowledge are appropriately protected and payment is charged when they are used by others, then knowledge reproduction brings benefits. Knowledge can be more valuable for an organization, when it is used "far from" an organization that generated it (Nonaka and Toyama 2015, pp. 95–110).

The flow of knowledge that is negative for an organization is as fast as the flow of positive knowledge. This is the case when values are generated as a result of independent and unpredictable thinking of individuals reacting to the flow of knowledge in a way that is not only positive but also negative for an organization. For instance, brand can be damaged by dissatisfied groups of customers communicating by means of the Internet. This requires immediate response, e.g., launching loyalty programs for consumers. In order to coordinate the flow of knowledge, trust and trust-based bonds are also needed. The flow of knowledge is regulated by the market, and more specifically by prices, but in the case of such resource as knowledge, lowering prices sometimes leads to obtaining greater value from knowledge. In this area, hierarchical structures can make it more difficult to take advantage of the opportunity to increase the values obtained from knowledge. Limited access to knowledge can decrease an organization's capability of quickly responding to market changes. Greater benefits are achieved when the flow of knowledge is based on trust, when an individual can have access to knowledge sources and when an individual monitors its usefulness. Long-term bonds that are built on the basis of shared values are more valuable than those established by contracts.

Another aspect concentrates around the concept of coevolution of knowledge and is based on the metaphor of "knowledge landscape." Coevolution is the driving force of a learning system. This concept can be used in studying organizations. There is a phenomenon of joint adaptation of organizations as a result of each of them learning within a certain "population." The impact of collaborative learning can be noticed, e.g., in changes in technology, key procedures or features of products. The survival of an organization depends on its intelligence, which is manifested in its reactions to changes in its environment, i.e., appropriateness of reactions to changes in the "landscape of knowledge." Even if an organization chooses the right way of reacting, the sector as a whole, as a result of natural selection, may record a much greater improvement in results than a single organization. The positive thing here is that adaptation to the sector becomes easier when the landscape is less "ragged," and the differences between what we do and what we should do are not very large. In other words, organizational knowledge has an important impact on the organization's ability to achieve successes, but this ability is to a large extent connected with the dynamics of changes in knowledge at the level of the sector. Strategic thinking requires finding a way to deal with high instability of the "landscape of knowledge," which forms the behaviors of market players in a given sector and at the same time impacts this landscape through such behaviors. The more the companies in a sector learn and acquire knowledge, the more difficult it is for a single company to identify its knowledge gap and specify the payback period for investments in knowledge acquisition. Studies show that successful organizations are willing to use knowledge obtained from outside, sometimes from organizations operating in different sectors (Kühne 2017, pp. 619–637), but there has to be a balance between used knowledge on the one hand and discovered and acquired knowledge on the other hand in order to catch up with the sectorial knowledge and the technology connected with it.

Propensity to seek new knowledge (i.e., explore the "landscape of knowledge") usually depends on external factors; e.g., when an organization is in crisis, it shows greater propensity for exploration, acquisition and internalization of external knowledge than when it is in a relatively stable situation and tends to gradually develop the knowledge it possesses. A strong push for changes may be then more determined by the management's policy than by external factors, e.g., consumers' opinions. Another potential important factor is costs—descending from the peak and climbing a new peak of knowledge are sometimes costly, especially when the scope of necessary unlearning is larger. These unlearning and learning new things impact the offer of products, and consequently the demand it creates. Therefore, an organization's responses to knowledge-related problems that arise in its environment cannot be intuitive, but have to be a subject of serious strategic considerations. There are numerous implications of creating a knowledge-based strategy (Figure 1.10).

An organization should also be able to absorb such knowledge from its environment that is useful to it in terms of its competitive potential and is compatible with its own knowledge. An organization's own knowledge is in this case knowledge base, while external knowledge is acquired through various ties of an organization with its environment. The broader the knowledge, i.e., the vaster our "landscape of knowledge" is, the more links with the environment are needed, the higher the costs of integrating new knowledge with the organization's knowledge. If our "landscape of knowledge" is the basis for decisions about absorbing knowledge from the environment, then the actions taken to acquire new knowledge should depend on the factors mentioned in Figure 1.11.

The greater the ability to absorb new knowledge, the greater the possibilities of making changes (El Elmary Ibrahiem and Brzozowska 2018, pp. 377–385). There are two types of absorptive capacity: potential and realized.

Potential absorptive capacity is the ability to acquire and assimilate potentially useful knowledge. Processes of acquiring and assimilating new knowledge are triggered by internal or external factors. Although knowledge acquisition can be extensive at the level of explicit knowledge, its assimilation requires some tacit knowledge. Potentially, absorption of knowledge opens up broad prospects, which depend on the adopted strategy, i.e., intelligence in competing or intelligent competing based on a strong learning culture (Santoro et al. 2018, pp. 347–354).

Realized absorptive capacity is the ability to obtain expected values from knowledge by transforming potential capabilities into operationalized ones, which contribute

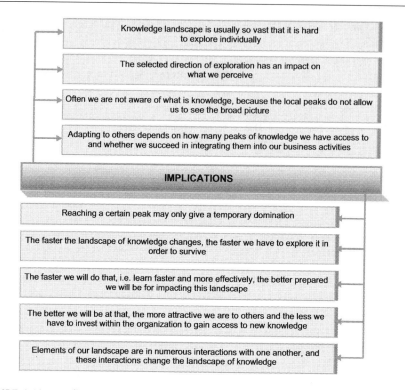

FIGURE 1.10   Implications of generating a knowledge-based strategy. (Own work based on: Lang M., Scherber S., *Der Weg zum agilen Unternehmen–Wissen für Entscheider: Strategien, Potenziale, Lösungen*, Carl Hanser Verlag GmbH Co KG, 2019, pp. 307–311.)

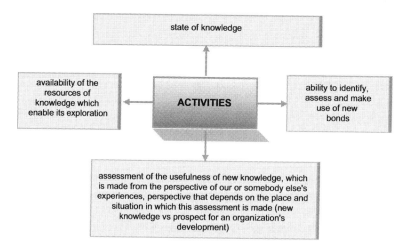

FIGURE 1.11   Activities dedicated to absorb knowledge from the environment. (Own work based on: Nonaka I., Toyama R., The knowledge-creating theory revisited: knowledge creation as a synthesizing process, [in:] *The Essentials of Knowledge Management*, Palgrave Macmillan, London, 2015, pp. 95–110.)

to the achievement of competitive advantage. At the operational level, there are usually barriers that hinder knowledge acquisition, which are as follows:

1. Social
2. Structural
3. Cultural

Mahringer, Rost and Renzl present in a synthetic way the two types of knowledge absorption in organizations: potential and realized. Development of absorptive capacity depends on (Mahringer et al. 2019, pp. 274–298):

1. Costs
2. Possible repayment of the costs as a result of increasing market share
3. Competitors' active engagement in learning
4. Predominant market logic (maintaining the status quo or willingness to make changes)
5. Attitude to uncertainty and risk (risk appetite)

The balance between the investment in potential and the realized absorptive capacity depends on the context of the knowledge in an organization as shown in Figure 1.12.

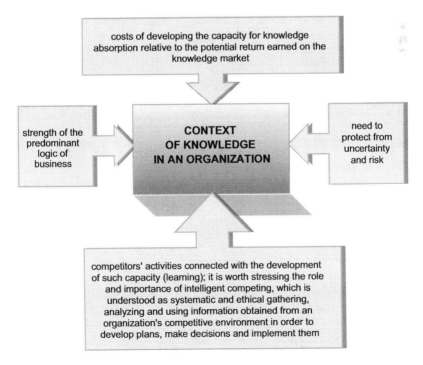

FIGURE 1.12   Balanced possibilities of knowledge absorption. (Own work.)

Proactive integration of knowledge is a critical success factor. External knowledge has to be integrated with the knowledge possessed by an organization. This integration is carried out at the level of competing, decision-making and learning.

Analyzing the issues of the contexts of knowledge in an organization presented in Figure 1.13 has to be taken into account.

The last issue presented in Figure 1.13 is particularly important here, as it expresses an economic perspective on knowledge management. The question is whether (Al Ahbabi et al. 2019, pp. 351–373):

Absorption and adaptation of knowledge will improve capacity for competing;
Products will deliver expected values to consumers; and
It will impact the way of strengthening the market position.

The right column illustrates what is the area of an organization's ignorance, which can be reduced through eliminating "dark spots" and product innovations (Al Ahbabi et al. 2019, pp. 351–373). The left column covers those areas in which values can be generated.

Both these areas should enable the creation of complementary products defining sectorial standards and achievement of a good return on investments.

Exploration of new potential of knowledge involves (Al Ahbabi et al. 2019, pp. 351–373):

- Assessment of exploratory activities aimed at adaptation to the turbulence in the environment
- Determining what knowledge should be absorbed and what knowledge should be shared with the environment

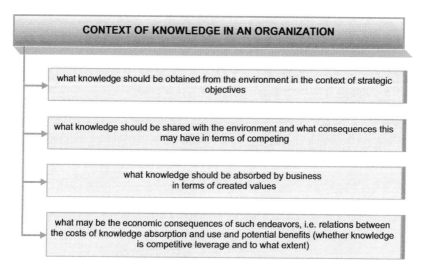

FIGURE 1.13   Issues of the contexts of knowledge in an organization. (Own work based on: North K., *Wissensorientierte Unternehmensführung: Wissensmanagement gestalten*, Springer-Verlag, 2016.)

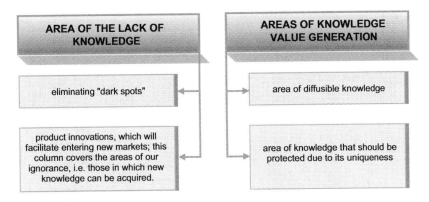

FIGURE 1.14   Strategic areas of knowledge as value. (Own work.)

Reduction of "dark spots" is about seeking knowledge which an organization does not possess and which will be essential in the future. The matrix in Figure 1.14 indicates what knowledge should be protected due to its uniqueness and how to use knowledge to develop products and increase market shares (Al Ahbabi et al. 2019, pp. 351–373):

1. *From the environment to an organization* (*two fields on the right side of the matrix*)—what an organization can do to develop appropriate activities and to integrate those values that are obtained through feedback loops from external knowledge to own businesses.
2. *From an organization to the environment* (*the fields on the left side of the matrix*)—what an organization can do to control its own activities that are expected to impact the change of external conditions.

The flow of knowledge from the environment to an organization is inspired by an organization's managerial staff as a result of strategic decisions, or incrementation occurs as a result of day-to-day contacts of members of an organization with its environment. The latter usually leads to the creation of tacit knowledge, which can become explicit as a result of particular activities, e.g., community of practice.

Knowledge obtained from outside of an organization is a result of a variety of activities (Figure 1.15).

A system of these assessments comprises the so-called knowledge audit, which enables the identification of knowledge gap and the way of its elimination, i.e., finding out (Donate and De Pablo 2015, pp. 360–370):

- Whether the knowledge that would close the gap exists in the environment at all
- Where it is (potential sources of knowledge)
- How to acquire it (who to cooperate with to acquire it)

A knowledge audit is based on the assumption that an organization "knows what it does not know." However, it is also possible that an organization "does not know what it does not know"; i.e., external knowledge is within the area of an organization's ignorance.

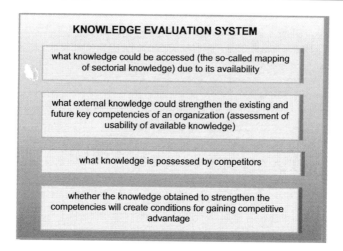

FIGURE 1.15   Diagnosis of knowledge evaluation system. (Own work based on: Donate M. J., De Pablo J.D.S., The role of knowledge-oriented leadership in knowledge management practices and innovation. *Journal of Business Research*, 2015, 2.68: 360–370.)

This is rather theoretical situation. It is more likely that the knowledge that lies within the area of an organization's ignorance is possessed by one of the competitors or even by somebody from a distant sector, which makes the state of ignorance short term. If it lasts longer, the following may be the causes (Girard and Girard 2015, pp. 1–20):

- Too much self-confidence (e.g., an organization only thinks that it is the best)
- Insufficient capacity for knowledge absorption, which causes an organization to be uninterested in what could be cognitively important to it
- Poor monitoring of the environment

In the first case, it is necessary to immediately define the organization's dominant logic and start a long-term process of rebuilding organizational culture. The second cause can be eliminated through appropriate learning. The third cause can be reduced by systematically monitoring the environment.

By absorbing knowledge that is obtainable in the environment, an organization can take advantage of the opportunities that emerge in it. This allows an organization to generate certain behavior patterns, the results of which are important to consumers. Approaches determining the forms of an organization's behavior are shown in Figure 1.16.

Knowledge obtained from an organization's environment is a source of creation of new values only when it is skillfully used, i.e., transformed from knowledge sources representing an organization's competitive potential into a knowledge resource used at the strategic (new prospects) and operational level (new possibilities of use).

The problem of exploring knowledge from the environment is, however, much more complex than it was presented above. If we were to apply here the "knowledge landscape" metaphor, it would be presented as follows: Reach the "peaks" step by step (incrementally) or rather conquer "new territories?" In other words, go in the direction

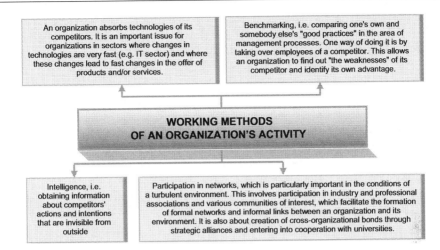

FIGURE 1.16 Aspects determining the forms of an organization's behavior. (Own work based on: Mertins K., Kohl I., Orth R., Ein Referenzmodell für Wissensmanagement, [in:]: *Wissensmanagement im Mittelstand*, Springer Gabler, Berlin, Heidelberg, 2016, pp. 31–40.)

of incremental development of the possessed knowledge or conquer new areas of knowledge? Which is more valuable to the organization? Which path of development is more risky? Experience shows that in the conditions of a turbulent environment, successes are achieved by those who are able to integrate knowledge that is diverse, sometimes very remote from the organization's knowledge base and obtained from a range of different sources that exist not only in the organization's sector but also in sectors that are very distant from this sector, even distant from the sectors offering substitutes.

Therefore, it seems important to understand the significance of data, as it enables the identification of behavior patterns in data sets. Data on customers participating in loyalty programs or using credit cards, and data on the Internet-based businesses are a rich source of consumer data. Understanding the "wealth of data" enables discovery of possibilities that individual consumers are not even aware of. It may facilitate the improvement of an organization's offer of products. On the other hand, identification of market distortions, which usually occur when suppliers or buyers do not have stable bargaining powers, manifests in price chaos. In this case, brainstorming could help to find mutually beneficial relationships (for suppliers and buyers). It is important to create scenarios, treated as a method of a prospective approach to the development of knowledge in the future, and enter into cooperation that is based on cross-organizational bonds in the form of joint venture alliances with partners possessing alternative or complementary knowledge, which may enable the creation of new opportunities based on new knowledge and risk diversification. It is also necessary to closely follow the development of technology that uses early warning systems in order to predict the possibility of emergence of the so-called technological leaps, i.e., abrupt, not linear technological advance.

García et al. (2015, pp. 179–196) noted that even innovative organizations show a tendency to stimulate the flow of their knowledge outside in order to intensify their learning, their learning cycle. An organization with learning capability above the sectorial average can develop capacity for gaining a strong advantage by "leaking" its own explicit knowledge to the market and intentionally causing turbulence in the landscape of sectorial knowledge. A strong organizational culture and environment that is favorable for an organization stabilize the staff and protect tacit knowledge. At the same time, they make it difficult to implement radical changes, but facilitate better use of learning capability and faster exploitation of opportunities than the competitors.

Although an organization should be careful when deciding what knowledge and to what extent it should share with others, it can use intentional leaks of its knowledge to make others dependent on it, and at the same time effectively protect its unique portion of knowledge. By doing so, it can significantly impact the sector and the market. An example can be companies that rely on franchising in some businesses, but maintain dependency relationships in other business areas.

There are the following ways of generating value through the flow of knowledge to an organization's environment (Fischer 2015, pp. 331–339):

1. *Cooperation in the area of supply*—entering into a knowledge-based cooperation in this area with other organizations reduces suppliers' bargaining power.
2. *Signing outsourcing contracts*—an organization may benefit from outsourcing the maintenance and development of knowledge that is not strategic to it, or knowledge that requires significant investment to develop and that can be used by others as generic service.
3. *Buying in complex components of knowledge*—this applies to high-technology sectors (e.g., aviation) where the individual elements of the final product are so complex that they require high specialization. Buying in at the level of component production and maintenance of knowledge on the integration of whole systems may contribute to the generation of greater values. For it to be cost-effective, it is important to retain in an organization more knowledge than the knowledge that is directly used in the area of key technologies that are applied to manage risk connected with coordination of product development and with future innovations. This is an example of a positive feedback loop, in which return on investment in knowledge can be increased by appropriate management of its flow. It is important here that the value-generating knowledge delivered outside of an organization is not the entire knowledge of the organization, and transactions are not on a continuous basis. There are many ways of "leaking" knowledge and thus achieving greater market values in the long term, but this involves difficult strategic decisions.

It should also be stressed that introducing loyalty programs for consumers involves the flow of knowledge outside of an organization. The more knowledge is embedded in products, the stronger this flow. It can be seen, e.g., in the banking sector, where loyalty programs are designed for both individual customers and businesses. In the latter case, knowledge feedback loop is necessary: The more specialized products are offered to loyal customers, the more knowledge they have to have about them. Experience demonstrates that such programs bring economic benefits to companies, and their number is on the rise in a variety of sectors (e.g., in trade, services).

Individual tacit knowledge is created as a result of individual experiences, is difficult to express verbally and is thereby difficult to identify, unless situations occur when it is revealed as a result of actions by individual persons. Its protection involves an appropriate system of human capital management, a policy of incentives and ensuring that people valuable for an organization do not leave it. Collective tacit knowledge is deeply rooted in an organization and manifests in activities undertaken in situations not foreseen by explicit knowledge. Its protection is connected with the fact that it holds together groups of people who see an important value in the organization for which they work. This knowledge is subject to rejection when an organization's social structure becomes disturbed. It is relatively easy to protect.

Explicit knowledge is rooted in the formal organizational structure and management system. It is protected by legal regulations and various security systems. It is a difficult problem, as it involves certain costs that increase as the turbulence of the environment increases. This figure also presents potential strategic directions of exploring various opportunities. The priority is to identify "dark spots," because they represent potential threats. Meanwhile, accurate identification of the knowledge used in the sector provides the answer to the question of whether an organization should develop such knowledge. The more turbulent the environment, the more likely it is that the vision of an organization's development is imperfect, which may increase risk: There is a knowledge gap against the sectorial knowledge and certain capacity for absorbing external knowledge, so the problem is how to effectively use this knowledge relative to the cost of its acquisition. Thus, the first step is to identify the actual gaps in an organization's knowledge and determine whether and how to eliminate them.

The next step depends on the degree of balance between the knowledge that is exploited and that part of the knowledge that is sought, which is necessary for the former and has to be acquired. If the exploited knowledge is more important (when the market is stable), then it is necessary to compare it against potentially available knowledge in terms of increasing return that can be achieved from the exploited knowledge and the costs and benefits of its protection. More generally, if an organization operates in a well-developed market and there is a threat of technological disruptions, then integrating knowledge around old technologies is not a good strategic solution. In this case, a better strategy is to get rid of the old technology or to find ways to use it outside of the organization, e.g., handing over to consumers or outsourcing to other organizations. When an organization makes both evolutionary (incremental) and rapid changes, it is better to integrate knowledge around those resources that are more important in terms of rapid changes (North and Maier 2018, pp. 665–681). The decisions about which knowledge should be integrated and which one transferred outside depend on the dynamic of changes in the environment. However, this does not mean resignation from seeking new opportunities connected with new knowledge. The following problem arises when to allow the knowledge to flow to the sector; it is better to be the first and set knowledge standards for the entire sector or to first use the knowledge inside the organization and transfer it directly—embedding it in the products and services offered to consumers. Various tensions occur here, as these processes can only partially be controlled. It seems that it is much easier to control the flow of knowledge from the environment to an organization, although problems arise here as well; e.g., absorbing too much knowledge from the environment without critical assessment excludes the possibility of fully integrating it with the organization's knowledge and using effectively; this means waste of time and financial resources. Excess of new knowledge also causes tensions within an organization, which manifest in states commonly referred to as mess. Thus, an appropriate level of knowledge absorption is needed. This must be knowledge that is most valuable for an organization in terms of its vision and objectives and makes it possible to close the gap between the current achievements and future strategic plans.

An uncontrolled flow of knowledge from an organization to its environment can increase the risk connected with carrying on business activity and cause a loss of values that could have been generated by means of those knowledge resources that were shared in an uncontrolled way with the competitors.

Summing up, the flow of knowledge from an organization to its environment can take place by directly informing the environment about possessed knowledge and sharing knowledge with suppliers, general partners, consumers and cooperating partners. Protection of an organization-unique knowledge encompasses intellectual property, key competencies, own culture and most talented employees. This knowledge should be used within an organization and reproduced. The flow of knowledge from the environment to an organization can be indirect or direct and is a result of the process of knowledge absorption and learning with the support of new structures, new intraorganizational bonds and new philosophy of operation.

An organization is a network of entities, groups and institutions of the environment that create and use knowledge. The values generated by a network depend on the quality of the links between them. The structure and operations of a network have a significant impact on the real values it generates. Possession of the entire knowledge by an organization is not the best solution in the ever-changing reality, as it is too costly and may have a negative impact on its flexibility. At the same time, creating and maintaining knowledge-based networks is an important competence of a knowledge-based organization in the long run, as the more changes in the environment, the more links an organization should have. On the other hand, the more the links, the more likely are conflicts and tensions among the members of the network, which has a negative impact on an organization's strategy. In order to use the potential of the intelligence of a knowledge-based network, one should aim to maintain cohesion with the network of own organization by strengthening its identity, raison d'etre and objectives.

Intelligent knowledge management refers to systematic and ethical collection, analysis and use of knowledge from the environment and within an organization in the processes of managing organizations and their networks. From the economic perspective, there is a problem: How to maximize the transactional value of ties by increasing their effectiveness, rather than by only minimizing the costs of transactions concluded with external organizations? Alliances are thought to be the classic form of interorganizational ties. Cooperation among organizations is a special form of ties that requires a more effective management of knowledge. It can take on very different forms, from licensing to franchising, to technology sharing and establishment of consortia. All these forms of ties result in the blurring of an organization's borders, as the competitors become cooperating parties, manufacturers advise consumers and bonds with suppliers are built for joint development of innovations. Business decisions in the area of knowledge cannot be taken in isolation, as this increases situational uncertainty and ambiguity exponentially. As the principles of competing change, the principles of organizing knowledge-related activities also need to change. If the changes in competition principles are fast, there is no point in investing in permanent knowledge resources, as they may quickly become a barrier to increasing the flexibility of operations and implementing strategic reorientation. In such conditions, it is more reasonable to develop awareness, proficiency and agility in organizations. By strategically positioning an organization in the center of an appropriately flexible network, more knowledge can be acquired than when knowledge is protected and prevented from leaking outside. Each member of a network contributes to the creation of the intellectual capacity of the entire network. Finding out how to integrate the knowledge that is available to the entire network becomes the main factor in its diversification. Changes in the environment or emergence of the conditions for such changes, activities undertaken within the network and observing the behaviors of other members of the network allow an organization to significantly diversify its own knowledge. The individual ties can be adapted to the flow of knowledge in the network to a greater or lesser extent. Moreover, it is possible to react more intelligently to change of a situation in the case of greater diversification of knowledge than when an organization operates independently. Thanks to knowledge diversification, organizations in a network become more flexible, adaptive and learn faster. Diversified networks are open, because the ties can be directly managed, but at the same time, this diversification is the main cause of mistakes made by numerous global alliances (Winkel 2019, pp. 128–138).

Brand image is the external perception of an organization, rather than its single product, although it is through products that the environment perceives the entire organization, constructing its image. This type of intellectual capital essentially depends on two factors: beliefs and values espoused by the people in an organization and how they communicate with their environment, and on the coherence of the portfolio of products and services and possessed operational capabilities. Image is closely connected with reputation. Its value can be increased by the two factors described in Figure 1.17.

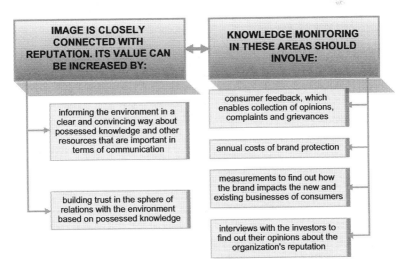

FIGURE 1.17 Aspects of monitoring knowledge in an organization. (Own work based on: Brzeziński S., Bubel D., Asymilacja standardów funkcjonowania organizacji inteligentnych w procesach zarządzania na przykładzie niemieckich przedsiębiorstw. *Studia i Prace Kolegium Zarządzania i Finansów/Szkoła Główna Handlowa*, 2016, 148: 85–97.)

Patents, publishing rights and protection of trademarks also comprise intellectual resources that affect the values generated by organizations. They also represent a factor restraining other organizations' access to our knowledge. The subject of monitoring should be the number of products and services with more than one patent or publishing right and how many times one patent is used to generate new products and services.

By coordinating and binding intellectual capital components, this capital is integrated, which impacts the stability of organizational knowledge. Coordination can take place through processes and infrastructure, which constitute elements of an organization whether or not people are in the workplace or outside of it; through organizational culture, which impacts behaviors; through communities of practice, which transform an organization's experience into future learning; through management of relationships, which aims to achieve a beneficial flow of knowledge and learning effects; and through the quality of leadership, i.e., effective coordination of decisions and accomplishment of objectives. They create a feedback loop, which enables assessment of the flow of knowledge within an organization and between an organization and its environment.

Organizational culture creates a context for people to interpret their tasks, and relying on knowledge resources, it contributes to an increased effectiveness of operations. It also has a big impact on decision-making processes, allowing decision-makers to collectively perceive the identity of the organization, its values, character of human relations and leaders' behaviors. The subject of monitoring can be the level of cooperation, by measuring engagement in it or the extent of knowledge sharing.

The discussion about ties leads to a conclusion that there are two factors impacting a network's potential and intelligence (Hänel and Felden 2016, pp. 259–281):

1. Social capital, its strength and character, which stems from the structure and configuration of the ties, compatibility of the network's participants in the cognitive sphere and the quality of relations manifested in trust and engagement;

2. Combination of applied coordination mechanisms that enable knowledge-based ties to be created. It is necessary to take into account the extent to which the existing common goals, structure of governance processes and trust impact the types of knowledge flow and cohesion of actions. Every structural form leads to a different level of the coherence of actions depending on the network and flexibility in reacting to changes in the turbulent environment. By choosing an appropriate coordination mechanism, the full potential of a network can be exploited.

A knowledge strategy requires answering the following questions: What value do the members of a network add? How many ties in the area of knowledge are established by means of possessed resources? Where do close ties that involve knowledge sharing in cooperation processes generate value increase, and where do loose ties involving cooperation improve the knowledge potential of an organization as a whole? When creating a knowledge strategy that is based on close ties (the so-called close networks), attention should be paid to acquiring knowledge about relationships with consumers, suppliers, competitors and other partners, and appropriately allocating the responsibility for coordinating the ties, especially in the case of relations engaging significant resources (e.g., alliances). Close ties enable a substantial flow of knowledge among the participants of a network, especially tacit knowledge. When developing a knowledge strategy that is based on loose ties, attention should be paid to outsourcing ties as well as performance monitoring, identification of opportunities and generation of knowledge that enables tightening of the relationships in the future.

The ability to appropriately adapt both types of ties (loose and close) enhances an organization's capabilities to adapt to changes in a turbulent environment. However, when such relationships are burdened with opportunistic behaviors of the network members, there is an increasing risk that close relationships may reduce access to potentially valuable new knowledge, while too loose relationships may result in the availability of only fragmentary, less valuable knowledge. Creation of close ties requires higher investment expenditures. In the case of loose ties, the flow of knowledge is rather limited. Thus, it is important to achieve an appropriate balance between these ties. Capability of cooperation is the basis for a dynamic management of a set of different ties by allocating specific responsibility for active management of external ties, constantly assessing and reconfiguring knowledge potential through the use of the knowledge opportunities matrix and adopting cooperation management styles in terms of three dimensions: complexity of tasks, number of barriers in communication that need to be overcome and the quality of ties that are necessary for the flow of knowledge between partners.

Organizational Culture Management in Terms of Knowledge Accumulation

2

2.1 KNOWLEDGE VERSUS ORGANIZATIONAL CULTURE IN MANAGEMENT

In today's turbulent environment, knowledge is becoming a key resource of modern organizations, with knowledge management turning into a key skill of not only the managerial staff but also most employees whose job requires direct contact with other people. It is especially important in designing internal processes in an organization as well as processes connected with product design and production and service delivery. This knowledge is usually concentrated in plans, procedures, methods of operation and economic processes, and its management is determined by a variety of internal and external factors (Kiełtyka 2013, pp. 119–130).

Organizational culture is one of them. Identifying and transforming the culture of a given organization may contribute to a more effective acquisition, sharing and, most importantly, use of knowledge. Wider interest in organizational culture, especially among organization management researchers and specialists, started in the 1980s. It was connected with a belief that organizational culture was a new key to improving an organization's efficiency and identity, improving human relations and winning new markets, in other words, a key to success. The management literature provides a variety of definitions of the term "organizational culture," which is connected with different understanding of the construction of certain meanings applied in social and economic sciences. We can distinguish three distinct approaches in the research literature that gave rise to the definitions of organizational culture.

The first, which draws on cross-cultural research in management, treats organizational culture as an independent variable that cannot be changed by an organization (Achouri 2015, pp. 217–260). Organizational culture is defined as something that is created outside of an organization and brought to it from outside (Voigt 2013, p. 45). Thus, it becomes an element of the background, a factor explaining and impacting certain elements of the management process. The researchers representing this way of thinking about organizational culture were mainly interested in the possibility of increasing management effectiveness in different cultural contexts (Voigt 2013, pp. 29–106). In the second approach, organizational culture is regarded as one of the elements of an organization or its internal variable that acts as a link between other elements and holds them together at the same time, thus determining the effects of operations. In this approach, organizational culture constitutes ideas that have an impact on the behaviors of people and whole organizations, and the results of such behaviors that have an impact on organizational, technological, economic and political systems that are present in organizations (Ackermann 2015, p. 9). Organizations can manipulate, manage their culture or generate it as a side effect, and thus, they can use it as a competitive advantage. This way of perceiving organizational culture is consistent with the definitions formulated by Christoph Barmeyer, Laurence Romani and Katharine Pilhofer, among others. According to them: "Organizational culture is unwritten, often subconsciously perceived principles that fill the gap between what exists formally and what actually happens" (Barmeyer, Romani, and Pilhofer 2016, pp. 63–84).

According to Engelen and Tholen (2014, pp. 215–227), organizational culture is how an organization learned to cope with its environment, and more specifically how people learned to solve more or less complex problems in a certain way.

It is noteworthy that certain levels of organizational culture are easily observable in an organization, while others are less visible or completely invisible. They are also to a varying degree related to different types of knowledge. Organizational culture is sometimes compared to an iceberg, where the first level is its top—emerging above the water and clearly visible. However, interpretation of the whole organizational culture based on observable artifacts requires appropriate reading of their meanings. The second level is only partially visible. This is because apart from the norms and values written down in an organization's mission, various regulations, charters and other normative acts, there are also unwritten rules of conduct that define interpersonal relations and guide people's behavior. Under the surface, there is a completely hidden third level, which refers mainly to informal aspects of an organization's life. It is related to people's tacit knowledge, expressing not only their cognitive potential but also their emotional attitude to various phenomena, notions and experiences. This is where attitudes and feelings, as well as values concerning human nature and the essence of interpersonal relations, and what an organization knows and may know are written (Lang and Baldauf 2016c, pp. 1–38).

The above-presented approaches to organizational culture draw on the functionalist paradigm and causal relationships, and so they do not go beyond an instrumental approach to managing an organization.

The third approach, in contrast to the previous two, is based on the non-functionalist paradigm. Culture is seen as a root metaphor for conceptualization of an organization (Lang and Baldauf 2016b, pp. 40–47). From a distinct element of an organization, with clearly defined attributes, it becomes an organization. According to the supporters of this way of defining organizational culture, it is not a system of distinct variables, such as beliefs, messages, norms or rituals, which can be managed instrumentally and by extension fully controlled. Instead, it is a construct independent from the impact of external and internal factors, pervading the activities of an organization, which means that an organization is a self-existent cultural phenomenon (Lang and Baldauf 2016a, p. 92). In this approach to organizational culture, all aspects of managing an organization, including economic and social ones, have cultural meaning, and organizational culture is the social space, collective identity in which and through which a human being sees the world, including an organization's internal life. It is a process, a collective framework that defines the scope for various activities. It is a form of interpretation, expression and manifestation of human consciousness, various myths, meanings and symbols (Nica 2013, p. 179).

In this sense, organizational culture serves to organize activities and gain experiences. In the non-functionalist approach, we can distinguish three areas of studying organizational culture, namely (Zheng, Yang, and Mclean 2010, pp. 763–771):

- Cognitive perspective, which assumes that culture is a framework of knowledge, a cognitive endeavor
- Symbolist perspective, which treats societies, organizations and cultures as a system of common symbols and meanings
- Structural (psychodynamic) perspective, which refers to subconsciousness, treats culture as the expression of subconsciousness, with its superficial manifestations, any activities and practices being projection of deeper, unconscious processes

Martina Linnenluecke and Andrew Griffiths (Linnenluecke and Griffiths 2010, pp. 357–366) see the significance of images, language, symbols, beliefs, stories, celebrations and other attributes as important tools that can be used in the process of management. They claim that the dress code and attitude, the decor of various rooms, especially director's offices, formulation of thoughts, as well as flexibility in contacts with other people, or even the skills and cleverness in applying the rules of the interpersonal game, have a significant impact and are meaningful in various interpersonal situations. They can shape employees' behaviors and patterns of organizational culture and subculture, helping the managerial staff to achieve desirable objectives. However, these authors note that managing and transforming organizational culture by imposing rigid rules of behavior on people, especially values and the way of thinking, is a form of manipulation, which can be met with employees' resistance, aversion and distrust. As a result, organizational culture becomes a tool of manipulation and control instead of expressing the nature of a human being (Tseng 2010, pp. 269–284).

In this approach to studying the management of an organization, organizational culture is usually described in a nonevaluative way. Thus, there is no good or bad, and high or low culture. One can only say that in a given organization, it is more or less visible (Hogan and Coote 2014, pp. 1609–1621). Summing up the discussion above, it is worth stating (Nguyen and Mohamed 2011, pp. 206–221) that most scholars concerned with organizational culture, despite differences in how they understand it, agree on the following points:

- Culture exists in every organization.
- Every organizational culture is unique, exclusive and exceptional.
- Culture can create desirable organizational behaviors, the internal identity of an organization and its external image.

In the theory and practice of managing an organization, the predominant approach to organizational culture sees it as a separate construct that is subject to evaluation. Consequently, culture can be high or low, and good or bad, depending on its impact on the organization and the implementation of its goals. In this sense, organizational culture is a system of patterns of thinking and acting established informally in the social setting of an organization that has an impact on the implementation of an organization's formal objectives (Prajogo and Mcdermott 2011, pp. 712–735).

There are multiple factors influencing the character of organizational culture. The scientific literature lists various dimensions of cultural differences, which refer to the degree of intensity of certain characteristics that have a strong impact on the character of a given organization's culture. These characteristics form certain cultural patterns. The best known systems of cultural dimensions include the systems created by F. Kluckholn, G. Hofstede and Ch. Hampden–Turner and A. Trompenaars (Asree, Zain and Rizal 2010, pp. 500–516).

The authors of the first system list five cultural dimensions distinguished based on attitude to nature, temporal orientation, human nature, attitude to action, locus of responsibility and social space. Meanwhile, G. Hofstede distinguished the following sets of cultural dimensions:

1. Large power distance–small power distance
2. Individualism–collectivism
3. Masculinity–femininity
4. Low degree of uncertainty avoidance–high degree of uncertainty avoidance

The last reference framework presents the following cultural dimensions (Sanz–Valle et al. 2011, pp. 997–1015):

- Universalism–particularism
- Analysis–synthesis
- Individualism–collectivism
- Inner direction–other direction
- Succession–synchronization
- Achieving a post–receiving a post
- Equality–hierarchy

The above characteristics have a significant impact on managing organizational culture in every organization and on its character that distinguishes it from among the organizational cultures of other organizations.

2.2 KNOWLEDGE AS AN ELEMENT OF SHAPING ORGANIZATIONAL CULTURE

2.2.1 Shaping Organizational Culture in Knowledge Acceleration

In the context of the above aspect, knowledge is a resource without which no modern organization can function. Knowledge helps organizations to achieve a permanent competitive advantage, to function on the market and to develop (Ziółkowska 2003, pp. 741–749). Moreover, knowledge is a resource that, in contrast to other resources, especially the material ones, does not decrease but expands.

Rajnish Kumar Rai (2011, pp. 779–801) defines knowledge as a fluid composition of directed experience, values, useful information and an expert's perspective that provides bases for assessing and acquiring new experiences and information. He maintains that, for knowledge to be created, one needs data, which, put in the proper context, take the form of information, which in turn becomes knowledge, which is a combination of appropriately selected information, experiences and assessments of values as well as analytical insight into a given issue. The resulting knowledge tends to be written down both in official documents and in databases, practices, norms and procedures, and a human being's experiences, espoused values and previous knowledge in a given field play an important role in the creation of knowledge.

In microeconomic models, knowledge appears in two different contexts. The first emphasizes the process of knowledge creation, i.e., transforming data into information, and information into knowledge, while the second treats knowledge as an asset, placing it both under the category of competencies and results of innovations (Al–Laham 2016, pp. 67–82).

Moreover, knowledge is considered in terms of a product and a causative factor of many internal processes in an organization. As knowledge resources increased, a need arose to classify and even hierarchize it. In terms of the content, knowledge is divided into explicit and tacit. Explicit, or formal, knowledge can be presented in the form of figures, procedures, instructions, rules, documents, orders and norms, and is written in various carriers and forms of communication. It is thus easy to communicate, document, convert and transfer (Güldenberg 2013, p. 115).

In contrast, tacit knowledge, which is the most valuable mental resource of every organization, is an intellectual composition that is difficult to perceive and express; it comprises experiences of a human being, his/her intuition, feelings, various emotions and skills. It is an individual resource, difficult to formalize and created by combining the content of a human being's cognitive, emotional and psychosomatic spheres with the reality surrounding him/her (Zelle 2013, pp. 67–71). Possession of tacit knowledge depends to a large extent on an individual's intellectual potential, willingness to learn and experience, whereas its transfer is based on interpersonal contacts between knowledge owners.

A system of accepted interpersonal relations, practices, customs and rituals, status levels and fulfilled roles, and a system of principles and behaviors, in particular established norms, beliefs and values, have a decisive impact on the process of acquiring, distributing and using knowledge in an organization. There is a constant interaction between organizational culture and beliefs, which express attitude towards various processes in an organization and its environment, attitude towards various assumptions concerning the nature of a human being and his/her attitude towards various phenomena, towards learning as well as sharing and using knowledge, as on the one hand culture impacts the way people think and act, while on the other hand, their information and skills, intuitive understanding, thinking, conduct and assumed obligations give a shape to culture.

Organizational culture is essential for appropriate management of knowledge, especially culture that refers to values and norms, is people-oriented, unleashes drive and enthusiasm in them, emphasizes knowledge sharing and takes into account such values as openness, trust, fairness, acceptance of failures, respect for the contribution brought by different employees, generosity, mutual support and cooperation (Mertins, Kohl, and Orth 2016, pp. 31–40).

Among the above-mentioned values, which are necessary for the process of knowledge management, in particular knowledge creation, an important role is played by creativity, understood as coming up with proper novel individual and collective ideas, where, apart from employees' competencies, personality and work motivation, a priority role is played by such elements of organizational culture as participation in decision-making, delegation of responsibilities, effective communication and readiness for changes. Trust is a value that impacts the process of knowledge flow. This is because one cannot share knowledge with people one does not trust or receive knowledge from people who are not trustworthy. According to Christian Broser (2016, p. 71), trust reduces uncertainty that accompanies actions in the context of relations with other people, reduces the sense of risk and enables a more independent and effective activity, including acquisition, processing, transfer and use of knowledge in an organization.

In the process of knowledge management, of importance is openness to other people, their needs, expectations and problems, and openness to variety (Nowakowska-Grunt and Kabus 2014, pp. 7–19).

Openness increases the freedom of expressing thoughts and emboldens employees who are unwilling to share their knowledge, thus increasing employees' potential and their usefulness for an organization. An open dialogue allows people, on the one hand, to share information and knowledge with one another, while on the other hand, to overcome the differences between them that inhibit the process of learning and knowledge sharing.

Active listening facilitates the process of creating tacit knowledge, then using it in various planning, organizational and manufacturing processes as well as sharing it directly and indirectly with others. Thanks to openness, informal cooperation networks are formed, informal interpersonal contacts thrive, and a wide range of interests develops. Moreover, openness facilitates diagnosis and self-diagnosis of the gaps in knowledge resources, and thus makes one aware of the need for further learning and enriching the knowledge and experiences by completely new elements. Open people are more credible, which may increase their authority in an organization (Abecker et al. 2013, p. 87).

Knowledge sharing is also facilitated by cooperation-oriented interpersonal relations, when representatives of various subcultures find a common goal and jointly strive to achieve it, and by cooperation, which assumes the necessity of taking into account the needs of other social groups or individuals and having regard for their interests (Sauter and Scholz 2015, p. 99).

Organizational culture that promotes such values is clearly people-oriented, which means that it attaches significant attention to proper interpersonal relations, trust-based relations, activity, sensitivity and empathy and assertion of own rights without infringing the rights of other people. Such culture promotes openness and freedom in presenting one's views, eliciting enthusiasm about work, creativity and innovation as well as awareness of common goals that require new knowledge to be achieved.

Teamwork has a particularly positive impact on knowledge acquisition and sharing, especially when an organization actively encourages employees to espouse such values as the ethos of acting, coming up with ideas and solving problems jointly in an atmosphere of trust and free and open communication.

Strong commitment to teamwork requires that people help rather than hinder one another, and cooperate to achieve the common goal. It is impossible to effectively work with one another without sharing information and knowledge. Moreover, teamwork leads to the creation of new knowledge, which can be stored, converted or used during teamwork and individual work. This also generates new experiences: Part of the knowledge hidden in the minds of the team members becomes explicit knowledge, which can be codified and easily communicated.

However, while managing knowledge, one should bear in mind that people do not always want to share it, both within an organization and with its environment. One cannot force employees to share knowledge. One can only create conditions, through appropriate atmosphere and system of incentives, in which they will be motivated to think creatively and, against payment or free of charge, share knowledge. Thus, a phenomenon called "stickiness of knowledge" is observed in organizations. It means that knowledge possessed by one person is not transferred to another person, and knowledge accumulated in one organizational unit does not flow to others (Soukup 2013, pp. 112–115). It has to do, on the one hand, with the personality of people, who prefer keeping knowledge for themselves, while on the other hand with the process of management, in particular with power distance.

In an organization where the autonomy of an employee is limited, knowledge sharing is more difficult. According to Christina Matschke (2014, pp. 419–434), the following has a destructive impact on knowledge sharing: supervision based on the position in the hierarchy rather than on competencies; no possibility of subordinates negotiating with their superiors, e.g., about how to implement the goals; lack of clear, transparent principles of promotion, in particular failure to take into account employees' engagement in the organization's affairs when considering promotion; failure to assign decision-making powers to employees concerning productivity and quality standards, i.e., lack of real participation in management.

A relatively important factor in inhibiting knowledge flow is organizational culture based on the principles of competition. This is because employees are unlikely to share knowledge if they work in an organization where confrontation dominates in interpersonal relations, and sometimes even intimidation and fight, especially between individual employees and groups of employees, in an organization where there is a clash between different cultural patterns, different individual and team interests, needs and expectations, which are not always in line with the organization's objectives. In order to gain an advantage over others, employees or teams protect their knowledge resources and refrain from sharing their experiences and skills. Stefan Voigt (2016, pp. 107–113) adds the following to the list of factors inhibiting the flow of knowledge: lack of an organization's vision, lack of visible chances and possibilities of development, in particular rigid principles and routine in an organization. Moreover, large power distance causes the managerial staff to not only refrain from sharing knowledge with employees, but also be unwilling to accept knowledge from their subordinates.

Activities in an organization aiming to acquire new knowledge and continuously update, verify and share it are determined by a number of factors, among which organizational culture comes to the forefront. Organizations differ in terms of culture, but also within an organization itself, especially when it starts functioning or undergoes a deep transformation, there are different types of culture. One can also observe a division of organizational culture into public one, often for appearances' sake, and internal one, experienced by all the employees and also encountered by customers, suppliers and other stakeholders. Not every organizational culture facilitates learning and knowledge sharing to the same extent, especially the use of knowledge. The least mobile is tacit knowledge, which is not easily subjected to various procedures of codification, a process that is necessary for sharing it.

Organizational culture that facilitates the process of knowledge management requires realization that every organization is different and has different objectives and tasks. This in turn requires not only diagnosing the current state and defining the consequences of certain artifacts, attitudes, cultural behaviors and beliefs, but also a skillful identification and application of instruments that shape a culture that is conducive to the process of individual and collective learning as well as sharing and using knowledge at work.

2.3 KNOWLEDGE DIFFUSION IN ORGANIZATIONAL CULTURE MANAGEMENT

Traditional resources such as labor, land and capital are often perceived as obstacles to rather than a driving force for the development of organizations. It is knowledge that becomes the key factor in their creative functioning. Knowledge constitutes intangible resources of organizations related to human activity.

Knowledge management can be understood as a process of identifying, acquiring and using knowledge for improving an organization's competitive position, which is

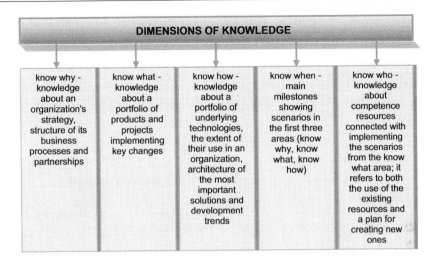

FIGURE 2.1   Knowledge dimensions. (Own work based on: Mäntymäki M., Riemer K., Enterprise social networking: A knowledge management perspective. *International Journal of Information Management*, 2016, 6.36: 1042–1052.)

supported by four factors: leadership, organizational culture, technology and measurement system. Figure 2.1 presents a model of such a solution—knowledge management system (KMS).

In accordance with this model, five dimensions of knowledge can be distinguished (Figure 2.1).

The widespread use of ERP (Enterprise Resource Planning) systems among organizations managed in a modern way suggests that such solutions are becoming a basic element of an organization's IT infrastructure and a sort of genetic code, which practically determines its effective functioning.

ERP systems undergo evolution, driven, among other things, by new business requirements, technological changes in IT solutions and dynamic evolution of the technical infrastructure. They are characterized by a strong focus on building relationships with customers and business partners, and system intelligence. This means that sales and distribution modules are extended to the level of customer relationship management, and supply and production logistics is integrated within supply chain management (SCM).

Evolution of integrated IT systems gave rise to the concept of Enterprise Content Management. It is a result of functional and technological integration of such solutions as enterprise applications integration, workflow management, integrated document management and web content management. All of these elements provide numerous benefits when applied separately, but have many limitations resulting from increasing functional requirements, problems connected with updating, compatibility and servicing, among other things. These solutions are based on specific types of documents and sets (electronic documents, electronically generated drawings, scanned images, multimedia records, transactional data, website content, etc.), but they rely on data presented/generated in ERP systems and other dedicated business applications.

In practice, these solutions constitute a basis for ensuring a full informational service of an organization in three functional dimensions (Cerchione and Esposito 2017, pp. 1551–1562):

- *Whenever*—enables online information exchange, i.e., making data available on an ongoing basis, e.g., delivery status, stock levels, progress in order execution.
- *Whatever*—enables access to all relevant data in terms of logistics processes, which allows them to be fully controlled to comply with the quality requirements; any disturbances trigger remedial actions and actions designed to control their effectiveness; there is a sort of feedback loop within supply chain event management.
- *Wherever*—enables a full review of the information used in the supply chain; it includes significant data about completed processes, e.g., the current location of the load, its status or planned route of transportation; this is possible thanks to the use of mobile and online solutions.

The above-mentioned functional dimensions are realized mostly through ERP applications, but also through advanced warehouse management.

The practice of the functioning of organizations in the so-called extended supply chain, which includes integrated business processes of cooperating organizations, "merges" with information processing tools and processes, and many elements comprising "the informational architecture of these organizations" (computer networks using ERP systems) have the features of IT infrastructure, which is in line with the trends to integrate and optimize business processes of all the partners cooperating in the chain. In practice, this is realized by means of APS (advanced planning systems), which are designed to synchronize procurement, production and distribution plans along with C systems.

Among many IT solutions, special attention should be given to KMS, which aims to integrate all processes connected with acquiring, managing and distributing knowledge within an organization (Girard and Girard 2015, pp. 1–20). This is achieved by means of dedicated tools, which gather information that comes both from the environment and from internal resources of an organization. The most important IT solutions that support knowledge management are shown in Figure 2.2.

The process of creating knowledge as an element of an organization's strategy is based on four main elements (Raupp 2017, pp. 143–163):

- Managerial staff
- Organizational culture
- Information technology
- Measurement system that examines the effectiveness of the solutions implemented

These elements enable the elimination of various pathological phenomena resulting from information monopolies existing in individual groups of employees or overcoming of the barriers to information exchange, which make information inaccessible to

FIGURE 2.2 The most important IT solutions that support knowledge management. (Own work based on: Döbler T., Wissensmanagement: Open Access, Social Networks, E-Collaboration. *Handbuch Online-Kommunikation*, 2018, pp. 1–30.)

certain people. It is worth adding that technologies based on XML (eXtensible Markup Language) are especially popular in KMSs today. This is because thanks to them, documents can be converted into XML format and transferred between various IT systems, and individual employees of an organization can correctly read data, which undoubtedly increases the pace of information sharing.

In the case of KMS, of importance are trust and an organization's openness to experimenting and employee learning. Without these factors, any initiatives aimed at improving the operation of an organization or increasing its competitive capacity are doomed to failure from the start. This is because lack of trust hinders exchange of knowledge, prevents the creation of employee teams and even leads to the loss of corporate image in the eyes of the organization's business partners.

The task of KMS is to close the gap between the existing and needed resources in order to achieve the biggest value added. This is because almost 90% of an organization's intellectual resources are hidden in various types of reports, tables and periodic summaries, while only 20% of them are ready for multiple use. It is no wonder then that over 90% of CEOs of various organizations admit in surveys that implementing

KMS is a condition for achieving and sustaining competitive advantage on the market (Nonaka and Toyama 2015, pp. 95–110). This is because such systems enable a marked improvement in access to information, as they handle the whole process of acquiring information from various sources, storing it in a database (databases) and sharing with all interested users.

KMS offers unquestionable benefits to an organization, as it increases its flexibility and ability to better cope with dynamically changing market conditions, among other things. This is important, because the inevitably increasing market competition forces organizations to search for new ways to gain competitive advantage and diversify their operations. KMS also impacts the process of creating internal governance in an organization, resulting in an increased pace of the flow of information among individual units of an organization and easier access to aggregated data.

The implementation of KMS is a complex process that is connected with high implementation risk. The most important factors determining success are shown in Figure 2.3.

This means that any changes in an organization should have their source in the new concept of management—a cooperation-based strategy, which has become a standard of functioning in e-business.

The key element of successful implementation of KMS is organizational culture that shapes the staff's attitudes in the area of knowledge sharing. The most important characteristic of KMS-based organizations is atmosphere of mutual trust, which is not a common case. Individual employees treat their knowledge as an element of competitive advantage on the labor market. Therefore, sharing knowledge with coworkers is perceived by them as getting rid of their assets. A difficult-to-overcome psychological barrier appears in organizations whose organizational culture concentrates around systems promoting individual performance. In such cases, knowledge management is reduced to the development of systems designed to organize organizational knowledge. Thus, a determinant of an effective implementation and functioning of KMS is having an employee motivation system in place that not only facilitates knowledge sharing, but also stimulates creativity and innovative activities.

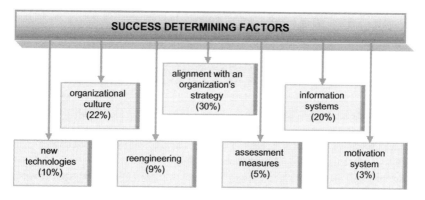

FIGURE 2.3 The most important success-determining factors. (Own work based on: Milosevic I., Bass A.F., Combs G.M., The paradox of knowledge creation in a high-reliability organization: A case study. *Journal of Management*, 2018, 3.44: 1174–1201.)

Well-functioning KMSs cannot be created in detachment from an organization's natural resources and external environment, but they should enable the creation of a learning organization, allow it to take up new market challenges and strengthen its competitive position.

Further discussion will be based on the general knowledge management model (Inkinen 2016, pp. 230–257).

The main idea of the model can be described as follows: Knowledge, as a resource existing both outside and within an organization, becomes a subject of management, which comprises stages adequate to the specificity of this resource, with management meta-instruments acting as an intermediary. These meta-instruments include the vision, mission and strategy of an organization, formal procedures, organizational structure, IT systems, organizational culture and leadership. Meta-instruments are a kind of vehicle of the elementary activities comprising the different stages of the knowledge management process, i.e., mechanisms that determine the existence and shape of such activities. Thus, the individual stages of the knowledge management process are implemented through a certain set of elementary activities, which in turn are embedded in meta-instruments.

Organizational culture is a special element of an organization and a special instrument of management. It shapes the other elements and instruments, acting as a kind of prism through which the rightness of the actions taken in an organization is assessed. This is also how the role of culture as a meta-instrument in the process of knowledge management should be understood. The fact that the elementary activities of knowledge management are reflected in it means that organizational culture approves of these activities, regarding them as right. These activities should also be seen in terms of adaptation of the knowledge management process to the existing organizational culture, although both the implementation of these activities and the overlap between organizational culture and the other instruments of management mean that these instruments impact the culture itself. As a result, the following is true: In order to manage knowledge, it is necessary to carry out activities that are appropriate in a given organizational culture, which in the long run helps to create organizational culture that facilitates knowledge management.

The stages of knowledge management identified in the model as well as the elementary activities comprising these stages are to a varying degree inscribed in organizational culture. They also vary in terms of the extent to which they relate to the culture, as shown in the reference model. In practice, these activities and their importance vary even more, due to the diversity of organizational cultures themselves. Some activities do not have to be assessed or approved in terms of organizational values. The other instruments can be effective vehicles for them.

Knowledge location is a set of actions that aim to identify the sources of knowledge that an organization needs in order to achieve its goals. This includes determining both subject and object sources of knowledge, residing both within and outside of an organization. The seeking of such sources can be constrained by organizational culture, which assigns values to the sources of knowledge used in an organization. Therefore, culture, as a meta-instrument of knowledge management, should reflect activities that involve numerous and varied knowledge sources. Effective knowledge management requires giving adequate importance to all potential sources of knowledge.

However, organizational culture does not have to be a vehicle for all activities connected with knowledge location. Activities regulated by other meta-instruments include actions involving certain sets of information (creating and updating thematic databases) covered by procedures, structure and IT systems, and establishment of contacts and cooperation with external knowledge owners addressed in the vision, mission and strategy.

The stage of knowledge acquisition can be equated with the stage of knowledge location, because the latter is unlikely to stop at the identification of knowledge source—the source will be explored in the next step. The rationale for inscribing these activities in organizational culture is the same as with knowledge location—the number and variety of sources and the ways of knowledge acquisition should be accepted in an organization so that they can be regarded as important and valuable. Apart from that, the stage of knowledge acquisition comprises such activities as purchases of publications, licenses and databases as defined in procedures, and systems for controlling the processes in an organization, which should be addressed in both procedures and IT systems.

Knowledge development, which is another stage in the knowledge management model, can partly represent the "continuation" of the activities comprising the preceding stages. This is because knowledge that has been located and acquired naturally leads to the development of the already existing knowledge. However, apart from the activities connected with the earlier stages, knowledge development also has to encompass other activities, without which it would be impossible to fully develop and create new knowledge. These are activities that should be strongly embedded in the system of organizational values, because there must be authentic conviction as to their appropriateness. They include, among other things, analysis of experiences referring to both external and internal interactions. Although organizational culture is partly an effect of the common experiences of organizational members, a conscious analysis of such experiences and learning from them is not necessarily automatically regarded as important or needed. Thus, learning from one's own experiences (successes and failures) should occupy a high position in the hierarchy of organizational activities. However, some reservations should be voiced at this point. Experiences, which make up the memory of an organization that is reflected in the habits of unknown origin, stories about how things always were in the organization and standard operating procedures may substitute wise actions. This is a result of a surprising phenomenon where if people do something in a certain way even once, then even if it turns out to have been done in a wrong way, people will tend to treat that as an automatic instruction for future actions.[3] Mindless reliance on traditional ways of doing things makes learning and implementation of changes difficult. Therefore, it is very important in organizational culture that people feel free to admit mistakes and accept them as a natural path towards improvement.

Organizational culture as a meta-instrument of knowledge development should also give high priority to employee learning and development, understood as improvement of qualifications. By prioritizing the undertaking of education in various forms, it should motivate employees to engage in such activities. This should be supported by HR (human resources) policy tools, also accepted in the organizational culture—employee evaluation system and promotion paths that take into account the efforts to develop individual and organizational knowledge. Knowledge development in an organization is strongly determined by collective forms of problem-solving. Although they can be regulated through appropriate procedural and structural solutions, their actual effectiveness is strongly related to how they are reflected in organizational culture. The leadership should formulate ambitious tasks, whereas the vision and strategy of an organization should include research and development and diversification of operations. The above-mentioned activities unrelated to organizational culture seem to form a basis, a kind of organizational infrastructure for knowledge development, but taking deliberate efforts with authentic engagement requires appropriate organizational culture.

Knowledge codification, which is another stage of the process of knowledge management, involves activities aimed at converting tacit knowledge into explicit knowledge. As a result, knowledge becomes more available in the form, at the place and time suitable to the employees who need it. Naturally, not every type of tacit knowledge can be codified, nor is it always necessary. Sometimes, codification can be dangerous, making it easier for knowledge to be copied and leak out from an organization (Pietruszka-Ortyl et al. 2019, pp. 20–24). The overwhelming majority of codification-related activities can be governed by appropriate procedures, IT system solutions or organizational structure. These include creation of databases and knowledge maps, financial, planning and HR documentation, etc. Giving appropriate priority to keeping a record of what is not obligatorily documented, i.e., external relations, internal reports, minutes of meetings, should be consistent with organizational culture. If such records are not treated as important or useful, then even if they are enforced by, e.g., internal procedures, they will not be a valuable tool for codifying organizational knowledge.

The next stage of the knowledge management process is knowledge storage. The activities at this stage basically refer to codified knowledge, i.e., one that has already been turned into explicit knowledge. With tacit knowledge, which resides in the minds and common experiences of the members of an organization, knowledge storage should be understood metaphorically in some sense. Storing tacit knowledge in an organization means preventing the people who possess it from leaving the organization. It is thus an area of activities akin to knowledge protection. Storage of codified knowledge, no matter whose responsibility it is, should be reflected in procedures, structure and IT systems. The activities undertaken at this stage boil down to defining who and where should gather and store specific carriers of knowledge. However, for these activities to be fully effective, they need to be given appropriate priority, and above all, the organizational culture needs to accept the collection and storage of such knowledge and its carriers, which otherwise may not be automatically perceived as needed. This involves, in particular, documenting experiences, the documentation of which has been indicated as one of the elements that should be reflected in organizational culture, and documenting "innovative" events and processes.

Knowledge sharing (knowledge diffusion) is a stage of the knowledge management process that is particularly important and very strongly determined by organizational culture. Of the elementary activities in that area, only three do not need to be reflected in organizational culture (Figure 2.4).

The other activities undertaken as part of the knowledge-sharing stage, which are also contained in the other instruments, should be reflected in organizational culture. These activities can be boiled down to two main objectives to facilitate the sense of belonging and team spirit and to stimulate creativity as a result of mutual inspiration.

These objectives are accomplished, among other things, by shaping organizational structures (towards the matrix structure, process structure, and task structure, which

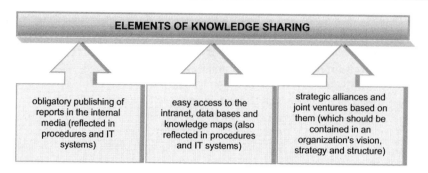

FIGURE 2.4   Elementary activities in the process of knowledge sharing. (Own work.)

also should be accepted in the organizational culture), implementing the concept of Total Quality Management (TQM) and project management (both strongly connected with organizational culture), promoting teamwork, using inventive problem-solving methods and creating a climate that fosters innovation. Organizational culture should accept and consider as appropriate forms and channels of knowledge sharing, e.g., informal discussion forums, informal meetings or common seminars. Combining these and similar activities should result in concentration on innovation, which will be implemented through teamwork, which naturally requires employees to share the knowledge they possess. Apart from that, an important activity in the area of knowledge diffusion is stimulating open communication, e.g., encouraging employees to make comments, even critical ones, and admit their mistakes. The elementary activities that support that must necessarily be inscribed in the existing organizational culture. Open and honest communication is also a competence of leadership as a meta-instrument of knowledge management. Another competence of leadership, but also an element of vision, mission and strategy of an organization, should be the development of an organization's identity and "patriotism," which—if consistent with the organizational culture—can be one of the most important knowledge-sharing activities in an organization.

In many cases, knowledge sharing results in the use of such knowledge. Exceptions are cases when it is individual knowledge that should be used. Such use should also be appropriately stimulated. That is why knowledge use constitutes a separate stage. Nevertheless, because it is connected with knowledge diffusion, the elementary activities identified for that stage also refer to the stage of knowledge use. Consequently, the impact of the organizational culture is also strong, making it one of the most important meta-instruments at the stage of knowledge use. Apart from the activities related both to diffusion and to use of knowledge, the latter stage involves activities that stimulate individual creativity understood as seeking new solutions and rationality in knowledge-related activities (i.e., using it for the right purpose, at the right time, at the right place and by the right people). Appropriate organizational culture can also be an element of the pursuit of development through innovations resulting from a proper use of knowledge in an organization (activities such as reward systems and rankings promoting individuals who appropriately use knowledge should be reflected in the organizational culture).

Knowledge updating and verification is the next stage, after knowledge use, of the process of knowledge management, although these functions are partially fulfilled by the earlier stages. Acquisition, development, codification, storage and diffusion often lead to updating of the existing knowledge, whereas the effects of knowledge use constitute verification of the existing knowledge. Nevertheless, certain activities can be identified that directly serve knowledge updating and verification. These activities are mainly related to organizational procedures and include systematic reviews of the existing knowledge resources, employee evaluation and self-evaluation, internal and external audits, etc. Selected activities should also be reflected in meta-instruments other than procedures, with organizational culture being in this case a vehicle for only a small group of them. Undoubtedly, a system of beliefs and values of an organization should embrace evaluation and self-evaluation of the knowledge possessed by employees as well as systematicity in updating knowledge from various sources. It is also important to accept modern performance measures (adequately to the methods adopted in a given case) and link them with the existing knowledge.

Knowledge protection is a stage that can include a range of activities, which—depending on the character of the knowledge subject to protection—can be embedded more in procedures and IT systems (especially in the case of codified knowledge, e.g., "removing vulnerabilities" in IT systems) or in procedures and the vision, mission and strategy of an organization (protection of the knowledge residing in an organization's competencies). It seems, however, that activities closely connected with organizational culture (but also with the vision and leadership), namely, developing employee loyalty and identification with the organization, are key in that area. Without being supported by organizational values, most security measures of more formal character are of little use.

Cultural Value Diversity in an Organization in the Context of Changes

3

Social, demographic, economic and cultural changes that have occurred worldwide in recent years pose new challenges in the field of organizational management. The increasing globalization and integration processes have a strong influence on the conditions and effectiveness of management. The environment in which most organizations now operate is a place of interaction between people with different cultural backgrounds. This results in differing beliefs and views, work styles, ways of perceiving the reality, conflict resolution methods or preferred values in organizations. As a consequence, organizations are increasingly forced to operate in a multicultural environment, and at the same time create a single organizational culture. One of the most important forms of cultural diversity is religious diversity, which is increasing, mainly due to increasing migrations worldwide. As a result of migrations, we see different faiths in one organization.

3.1 AN ORGANIZATION'S CAPACITY FOR CHANGE

Change in an organization is a multifaceted phenomenon, as it encompasses social, organizational and technical issues. Traditionally, there are a few approaches to looking at change: result-oriented approach, which focuses on the effects of introducing changes; process-oriented approach, which refers to the occurrence of changes over time; and behavioral approach, which is concerned with changing employee attitudes and behaviors. Implementing change projects in an organization requires combining all of these approaches. It involves, among other things, breaking down the process of changes into certain stages, i.e., recognition of the need for changes, planning, implementation and control. The structuring of a change process should be governed by the expected results of the change, including the change in how an organization operates, which can be achieved by changing employee behaviors and attitudes. Change is often treated as a project that should be implemented by skillfully combining the hard and soft elements of management. However, the variety and scope of changes as well as the pace of transformations occurring in the environment make it necessary to verify the approaches to and methods of change management applied in an enterprise. The way in which changes are implemented can be a source of valuable experiences enhancing the competences of employees and the organization, but also a factor that blocks subsequent change processes. Therefore, it is necessary to expand the perspective of the phenomenon of change and include in the analyses the dynamic resource, which is an organization's capacity for change. An organization's capacity for change involves the effective management of both single change projects and changes implemented concurrently or sequentially. It applies to various types and forms of changes occurring in an organization. Rockstuhl and Ng define it as a dynamic organizational capacity that allows an enterprise to adapt its capabilities to new chances and threats, and enables it to create new capabilities. Focusing on an organization's internal potential, they distinguish the following components of capacity for change (Rockstuhl and Ng 2015, pp. 224–238):

1. *Reliable leadership*—the ability of the management to gain the trust of other employees and to show the organizational members how to achieve common goals
2. *Trust of the followers*—employees' capability of constructive opposition, and following a new path recommended by the leaders
3. *Talented masters*—an organization's ability to attract, retain and empower change leaders
4. *Involvement of mid-level managers*—the ability of mid-level managers to create a bridge between the top management and the other employees
5. *Innovative culture*—an organization's ability to establish the norms of innovativeness and encourage innovative activities
6. *Culture of responsibility*—an organization's ability to carefully manage resources and complete tasks on time
7. *Effective communication*—an organization's capability of vertical and horizontal communication as well as communication with the customer
8. *Mindset*—an organization's ability to focus on the causes of phenomena and achieved results, and to recognize such relationships inside and outside of the organization

According to Ashikali and Groeneveld, change can take place through adaptation, which involves adapting to the changes occurring in the environment, and through proactive actions connected with strategic choices and the impact of an organization on the environment in which it operates (Ashikali and Groeneveld 2015, pp. 146–168). They believe that focusing merely on an organization's internal potential is insufficient. Instead, they propose that the analysis of an organization's capacity for change includes contextual factors (organizational conditions), process-related factors (connected with how change progresses) and structural factors (related to the process of learning and knowledge transfer).

An organization's capacity for change in this sense points to three crucial areas that impact one another. The first can be referred to as infrastructure for changes (contextual factors) and is based on the values, the way of communicating in an organization, joint problem-solving, etc. This infrastructure, on the one hand, impacts the process of changes, and on the other, it evolves as a result of implementing new solutions in an organization or improving the existing ones, which is possible thanks to the ongoing processes of learning and knowledge transfer.

Thus, a challenge is to look at the implementation of changes in an organization from the perspective of its dynamic resource, i.e., capacity for change, which involves solving many dilemmas connected with the moment of introducing changes, their pace and the proportion of time and effort devoted to planning and later implementation. Moreover, change in an organization loses its character of a single phenomenon, as many change projects that impact one another are initiated simultaneously. Thus, another challenge for managers is to appropriately manage the stream of changes so that the ongoing process of changes does not become a barrier to future change projects, but is a factor that increases an organization's capacity for change.

Change can be approached in different ways. Although there are many distinct methods, each of them can be classified into one of three categories or change faces: turnaround, tools and techniques, and transformation. Turnaround can involve both acquiring additional assets and reducing the existing ones in order to improve short-term financial results of an organization. The second face of changes is tools and techniques. The third face, called transformation, refers to employee behaviors and interactions. Thus, transformation is understood as change of behavior that enables the development of competences.

According to Elsner, it is important to distinguish between change management and transformation management, because the causes of the problems with change implementation are not so many changes as transformations (Elsner 2018, pp. 73–82). Change has a situational character, whereas transformation a psychological one. Situational change refers to what is new, whereas psychological transformation requires rejection of the previous organizational reality and identity. If the effects of this process are not taken into account, no real changes can take place in an organization. According to Elsner, the aim of change management is to understand the desired result and how it should be achieved, whereas transformation management involves the elimination of the existing operation and behavior patterns (Elsner 2018, pp. 73–82).

Transformation begins with a certain end, and ends with a new beginning. In a model, three phases of "going through change" are distinguished (Figure 3.1).

In the first phase, organizational members give up the previous identity and ways of acting, i.e., leaving behind the so-called comfort zone (let go of the past and accept the losses incurred). The second phase is a transitional phase—"the old" no longer exists, while "the new" is not fully functioning yet. It is a time when patterns are established anew, and critical changes and psychological reorientation occur within people. In the third phase, change participants receive a new identity, experience a new energy and regain a sense of meaningfulness in their work. The transformation phases are

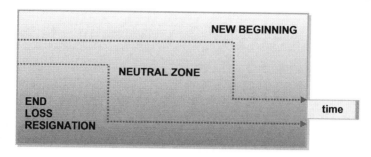

FIGURE 3.1 Three phases of the process of transformation. (Own work based on: Kirch J., Interkulturell besetzte Teams in der Pflege–eine konflikttheoretische Analyse, [in:] *Digitale Transformation von Dienstleistungen im Gesundheitswesen III*, Springer Gabler, Wiesbaden, 2017, pp. 187–199.)

not separate stages with clear-cut boundaries. Each of these processes starts before the previous process comes to an end. Therefore, it is possible to be in more than one phase at the same time. This is because the process of transformation is about changing the dominance of one phase over the others rather than a complete transition from one phase to another (Kirch 2017, pp. 187–199).

The need for transformation management is particularly important under the conditions of continuous change, characterized by a multitude of successive or simultaneous mutually conditioning changes. The condition of embracing continuous change is awareness that the aim of changes is to protect what is unchangeable. This is because for an organization to continue operating and develop, it has to make changes (Kirch 2017, pp. 187–199).

Introduction of changes in an organization provokes various reactions. These reactions are usually ambivalent. On the one hand, change gives a promise of achieving certain benefits, improvements, breaking the routine, developing competences, fulfilling professional ambitions, etc. On the other hand, however, it involves resignation from the established ways of acting and the sense of security that comes from repeatability, predictability and established relations. Therefore, it is a source of anxiety, concern, fears and negative emotions. During their research, Klaus and Schneider identified a mechanism they called competing commitment mechanism. The effect of competing commitment is a dynamic equilibrium. Klaus and Schneider developed a three-stage process that can be used in an organization to identify the mechanism of competing commitment, to explore the reasons behind certain ineffective behaviors and to change them (Klaus and Schneider 2016, pp. 185–207).

The phenomenon of competing commitment refers, among other things, to participants of an organization who openly declare their support for changes and in the initial phase are actively engaged in the process of changes. However, we can also observe behaviors in the organization that are a manifestation of passive resistance of its members. This resistance is hidden and involves refraining from taking actions that could contribute to the completion of a project, as well as avoiding speaking up when significant problems are noticed in the functioning of the organization, or when chances or threats are perceived in the environment. Such behavior can bring about negative consequences for the organization in the form of organizational spiral of silence. The causes of this phenomenon are believed to be social and organizational factors, such as conformism, diffusion of responsibility or organizational culture based on confrontation avoidance (Gümüsa 2019, pp. 93–104).

There is a variety of reasons behind the resistance of organizational participants to change. Therefore, a modern organization should look beyond stereotypical reasons for resistance and include into the process of transformation and change management the knowledge about the psychological mechanisms behind behaviors during the process of change. This will allow it to predict difficulties in the process of change and take preemptive steps in order to break the barriers within organizational members, thus enabling their personal development.

The changeability of the conditions under which an organization operates makes it necessary for its members to assume new organizational roles, and thus face new tasks and greater responsibility. The ability of taking on new organizational roles is connected with the level of the self-awareness of own needs, values and motivations and with emotional literacy. This self-knowledge, awareness of the mechanisms behind one's conduct, can be a source of change of the behaviors and attitudes that are no longer adequate to the changing conditions of the functioning. Another tool that can be used in the process of change and transformation management in an organization is the concept of Graves' value levels/systems (Van Marrewijk and Werre 2003, pp. 107–119).

This concept assumes the development of the self-awareness of a human being and humanity as a collectivity, which is also manifested in organizational culture management. At each of the levels (see Table 3.2), which also represent a certain system of values and needs, an individual manifests behaviors, motivations, emotions and ways of adaptation that are specific to that level. The system of values determines what organizational members who are guided by that system consider important or less important. Thus, each of the systems is a response to the external environment, the threats coming from it as well as the chances and changes in that environment. An individual has all of the levels of awareness active, but to varying degrees. Low activity of a given level allows an individual to make use of associated characteristics and potential to a small extent, whereas high activity does so intensively. Awareness of the activity of the different levels, identification of the group of dominant values and development of these levels enable improvement of work effectiveness and internal balance (Becker and Pastoors 2018, pp. 43–49).

The concept of Graves' value levels can be used in the process of introducing changes in an organization. It gives space for understanding the behavior of people and teams in an organization. Organizational members are located at different levels of awareness, which determine their needs, motivations, actions, engagement, etc. This should be taken into account when communicating the need for change, its objectives and proposed solutions.

Thus, another challenge for a modern organization is to understand which value systems are followed by its organizational members, and to skillfully use this knowledge in the process of transformation and change. This style of management requires from an organization a high level of awareness and readiness to (Krell, Ortlieb and Sieben 2018):

- Ask questions to encourage creative thinking, assumption of responsibility for tasks
- Identify values, needs and motivations
- Support the discovery of potential
- Tap the potential of organizational members in task execution
- Build work climate that encourages members to share their experiences, develop, get to know oneself and take care of their needs and values

Using the concept of Graves' value levels, it is possible to build awareness of values and how these values impact the functioning of an organization.

The implementation of changes in today's organizations involves resolving multiple dilemmas and managing not so much single change projects as streams of changes. This also requires taking a different perspective in perceiving and understanding changes and including in the analyses the dynamic resource of an organization, i.e., its capacity for change. Thus, a challenge is to flexibly navigate the space of changes and build organizational potential for changeability by combining factual knowledge, which enables the transformation of changes into a project as part of a larger program or enterprise, and the courage to draw on and use in practice the psychological knowledge about the mechanisms behind changes and behavior of organizational members in the process of implementing changes.

With reference to the above, it should be stressed that culture as an attribute of humans and the societies they create, just like change, are not homogeneous. It is not a single view or assumption, but a collection of interrelated views and assumptions. The cultural differences between the environments where organizations operate suggest that such differences occur even in organizations that are homogeneous in terms of management but decentralized territorially. Thus, organizations are affected by larger cultural systems. The differences in mindsets can be explained by means of four parameters (Sackmann 2017b, pp. 169–206):

1. *Power distance*—the degree to which members of a nation are ready to accept uneven distribution of power, goods and prestige.
2. *Uncertainty avoidance*—the way of coping with uncertainty learned by individual societies, e.g., constructing legal systems to protect property, freedom, and reputation.
3. *Individualism*—reflects the extent to which an individual belonging to a certain group is expected to act independently from the other members of the society. In some cultures, individualism is perceived as a source of happiness (e.g., America), while in others, it is regarded as something undesirable and alienating (e.g., in China, Italy or Mexico).
4. *Masculinity*—reflects the degree to which the roles of men have been separated from those of women in a society. In cultures characterized by a high degree of masculinity, men are expected to be more confident than women, and women to be more caring. The main focus is on professional career, salary and prestige.

Formal rules dictating how to behave do not have to exist—organizational members learn to comply with unwritten rules so quickly that certain behavior patterns become common in the organization, and can even distinguish it from other organizations, giving it a clear identity and specific character.

The culture process and the issues of change underline successive and causally related human activities and phenomena. They highlight the dynamic aspect of culture, i.e., changes, development and how its goods are used. This is mainly about the role of tradition in the development of culture and changes—progress, revolutions, crises, integration, acculturation, diffusion, propagation of culture and participation in it, issues of democratization and vanguardism (Sackmann 2017a, pp. 375–385).

Participation in culture is an all-important process, as people have an active attitude to cultural goods, use and contribute to them. Participation in culture has a large impact on working life and leisure time activities. Above all, it facilitates the comprehensive development of personality and establishment of core values in the life of a human being, and teaches how to live a life.

It can thus be said that organizational culture (Achouri 2015, pp. 217–260):

1. Extends our knowledge about the world and makes it easier to understand another human being
2. Intensifies personal experiences through contact with various cultural contents, especially art
3. Provides varied material to build own system of values
4. Creates a common ground for people from different cultures, thus contributing to the establishment of bonds between individuals and groups

Changing organizational culture, especially at the level of values and assumptions, is very difficult, but it is often a necessary condition for increasing organizational efficiency or successfully implementing required changes, e.g., restructuring of an organization. The principles that are worth following when attempting to change cultural patterns include (Wiedmann 2016, pp. 153–184):

- Understanding the old culture before you start to implement a new one
- Supporting the people interested in changes who are ready to be committed to them
- Making the most effective subculture a role model
- Avoiding directly attacking the old patterns, and instead, helping the people to develop new ones
- Treating the vision of the new culture as a principle of implementing changes rather than a panacea
- Accepting the fact that cultural changes are usually a long-term process
- Implementing the elements of a new culture instead of just talking about them

The condition for employing the methods of organizational management that are adequate to new situations is fundamental cultural change, which involves a shift from an organizational culture that promotes uncertainty avoidance to a culture that facilitates high tolerance of uncertainty. An organization can be expected to be able to cope with uncertainty and not treat it as something highly stressful or paralyzing its activities. It is claimed that cultural stereotypes can be a significant obstacle in implementing desirable changes. It is important to make sure that the shift in culture towards high tolerance of uncertainty does not result in new stereotypes established in place of the old ones, but in a critical approach to stereotypes generally. Organizational culture, even one undergoing change and transformation, should constitute a relatively stable anchor for an organization defining the area and style of its functioning (Bruhn, Meffert, and Hadwich 2019, pp. 945–1016).

The processes of organizational culture formation take place through acceptance of solutions that allow the organization to better cope with difficulties. When the proposed solutions are effective, the group consciously accepts the values related to them. Perceived successes determine acceptance and assimilation of the successful elements of culture. Over time, such values are accepted as natural and gradually removed from the consciousness. They become well rooted in the subconscious of the organizational members. Thus, the elements of culture that have been confirmed by experience achieve the status of its real components. This is experience gained during group problem-solving.

3.2 DIVERSITY OF CULTURAL VALUES IN ORGANIZATIONS IN THE CONTEXT OF CHANGES

The diversity of preferred social, economic and political values definitely has implications for management, in both homogeneous and heterogeneous environments. Cultural diversity, which also determines organizational culture in organizations, focuses around economic issues, such as the attitude to wealth and the approach to entrepreneurship, profit or unemployment, analyzed from the perspective of religion. Preferred social, economic and political values espoused by the followers of different religions are also very important. Therefore, it is necessary to create a concept of cultural diversity management in organizations that allows them to maximize the benefits of diversity and minimize the burdens. The idea of diversity management is, as it were, a response to the requirements of the environment, when organizations operate in a global environment. Cultural diversity is a double-edged weapon for an organization, as it can help it to gain a competitive edge, but it can also be a factor leading to numerous failures. It can be a precious resource contributing to an organization's success, and at the same time a source of many conflicts, caused, among other things, by misunderstandings during contacts between members of differing groups.

Religions, which are carriers of certain values, have shaped the culture of societies also in economic terms. The great monotheistic religions have had and are still having a significant impact on the attitude to economic activity and business ethics—through cultural influences and traditions, including among nonbelievers. In every religious tradition, there are preferences of certain values, norms and views, which determine human attitudes and behaviors. Followers of different religions bring them to the organizations in which they work. Religious norms in business resemble archetypes: They are passed down from generation to generation within the circles of the followers of different religions and end up in the collective consciousness, becoming its hidden element that determines the shape of the economic life.

Values are the central point of every organizational culture. As such, they are crucial for managers. The type and version of the religion adopted in a given country is a result of cultural patterns previously existing in a given territory as well as a culture-forming factor. The impact of religion on the process of the functioning of an organization is considered to be very significant, because work and religion, as well as the relations between them, are a fundamental component, a building block of human society (Franken 2019a, pp. 273–309). Research conducted so far (Von Au 2017) confirmed the relationship between religion and attitudes to an organization, and also found a relationship between religion and motivation, satisfaction and even the degree of commitment. In the social life, the role of religion is expressed in showing the followers a range of values that should guide their life, but this system of values also applies to organizational culture. Many business practitioners see the necessity of understanding the role of religion, as it has a strong impact on organizational life. The role of religion is acknowledged not only by practitioners, but also by theoreticians of management, who regard it as the second most important, after nationality, variable of the cultural dimension of individualism (Benhabib 2015, pp. 32–48). Nationality alone is insufficient in explaining all the differences in a multinational organization. Therefore, organizational management has to take into account values. The appropriate method of management would be here cultural diversity management. Cultural diversity management is based on the assumption that in most organizations, there are many different environments and cultural factors that are significant for an organization, and organizational members with different backgrounds can successfully cooperate for the benefit of the whole organization. The ability to manage cultural diversity is particularly important when a decision has been made to merge organizations, as the capability of solving problems related to cultural diversity is crucial in such a case. However, managing an organization culturally, in particular a multinational organization, requires the ability to make difficult strategic choices, efficient planning of structural changes and often the development of a new HR (human resources) policy and constant monitoring of organizational culture. Cultural diversity management is preceded by two steps. The sequence of this process is as follows (Franken 2019b, pp. 191–234):

1. *Acknowledgment of diversity*—a human being has to be exposed to it, experience it, gain knowledge about it and understand it better.
2. *Assigning value to diversity*—this refers to the importance and significance given to diversity. This appreciation and respect of differences can lead to *diversity management*, which involves planning, organization and leading of organizational members with different cultural backgrounds so that they can fully contribute to the achievement of the organization's goals.

Rather than being reactive and passively waiting for a crisis caused by diversity, organizations should introduce changes that will lead to approval of diversity and its active, anticipatory management. Diversity management guarantees the organization numerous benefits such as reaching new, varied market segments, or increasing creativity and innovativeness by creating teams composed of members with different experiences and patterns of perceiving the world. On the other hand, ignoring diversity in an organization prevents effective communication and can lead to conflicts, which will take time and effort to solve as well as putting an additional burden on the organization.

The basic aim of cultural diversity management should be to create such a work environment in which every organizational member, no matter how different he/she is, will be appreciated and respected and will be provided with the right conditions to fully use his/her potential (Eberhardt and Streuli 2016, pp. 7–25). Achieving this aim is a long-term, complex and relatively difficult process, but at the same time, it is a recognized imperative of modern management of organizational culture in the business world.

In today's world, many organizations devote a lot of time to the development and improvement of the qualifications of their members. This takes place as part of the process of human resources management (HRM), which is defined as a strategic, unified and consistent method of managing the most precious capital of every organization, i.e., its people.

HRM is a process that is carried out under certain conditions. This process, in turn, involves many aspects that impact not only specific tasks and processes, but also techniques. These aspects can be divided into those within the organization (microenvironment) and those outside of it (macroenvironment) (Gutting 2017, pp. 143–157).

Of the factors mentioned in Figure 3.2, the greatest differences and similarities can be observed with respect to the internal aspects of the functioning of an organization.

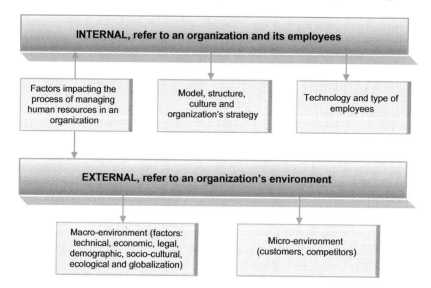

FIGURE 3.2   Factors impacting the process of managing human resources in an organization. (Own work based on: Eberhardt D., Majkovic A.L., Zukunft der Führung: Veränderung in Sicht oder bleibt alles beim Alten? [in:] *Die Zukunft der Führung*, Springer, Wiesbaden, 2015, pp. 87–100.)

Among them, the following are key: the aspect of an organization's strategy (with a special focus on the approach to managing international personnel), the aspect of an organization's model, the aspect of organizational culture and the aspect of technology. With regard to the aspect of technology, which encompasses organizational processes, of key importance are the issues connected with the motivation system and training courses.

According to Schröer, intercultural competences refer to knowledge about a given culture and cultural differences, interest in other cultures, as well as the communication process within the team around common goals and creation of common values (Schröer 2018, pp. 773–785). Intercultural competences serve effective cooperation with other cultures. According to Ebert's and Pastoors's model, these competences include individual, social, professional and strategic factors as well as those pertaining to international cooperation, such as the knowledge of the language, tolerance of uncertainty, polycentrism and readiness for multicultural learning (Ebert and Pastoors 2018, pp. 211–218). According to S. Magalia, multicultural competences should be perceived as metacompetencies, as they are a component of many characteristics, knowledge factors, experiences and skills that determine operation under the conditions of cultural diversity (Hermann and Erten 2018, pp. 157–177). Thus, intercultural competences refer to an individual's ability to effectively use his/her knowledge, skills and personality traits to work with people from different cultural backgrounds.

When defining the concept of intercultural competences, it should be noted that in the literature, they are presented as a sum of knowledge, skills and attitudes that enables an individual to understand representatives of cultures other than their own and to be understood by the representatives of such cultures. Intercultural competences include, among other things, the following factors (Krell, Ortlieb and Sieben 2018, pp. 71–86):

- The ability to perceive culturally different patterns as distinct from those of own culture without evaluating them in a positive or negative way
- The ability to identify own cultural standards and assess their effects during interaction with a different culture
- Awareness of the impact of culture on the human behavior
- Development of own patterns of cultural behavior through
- The ability to make rational cultural choices in specific situations
- The ability to adopt selected norms from other cultures
- The ability to use cultural rules in a flexible way
- Forming positive relations with people from a variety of cultural backgrounds and the ability to cope with conflict situations in a multicultural team

The study of the process of acquiring intercultural competences requires taking into account a number of factors that can impact them and lead to certain changes. These are both individual-dependent factors (motivator factors, personality traits, emotions and personal experiences) and individual-independent factors (conditions of the context, group stereotypes). Achievement of intercultural competences should be perceived as a process, with the starting element being attitudes towards other culture. It is only based on this element that the other components of these competences are developed: knowledge and skills that can be absorbed and effectively used in a situation of intercultural contact.

An enterprise's intercultural competences are created based on the competences of individual, culturally diverse employees, although they are not a simple sum of them. They are part of all of the organizational processes and impact the structure of the organization, constituting conceptualization of a new class of the resources of the organization. In many studies on this subject, intercultural competences represent a combination of knowledge and skills, which reflect both the wealth of basic knowledge and the skills required to take the necessary actions. Competences are based on the knowledge embedded in the skill sets of individual employees and at the disposal of individual companies. Since competences encompass three areas—knowledge, attitudes and values, and skills—intercultural competences are built at three levels. The first, cognitive, level is characterized by the knowledge of all of the organizational members regarding universal cultural issues such as cultural shock factors, culture models and culture dimensions and differences between the different cultures. At this level, of importance are such aspects as espoused values, respected norms and behavior patterns. The second, affective, level refers to organizational members' attitudes connected with emotions in intercultural contacts and the abilities to cope with own emotions. The third level is the level of specific skills expressed in specific activities undertaken by organizational members.

According to Lang and Baldauf, a model of intercultural competences should include knowledge (about the traditions, behaviors and customs), motivation (willingness to cooperate with other cultures) and skills (adaptation, empathy) (Lang and Baldauf 2016a, pp. 1–38). Fajen, in turn, defines intercultural competence as the ability to act effectively under the conditions of a different culture, in which an important role is played by cultural empathy, adaptability, knowledge of languages and kind attitude to other cultures (Fajen 2018, pp. 47–59). The author too indicates three dimensions of intercultural competence: emotions (attitude), cognition (knowledge) and skills (acting). It is important to be able to appreciate the value of other cultures and act effectively in cooperation with people from other cultures.

Based on the available literature, a model of intercultural competences consisting of seven competences can be built, namely, openness to otherness, the ability to manage emotions, intercultural communication competences, coping well with uncertain situations, cultural understanding, the ability to acquire and process information and the ability to solve conflicts, as shown in Figure 3.3.

In this context, it is worth pointing out that globalization, the changeability of the conditions under which an organization operates in its environment, increased competitiveness, disappearance of divisions and blurring of boundaries between different cultures as well as convergence—becoming similar, mainly with regard to "the hard elements of management," i.e., strategies, structures, procedures, and education standards—facilitate closer international cooperation. However, for such cooperation to be possible, it is necessary to create the right conditions for people from different cultures to understand and come close to each other. It should be mentioned that in the sphere of "the soft management tools," which encompass organizational culture, leadership style and decision-making process, i.e., where a human being plays the leading role, divergent processes dominate. Divergence also refers to the sphere of attitudes and motivations of a human being, how he/she perceives the world and himself/herself. However, despite cultural diffusion, national management styles seem qualitatively distinct. Due to

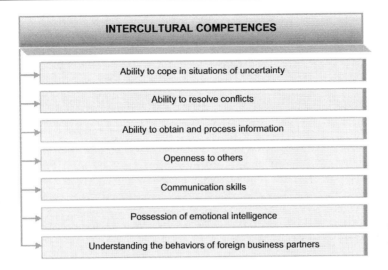

FIGURE 3.3   Model of intercultural competences. (Own work based on: Barmeyer Ch., Eberhardt J., Interkulturelle Kompetenz von Drittkultur-Managern in Schnittstellenpositionen multinationaler Unternehmen. *Interculture Journal: Online Zeitschrift für interkulturelle Studien*, 2019, 18.31: 31–52.)

cultural diversity, which results from the fact that individual organizational members see and understand the world and various situations differently and behave differently, a team functions under more difficult conditions. It is hard not to notice that the development of modern technologies and globalization trends, although they enable integration, often create a barrier separating people from one another and may lead to numerous cultural misunderstandings and conflicts. Many barriers and misunderstandings arise between cooperating people from different cultures, and the differences between them become more pronounced. In every culture, there are various institutions through which people pursue different interests, various customs that fulfill their inspirations, various legal and moral codes that reward virtues and punish shortcomings (Herzfeldt and Sackmann 2019, pp. 353–369).

Given that the survival of an organization depends not only on its ability to adapt and appropriately respond to the changes in the environment in which it operates, but also on people, their engagement in teamwork and better communication, it is obvious that organizations seek to increase harmony in the relationships between their members, especially that human resources are increasingly treated as a key determinant of an organization's success (Genkova 2019, pp. 351–364).

The internationalization of economic activity became one of the most important phenomena of the second half of the 20th century, although it should be mentioned that traces of cooperation between people from very distant areas can be found in many early civilizations. Cooperation networks, strategic alliances and employing people from other countries give international organizations an easier access to materials, technology, capital and workforce. Internationally oriented organizations can effectively tap the potential of the individuals comprising them. A good knowledge of national specificities of management can facilitate a better understanding, establishment of contacts and cooperation as well as effective competition. What is more, jointly developed technological and organizational solutions can much better cater to the specific needs of the local markets. However, many organizations have difficulty in coping with multiculturalism, which refers to any events and cultural differences where a multitude of senses and values emerge, where culture participants are driven by different customs and religions, or—more broadly—ideologies—when interacting with one another. The problems mainly result from the mismatch between management styles and management systems, lack of coordination and integration, technological changes, language problems and lack of deeper understanding of the reasons why people with different cultural backgrounds behave the way they do. Working together in one organization is not the same as concluding a transaction, in which one party is the purchaser and the other is the seller. The problems may exist because organizations operating internationally on a large scale lack departments responsible for intercultural management. However, the management in organizations are increasingly aware that the future belongs to organizations that know that appreciating human diversity and managing cultural diversity mean the highest level of management, and to the organizations that are able to create a vision of how to put that into practice (Muche 2020, pp. 25–37).

The perspective of multiculturalism better expresses and highlights the transcultural character of the processes of mutual learning and expanding the repertoire of own cultural standards and values by values of other groups in ways other than enforcement or assimilation. In order to ensure and maintain balance and harmony in an organization, an appropriate organizational culture is needed. The classic organizational culture is based on a single cultural system. However, the organizational culture of international organizations should take into account the values and norms of all of its members, regardless of their cultural background. By introducing the concept of a dialog as the principle underlying the functioning of organizational culture, it is possible to step outside of the framework of communication within one culture, which is necessary for mutual understanding, confrontation and cooperation. Focusing on the issue of a dialog in a culturally diverse organization, it can be noted that communication is the most important tool for executing tasks, as well as a condition for understanding and strengthening competences and good relationships between organizational members.

3.3 IMPACT OF CULTURAL DIFFERENCES ON THE DEVELOPMENT OF ORGANIZATIONS

The subject of culture at the macro level which addresses intercultural aspects is very broad in scope and impossible to analyze or assess as a whole. In the literature, there are many attempts to classify these issues. Such approaches differ in the number of the cultures they examine, the way they handle similarities and differences, and adopted methodology. Generally, we can distinguish two solutions in the application of the phenomenon of culture and its consequences for the study of organizations and management. The first (divergent or situational) is often referred to as dissimilarity orientation. The second approach (convergent) claims that no matter where organizations are located, there is one good way of managing them using structure and technology—in this pragmatic approach, culture does not play an important role.

D. Cray and G. Mallory develop a classification of cultural studies and propose categorization focused on the relationship between work and its underlying theory. They distinguish the following three approaches (Hermann and Erten 2018, pp. 157–177):

1. *Naive comparisons*—where culture is treated as the basic explanatory variable. It is perceived as the cause of the observed differences. However, culture is more often described than analyzed. The term "naive" refers to the lack of full explanation or clarity offered by the theory rather than the evaluation of the approach as of little value, as some of the studies from this category are very sophisticated, in both methodological and substantive terms.

2. *Culture-independent approach*—based on the contingency theory, which enables a comparison of various types of organizations across many structural dimensions. After comparing organizations in a given society, the next natural step was to compare societies. The proponents of the culture-independent approach think that the basic tasks of an organization are the same everywhere in the world. Under the same conditions, the structure of an organization—the fundamental patterns of control, communication or coordination—does not differ regardless of the location. In this approach, the key issue is structural similarities and relationships between structural variables.

3. *Culture-oriented approach*—whereas the previous approach focuses mainly on what is common for the countries, this one concentrates mainly on the differences between cultures. Another difference is that the culture-independent approach is based on single theories and a limited number of concepts, whereas the culture-oriented approach is based on numerous theoretical foundations, particularly from the fields of psychology and sociology. In this approach, like in the approach of naive comparisons, culture is treated as the key explanatory variable. In practice, of the three above-mentioned approaches, this approach seems to be the most important, as it treats culture as one of the determinants impacting behavior.

These approaches, though very significant in conceptual terms, can be problematic in terms of differentiation in practice. The authors also indicate the fourth approach—international management, which mainly focuses on effective management of international functions that have to be executed in different cultures.

The increasing globalization and integration that have been observed over recent years make it necessary to take a new look at the essence and role of organizational culture. Based on the review of the literature on intercultural management, Münzberg et al., point to the following three key research streams rooted in different conceptualizations of culture (2018, pp. 65–79).

a. Studies focused on international comparisons

The interest in international cross-cultural management first began in the United States in the 1950s and 1960s, and the intellectual foundation was concentration on the main research stream of international comparisons and on understanding culture as a national independent variable, which was driven by the need for deeper understanding of the national context and its impact on organizational management.

G. Hofstede wrote that "management is American invention." With increasing scientific interest, "nation-state" was adopted as a logical unit of analysis, as ersatz culture. Since nationality was regarded as a given, only and permanent characteristic of an individual, cultural identity was treated in the same way (Hofstede 2003, pp. 17–27).

The original aim of cross-cultural studies was to better understand the principles underlying the functioning of organizations in a given country. Attempts were also made to identify the specificity of a given country, and these studies can be regarded as the first cross-cultural studies conducted on such a wide scale. The conclusions concerning the issues of culture that were formulated can be presented as follows (Hofstede 2013, pp. 63–79):

- Cultural boundaries overlap with national borders.
- National, and then cultural, identity is a given, only and permanent characteristic of an individual.
- Managers' attitudes, not culture, is the dependent variable, as culture is not defined a priori.
- Culture is an independent variable.
- If significant differences were identified between nations keeping the other factors constant, these differences could be explained as cultural, although they are not clearly measured.

Thus, with the development of science, culture started to be treated as one of many independent variables.

b. Studies concerning intercultural interactions (impacts)

According to the representatives of this approach, most managerial actions concern interactions rather than comparisons. This view is represented, among others, by Buche, Jungbauer-Gans, Niebuhr and Peters (Buche et al. 2013, pp. 483–501), who mainly point out the increasing importance of these issues in the globalized business environment. The subject of the studies was interactions between people of different nationalities in the context of an organization, in particular the impact of national culture on the organization and its members.

c. Multiple cultures

The latest approach is based on taking into account the changes occurring in the environment in terms of the globalization of the economic activity, where we see a diverse workforce in terms of interests, education, nationality and experiences. Since culture is not an isolated phenomenon, it is worth analyzing its complexity more deeply. The theoretical implication is defining culture as a collective social phenomenon, which is not inherited but created jointly by members of a group (Steinle 2019, pp. 112–115).

This means that the character of culture is cognitive rather than symbolic or material. This definition also indicates that culture may exist or emerge every time a set of basic assumptions is shared by a group of people.

Therefore, the researchers representing this research stream were mainly interested in identifying these assumptions and defining groups. Apart from that, this definition stressed the individual nature of culture, as the carriers of culture are individuals, who at the same time belong to different groups. Of the above-listed approaches, the multiple cultures approach deserves special attention, as its contributions include the following (Weber, Kabst and Baum 2018, pp. 433–464):

- Indicating subcultures existing at different levels: suborganizational, organizational and national
- Raising awareness of the complexity of the phenomenon of culture and proposing how to use such knowledge

One important conclusion can be drawn. The aim of dealing with cross-cultural issues is not only to seek the bridges connecting national cultures, but also to draw on similarities to find common solutions. At the same time, despite numerous discussions, it is worth stressing the applicability of cross-cultural studies.

Continuing the above line of thinking, it is worth noting that cultural differences impact an organization's success on the domestic and international markets. Since the second half of the 20th century, we have been observing gradual internationalization of organizations. Over the years, this phenomenon has become increasingly important. Today, it would be difficult to imagine a world where large organizations only operate on one market. Growth on international markets is a huge chance for many organizations, but also a difficult process impacted by many factors. Companies employ various strategies—some are more formal, while others more flexible. An important factor for an organization's growth in the international markets is, apart from financial, technical or location factors, the culture of the country to which the organization plans to expand. That is why the role of culture is also important in the local and regional development.

After the end of the Second World War, a crisis ensued, and the main aim was to rebuild the economies of the countries. It took some time before the countries started to focus on the development rather than survival. In the post-war period, the emergence of trade promotion organizations facilitated internationalization, and the development of communication and transportation stimulated economic growth in the international markets. Towards the end of the 20th century, the world opened up to the development of business. And this continues to this day. Large organizations seek new markets beyond their home country, whereas local markets want to attract foreign investors. Today, successful introduction of a product to a new market is no longer simple—it is not sufficient to have a competitive product. It is also necessary to have a strategy that will allow the product to be launched in a new region despite numerous variables that make this process difficult, and the management have to be aware of cultural differences and know how to handle conflicts that may arise in that area.

However, before a strategy is developed, it is necessary to think about the philosophy that the company will follow. According to Sparrow and Hiltrop, a global strategy is "a business philosophy or mindset" (Sparrow and Hiltrop 1997, pp. 201–219). Thus, it is important to look at an organization's philosophy and see to what extent it is prepared to become a global company. ERPG model is one of philosophy categorization frameworks. It distinguishes four categories (Agrawal and Patgaonkar 2010, pp. 17–22):

1. *Ethnocentric philosophy*—there is preference of one's own country based on the conviction that the domestic industry is better. Foreign markets are perceived as worse than the domestic market. The adopted strategy will be the same as the strategy applied on the internal market; the same range of products will be offered.
2. *Polycentric philosophy*—it is oriented towards the host market (foreign market), but stresses adaptation to the local conditions in other places. The strategy of multiple internal markets that fully adapt to the requirements of the national markets will be implemented.
3. *Regiocentric philosophy*—it stresses orientation towards regional groups of countries, such as Europe, Northern America or the Far East. The strategy will be coordinated regionally, but not globally.
4. *Geocentric philosophy*—it assumes a global approach to business. A global strategy is developed, which is not determined by home country or host country factors.

The role of the management is to choose the company's philosophy and define the scope in which this philosophy will be adapted to carry out the process of internationalizing the company.

The role of culture in international negotiations or when a company enters a new market is often underestimated. It seems that in a globalized world, a company's global strategy and success on one market would be a sufficient factor to succeed in the international market. It turns out that the knowledge of the other country's culture has a large impact on the success of a business transaction. In recent years, researchers have been studying the similarities and differences between different cultures and their impact on human relations. The knowledge of a foreign language turns out to be an insufficient skill to feel comfortable in the foreign culture. Arnold developed culture models, which are described further in the text. Cultural differences are not only about choosing the right words, but also about choosing the body language (Table 3.1).

Learning about cultural differences enables understanding the reasons why the negotiations failed. Four culture groups are distinguished: deal-focused cultures versus relationship-focused cultures, formal cultures versus informal cultures, monochrome cultures versus polychrome cultures and expressive cultures versus reserved cultures (Arnold 2018, pp. 305–329). In the international business, two rules are generally applied: The seller conforms to the buyer, and the foreigner follows the local customs. In order to comply with these rules, it is necessary to learn about the cultural models of the potential trade partners.

For a relationship-focused culture, it is important to establish relationship with the business partner. An intermediary who knows both the parties, e.g., an embassy or trade organization, can be helpful. Fairs and exhibitions will also work. In the deal-focused culture, trade partners meet during formal meetings, at which they discuss prices, dates, quantities, etc. It is also an occasion to form an opinion about the other party. For people from relationship-focused cultures, this way of establishing

TABLE 3.1 Relationship-focused and deal-focused cultures

RELATIONSHIP-FOCUSED CULTURE	DEAL-FOCUSED CULTURE
Focus on the people with whom one cooperates—good relations Personal contact network—indirect contact Time and patience—trust needs to be won Maintaining personal ties with the trade partner Open, honest and direct communication	People are focused on task execution Are open to cooperation with foreigners—direct contact Ambiguous and vague communication
Arab world, most countries in Africa, Latin America, Asia	Northern part of Europe, North America, Australia and New Zealand

Source: Own work based on: Wagner A.S, Lose Zugehörigkeiten von globalen Identitäten (Glopats) in internationalen Unternehmen–Konflikte zwischen Nationalkulturen und Hyperkultur. *Gruppe. Interaktion. Organisation. Zeitschrift für Angewandte Organisationspsychologie (GIO)*, 2018, 49.4: 379–390.

cooperation is unacceptable—they first arrange a few social meetings with potential trade partners and engage in small talk to win their trust and only then arrange meetings to discuss business. For the deal-focused culture, a contract is binding and discussed item by item during a meeting with lawyers of both the parties present. People from the relationship-focused culture only call their lawyer during a break in the meeting, and renegotiation of a contract does not mean verification of the written provisions—it is necessary to meet with the other party to discuss the changes. The verification of contract provisions is considered to be an irresponsible behavior. Another difference is in communication style—in the deal-focused culture, one speaks what one thinks and one thinks what one speaks. People from the relationship-focused culture seek harmony and friendly relations; therefore, they don't directly say what they want, they don't use the word "no," and instead, they will say "it's difficult," "maybe" or "I will think about it" (Table 3.2).

The representatives of the formal culture may feel offended if their trade partners show too much familiarity. On the other hand, members of the informal culture may feel uncomfortable and think that the other party is condescending. In the formal culture,

TABLE 3.2 Formal and informal cultures

FORMAL CULTURE	INFORMAL CULTURE
Is based on hierarchy, differences in social status and power between people	Supporting egalitarian organizations where smaller differences in social status and power exist Equality in social status
Using complimentary closes	Direct expressions
Most countries of Europe and Asia, Mediterranean countries and Arab world, Latin American countries	The United States, Australia, New Zealand, Denmark, Norway, Island

Source: Own work based on: Wagner A.S., Lose Zugehörigkeiten von globalen Identitäten (Glopats) in internationalen Unternehmen–Konflikte zwischen Nationalkulturen und Hyperkultur. *Gruppe. Interaktion. Organisation. Zeitschrift für Angewandte Organisationspsychologie (GIO)*, 2018, 49.4: 379–390.

hierarchy is closely connected with showing respect. A representative of the formal culture may even break negotiations, if the party representing the informal culture does not make sure that high-ranking employees are present throughout the negotiations, which is perceived as a sign of respect for the other party. Therefore, to avoid mistakes, one should be extremely formal. In international relations, it is recommended to use complimentary closes and titles (Table 3.3).

Even within a single country, there are cultures with different approaches to time. For instance, people from larger cities will pay more attention to punctuality compared to those from small towns. In the monochrome culture, being late means a lack of discipline and may lead to a conflict. On the other hand, it should be borne in mind that trade partners from the polychrome culture should not be given rigid deadlines. A good solution is to give a much earlier deadline and frequently contact the trade partner to monitor the progress of the transaction on a continuous basis instead of agreeing on a rigid deadline at the beginning of the cooperation (Table 3.4).

TABLE 3.3   Monochrome and polychrome cultures

MONOCHROME CULTURE	POLYCHROME CULTURE
People attach importance to punctuality, schedule, lack of interruptions during meetings	Punctuality is not important; changes in the schedule are acceptable
Nordic and other German European countries, North American countries, Japan	Arab world, most African countries, Latin American countries, countries of South Asia and Southeast Asia

Source: Own work based on: Wagner A.S., Lose Zugehörigkeiten von globalen Identitäten (Glopats) in internationalen Unternehmen–Konflikte zwischen Nationalkulturen und Hyperkultur. *Gruppe. Interaktion. Organisation. Zeitschrift für Angewandte Organisationspsychologie (GIO)*, 2018, 49.4: 379–390.

TABLE 3.4   Expressive and reserved cultures

EXPRESSIVE CULTURE	RESERVED CULTURE
Speaking loudly and lifting up one's voice to stress something important	Punctuality is not important; changes in the schedule are acceptable
Interrupting others when they are speaking	Low-pitched voice
Avoiding "awkward silence"	Longer silence during conversations
Several people can speak simultaneously	Alternate participation in a conversation
Small spatial distance	Large spatial distance
Direct eye contact	Avoiding touch
Gesticulation	
European countries speaking Romance languages, other Mediterranean countries, Latin American countries	Countries in East and Southeast Asia, Nordic and other German European countries

Source: Own work based on: Wagner A.S., Lose Zugehörigkeiten von globalen Identitäten (Glopats) in internationalen Unternehmen–Konflikte zwischen Nationalkulturen und Hyperkultur. *Gruppe. Interaktion. Organisation. Zeitschrift für Angewandte Organisationspsychologie (GIO)*, 2018, 49.4: 379–390.

Cultures also differ in the way of communication, which includes both verbal and non-verbal communication. In the expressive culture, people speak loudly and more clearly lifting up voice to stress something important. In the reserved culture, this will mean anger. Gestures can be interpreted in a totally different way in each of these cultures. In the expressive culture, silence during a meeting is perceived as awkward, whereas people from the reserved culture often sit in silence. Interrupting somebody who is speaking is a common behavior in the expressive culture, whereas in the reserved culture, it will be considered rude.

Cultural differences are visible in every sphere of our life. It is important to be open to encountering another culture and prepared for such an encounter. In the business world, such knowledge can prevent conflicts, as differences in behavior result from different values adopted in different cultures rather than from personal dislikes.

Process of Stabilizing Changes in Organizational Culture Management

4

4.1 ORGANIZATIONAL CULTURE MANAGEMENT IN TERMS OF DECISION-MAKING

Managing organizational culture in terms of the functioning of an organization results from the function that culture fulfills in an organization and the impact it has on the organization's relationships with its environment. In this regard, the functions of organizational culture can be divided into two groups: internal and external (Camphausen 2013, p. 241). Internal functions include the integration function, which is about building cooperation and community, and forming bonds and relationships between employees. New members of an organization, in order to be accepted, are expected to learn a new way of doing things and proper behavior in the new setting. Bernd Camphausen emphasizes that proper identification of organizational culture requires participation. Despite certain differences in members' views, behaviors or objectives, organizational culture is expressed through what is common and results from participation in a given group. The integration function can also be treated as a way of identifying members of an organization who do not fit in the fundamental assumptions, norms and values of the organizational culture. On the one hand, the managerial staff, by preferring certain attitudes and behaviors, indicate the types of people that are sought, while on the other hand, people are allowed to consciously decide whether to belong a given community.

In an organization, the integration function is expressed through the process of creating shared thinking patterns, values, norms and experiences; learning; giving members of an organization the sense of stability, balance, peace and safety; and building organizational identity, as an organization consists of multiple personalities, characters and values that together make up organizational identity. According to Mathias Diebig, it is an identity that, through such elements as philosophy, history, name, traditions and values, differentiates organizations, makes them unique and gives their members the sense of belonging to a certain community. Identity can also be used to create and strengthen a positive image thanks to shared values (Diebig 2015, pp. 129–139). It also involves a shared language and conceptual framework—a common language and way of communication understandable to all members is necessary for integrating an organization as well as defining and shaping its boundaries, which has a significant impact on its efficient functioning. It is also important to mention the development of ideology, i.e., explaining incomprehensible events. In fact, culture facilitates perception of unexpected situations and gives sense to situations, thereby reducing the uncertainty of organizational members. It is further worth mentioning the identification of status symbols, i.e., the ways of achieving higher levels of power and the authority that comes with it, which in turn enables the definition of relationships in an organization, reduction of conflicts and misunderstandings and provides information about appropriate behaviors in an organization. The possibility of defining desirable behaviors as well as punishment and reward criteria allows organizational members to integrate more closely, whereas organizational culture management establishes common foundations for assessing behaviors and attitudes, which enables the specification of desirable and undesirable behaviors, values and cultural standards (Urbanowska-Sojkin 2015b, pp. 146–160).

Another internal function is the perception function, which relates to the ways of perceiving an organization and its environment, thus enabling gathering and sharing of knowledge, interpretation of events and formation of patterns in perceiving phenomena (Urbanowska-Sojkin 2015a, pp. 303–320). This function also makes it possible to define a common way of assessing the attitudes and behaviors in an organization by establishing uniform criteria for rewards and punishments. Members of an organization can easily find out whether their behaviors conform to the established standards or whether they should modify their actions. Such a structuring of processes, meanings, values and behaviors facilitates achievement of the objectives set by an organization (Bubel 2016, pp. 51–63). Thanks to this function, the principles of power and status can be defined. Organizational culture management enables the definition of clear criteria for maintaining and gaining authority, leading to the reduction of conflicts and establishment of the criteria for desirable and unacceptable behaviors.

The adaptation function, also classified under internal functions, involves the formation of behavior patterns during changes occurring within an organization and in its environment in the decision-making process. Proper organizational culture management reduces uncertainty and makes it easier to make decisions and to plan and predict events. As a result, there is a greater sense of security, which leads to greater motivation and willingness to act among members of an organization (Bubel 2015, pp. 253–263).

This function also relates to the vision, mission, strategy and criteria for assessing the operation of an organization when decisions are made. The most common ways of adapting include (Laux and Liermann 2013, pp. 77–86):

- Isolation, which involves the selection of irrelevant or incorrect information
- Passive adaptation, which enables the elimination of a specific element in the hierarchy of values
- Active adaptation, which involves maintaining the continuity of culture by passing on the norms and values to organizational members

The functions of organizational culture also relate to external adaptation, understood as an impact of internal mechanisms on external elements, and as an impact of the changes in the environment on the inside of an organization. These functions include (Schneeweiß 2013, pp. 181–193):

- Understanding an organization's mission, strategy and objectives
- Ensuring the integration of an organization's members to achieve the established objectives
- Creating uniform criteria for measuring the progress in the achievement of the established objectives to find out whether the objectives have been achieved and to what extent
- The possibility of collective formulation of a strategy of changes, ways of its modification as well as the directions and methods of improving the organization
- The flow of norms, values and attitudes from an organization to its environment and the development of a desired strategy in decision-making situations

Organizational culture management in decision-making situations differs from that in a stable and predictable environment. While no differences in defining organizational culture can be observed in the preparatory phase for decision-making, in the other phases of managing the decision-making process, organizational culture, unless it is subject to modification, needs to be understood in a broader context.

Organizational culture is often regarded as a stabilizer of organizational changes. However, in the case of a decision that may pose a threat to the existence of an organization, lead to the loss of control over the functioning of an organization, have a negative impact on an organization's resources and result in a limited time for reaction and a limited access to information, organizational culture should support the changes that are necessary. In a decision-making situation, organizational culture management often has to change. It is no longer an anchor for organizational members, but sets the direction of actions and represents a challenge. During the decision-making process, organizational culture management should enable changes, reduce uncertainty in the face of the unknown and give the members of an organization the feeling of flexibility and autonomy rather than providing the sense of stability.

This aspect also relates to organizational culture with high tolerance of uncertainty, in which it is a catalyst for changes and forces organizational members to shift from uncertainty avoidance to absorption, which requires overcoming aversion of stressful situations and acceptance of the changeability of the environment.

Managing organizational culture with high tolerance of uncertainty involves (Werner 2013, p. 215):

- Increasing resilience to uncertainty
- Acceptance of different cultural patterns
- Acceptance of the possibility of changing organizational culture
- Shift from hierarchy to heterarchy
- Replacing standardization by a diversity of actions
- Adaptation to various environments and forms of activity
- Openness to new forms of activity and interactions with other people
- Departure from the traditional approach to regulations and procedures and from the attachment to tradition
- Increased importance of the role of an employee, the scope of his/her tasks and responsibility

Given the increasingly turbulent environment and the necessity of decision-making in organizations, they should depart from bureaucratization and focus on human relationships and bonding. Matthias Graumann points out that traditional organizations concentrated on the community culture by being closed and isolating the members from the environment. This ensured internal integration and sense of identity, and enabled the members to react to situations in the environment. The opposite of the community culture is the networking culture, which allows for greater openness and autonomy, and is more flexible. It enables effective operation in decision-making conditions, allowing an organization to act creatively and react to phenomena in a fast and direct way (Graumann 2015, p. 128). So, with increasing openness and networking (Kościelniak 2015, pp. 211–219), organizational culture management changes.

The integration function, which was previously understood in terms of the sense of identity, building a common conceptual framework and ensuring stability, is now perceived in terms of integration of different groups. Rather than stability and internal integration, openness to building new relationships, integration of different groups and easy movement across groups are important now. The permanency of the established bonds is no longer so significant, because the conditions are changeable and it is necessary to make the structures more flexible, and establish relationships with other people.

The ability to establish bonds, make and break contacts should allow members of an organization to adapt more easily to proposed changes, seek solutions on their own and adapt more easily to the new conditions. However, such a perception of the integration function (Pachura and Kot 2005, pp. 193–198) of organizational culture requires appropriate norms and values that will allow members of an organization to resign from the need to belong.

Such approach to organizational culture management will enable a more efficient operation in the case of decision-making and reduction of fear among organizational members. The need to belong will be satisfied by the common conceptual framework, shared language and common norms, values and experiences, which will facilitate the integration of organizational members, who will now identify not with a specific group, but the whole organization.

Organizational culture management in terms of decision-making also relates to changes in the perception function. The essence of this function, as it is traditionally understood, boils down to the perception of the environment, group, models, norms and assumptions that determine operation in a specific environment. In the conditions of decision-making, this function can be interpreted as the ability to perceive facts, events and processes as they are. Such organizational culture management enables the reduction of generalizations and encourages relativism of judgments. Previously, the perception function meant interpreting an organization in terms of organizational culture management; i.e., it provided information about behavior patterns and perception of a certain order and reality. This led to the use of generalizations, mental shortcuts and faster assessment of the reality. However, in the decision-making situation, it is necessary to be able to expand rather than to reduce the set of information. It is necessary to have as much information as possible to ensure a deeper analysis of the situation in which decisions are made. The insight into the actual meanings and conditions will make the process of drawing conclusions and learning easier for an organization at the stage of decision-making. This is because a decision-making process requires verification and, in some cases, modification of the implemented strategy. The effectiveness of actions is determined by the information acquired at the individual stages of the decision-making process; therefore, the information cannot be processed in a fast and generalized way. New cultural patterns of expanding the set of information are necessary to overcome the anxiety related to cognitive dissonance. Members of an organization feel anxiety because they need to process a large amount of information. Therefore, organizational culture management must support the employees and compensate their fear by defining and creating new desirable behavior patterns.

Change in the perception of organizational culture management also relates to the adaptation function. We can see a transformation in the relationship between an individual and the environment, because previously it was an individual who sought to adjust the environment to the values and standards of the organization, while now an individual is required to adapt to the changing situation or create cultural patterns together with other social groups. Members of an organization have to be open, abandon stereotypical thinking and instead seek paradoxes and contradictions. It is a useful approach not only in managing a culture with high tolerance of uncertainty but also in managing a culture that facilitates decision-making. Such attitude among members of an organization is necessary at each stage of decision-making. Already at the preparation stage, when scenarios are developed or the environment is analyzed, it is necessary for employees to be open, get rid of cultural constraints and a narrow perspective of thinking. Such an attitude is also desirable at the stage of decision-making, when the necessity of creative thinking and seeking contradictions allows more effective methods of management to be developed. Overcoming cultural barriers and abandoning constraining thought patterns are also necessary during decision-making. The new perspective of the adaptation function should facilitate overcoming the fear of responsibility for one's own decisions and actions.

As can be seen, organizational culture management plays a huge role in the decision-making process. It determines how actions are carried out at different organizational levels. Proper understanding of the role of organizational culture makes it possible to define the functions it serves in the entire decision-making process. The shift in how the function of organizational culture is perceived forces organizations to manage the organizational culture in a way that will facilitate decision-making. Different approaches among scholars to the paradigms, definitions or typologies of organizational culture determine different views on the possibility of managing organizational culture (Fandel 2013, p. 22). Some authors claim that it is possible to have a conscious impact on organizational culture management. The differences in opinions result from the adoption of different temporal perspectives. In the short term, organizational culture was treated by scholars as an independent variable, as it is impossible to manage it effectively within such a time frame (Laßmann 2013, pp. 325–329). It was thus assumed that cultural intervention is possible even in a short period of time. Naturally, this does not mean cultural change at all levels. Still, one can begin with changing artifacts and developing norms and values, which will later become more deeply rooted. In the long time horizon, organizational culture can be considered as a dependent variable, shaped by culture-forming factors. In this perspective, it can be shaped and oriented in a deliberate way.

4.2 OPTIMIZATION OF CHANGES IN THE CONTEXT OF ORGANIZATIONAL CULTURE MANAGEMENT

The process of organizational culture management is time-consuming and multistage, and can take on the following forms (Krause 2015, pp. 57–59):

Vicious circle—when an organization does not learn from its own errors and experience, and makes routine decisions.

Cultural revolution—which is a fast, rapid and radical change involving organizational transformations.

Evolutionary changes—focused on introducing slow changes while preserving valuable elements of the culture; a change is preceded by diagnosing the existing organizational culture and drawing up a plan for changing it.

Thomas Lauer presented a different division of changes made to organizational culture management. He distinguishes regressive changes (based on the existing solutions, not providing additional value and not increasing effectiveness), adaptive changes (enabling adaptation to the environment by adding new elements to the existing culture) and innovative changes (where the aim is to implement new solutions and change the system) (Lauer 2014, pp. 3–12). A different course of changes is presented by Jean-Paul Thommen and Stefan N. Grösser. According to these authors, every change in organizational culture management has its beginning in a situation when a decision-making is to take place. There is a discrepancy between the existing and new norms and values proposed by the managerial staff. This leads to a situation of conflict due to cultural differences. If the employees accept the new norms, the culture will be adopted in the organization. It is, however, by no means simple, as the proponents of the existing norms often oppose the changes (whether individually or as an organization) (Thommen and Grösser 2017, pp. 27–29), which may also affect the other members of the organization.

Ralph Berndt presented a holistic approach to making changes in organizational culture management, which encompasses five stages (Berndt 2013, pp. 72–85):

Stage 1—diagnosis of the existing organizational culture—defining its characteristic features, profile, type and areas requiring improvement; this stage should be preceded by, or carried out concurrently with, the formulation of an organization's strategy; apart from the formulation of a strategy, it also includes the formation of leadership coalition.

Stage 2—defining the features of a desirable and ideal organizational culture— specifying the most desirable values and norms in an organization that can help it to accomplish its objectives; it is necessary at this stage to pay attention to the strategy, i.e., making strategic choices, designing necessary structural and procedural changes.

Stage 3—comparing the features of the existing and desirable cultures— identifying the differences between the expected and the actual culture, determining the scope and costs of changes, and taking into account the additional element, i.e., communication of the vision of changes and how they will be implemented.

Stage 4—proper management of organizational culture—it is important at this stage to ensure strong involvement of the managerial staff, who set an example for the other members of the organization, integrate employees around the new values and norms, and secure their approval and engagement, as well as implementing a proper human resources policy, which involves eliminating those who are adverse towards the changes and critical of the new attitudes.

Stage 5—monitoring, assessment of changes and reinforcement of the new dimension of organizational culture management—at this stage, it is necessary to continuously monitor the changes, introduce improvements and evaluate the effectiveness of the whole process, i.e., assessing the elements that have been successfully changed, to what extent they have been changed and whether the changes were complete; it is also necessary to conduct a periodical review and plan further changes.

A different aspect of organizational culture management, which integrates the above-described concepts, is presented by Holger Kleingarn, who bases it on two assumptions (Kleingarn 2013, pp. 288–295):

• Individuals are subjected to group values and norms.
• It is necessary to introduce and reinforce new patterns.

The author emphasized the second condition, namely, the necessity of inculcating and reinforcing new patterns in order to make a long-term deep change. The process of change in organizational culture management is long term and requires engaging all members of an organization. It is also necessary if a gap exists between the present and desirable situation. In the case of decision-making, if the changes that are introduced are not in line with the organizational culture, they may provoke resistance and aversion in employees, who may hinder their implementation. In the case of decision-making and the necessity of making deep changes at the level of the whole organization, it is necessary to manage organizational culture in a way that supports and facilitates decision-making. In order for changes to be implemented effectively, a few conditions have to be met (Kleingarn 2013, pp. 288–295):

- Developing plans
- Good communication; developing an appropriate form of information distribution and continuous and systematic distribution of information
- Engaging the managerial staff
- Stabilizing the relationships among colleagues
- Personal responsibility, since for a change to be possible all members of an organization must understand their responsibilities; it is also necessary to make sure that everybody is fully informed

Organizational culture management has an impact on the effectiveness of an organization by influencing the productivity of its members, boosting motivation and engagement, controlling and verifying organizational behaviors and cooperating with other subsystems of an organization. In this context, culture management may lead to a radical change of culture or reinforcing of the existing culture. However, in order for change to be profound and lasting, and the new norms and values approved and accepted by the members of an organization, appropriate methods have to be applied. The following dimensions of organizational culture management can be distinguished (Gergs 2016, pp. 189–203):

- Developing a vision and boosting engagement of the members of an organization; employees should identify with their organization, and a clear vision should help to achieve that
- Ensuring appropriate communication and education that should state the necessity of making changes and the benefits of the implementation of the changes both for the organization as a whole and for its individual members
- Creating systems and processes that facilitate the introduction of changes that support the implementation of a new culture

Hans Joachim Gergs (2016, pp. 189–203) presented the methods of shaping organizational culture, both directly and indirectly. The direct methods, on the level of an individual and group, include the following:

- Redefining the values of an organization
- Creating new normative rules
- Changing artifacts
- Adapting artifacts to the changing core of values

Among the methods indirectly shaping organizational culture are the following:

- Creating and changing the mission and vision
- Creating systems of communication and power distribution
- Changing job descriptions
- Meetings, discussions and employee training
- Shaping a desirable role of the managerial staff
- Developing motivation systems
- Changing selection criteria

Wöhrle also says about inspiring decision-making, which, on the one hand, should cause change to the existing values, while on the other hand represent an effective method of organizational culture management. In organizational culture management, it is also necessary to establish new rituals that will help to replace the old norms and values by new ones, and to create visible and tangible symbols (Wöhrle 2016, pp. 112–117).

Organizational culture management should begin with the change of behaviors, which in the long run should result in the change of norms and values. It is necessary to engage the managerial staff in the entire process of management. They should initiate changes, set an example for the other members of the organization and support and create changes. The tools that have the strongest impact on organizational culture management include motivation system, training, employees' participation in management, level of decentralization, management style and a common mission and vision. A very significant role in organizational culture management is also played by the process of motivation. "Motivating is a deliberate process whereby the superior impacts his/her subordinates, focusing their behaviors on performance of the tasks assigned to them" (Kriegesmann and Kley 2016, pp. 105–118).

Effectiveness of this process is determined by (Buchner, Hofmann and Magnus 2013, pp. 211–212):

- Defining the detailed objectives of motivation
- Using appropriate motivation tools, positive or negative incentives, which inform employees about the desirable organizational culture, motivate potential employees and, due to their individualized character, allow the behaviors of organizational members to be corrected
- Creating appropriate working conditions for an employee, i.e., where he/she feels that he/she can freely choose his/her behavior

There are a few principles underlying the effective use of incentives (Von Rosenstiel, Von Hornstein and Augustin 2013, pp. 34–47):

- Clear communication of expectations, which should be inspiring and positive Individualized approach to members of the organization
- Correlation of the incentives with the system of objectives for reinforcing the desired behaviors
- A clearly defined system of rewards and punishments
- Adherence to the rules of rewarding

- Correlating incentives with employees' performance so that the tasks for which they are to be rewarded are achievable and yet mobilizing
- Applying incentives immediately after an action
- Rewarding for effects over which an employee has control
- Creation of a coherent motivation system: a simple, comprehensible and accepted system that includes both financial and nonfinancial incentives, and positive and negative reinforcement

Training courses represent another aspect in organizational culture management. Figure 4.1 shows how training methods impact organizational culture management.

The mechanism of the impact of training on organizational culture management refers to both hiring new employees and shaping the existing values. A training can raise awareness among organizational members of the need for changes. This can reduce their resistance and fear. A training takes place when values are passed on and can be understood and reinforced. Training also allows organizational members to understand the goals of their organization and extend their skills.

An important element of organizational culture management is employee participation. It involves allowing employees to make real decisions concerning the organization. Such participation may result, e.g., from participation in profits or property, from operation of law or from a decision of management. It has a positive impact on the atmosphere in the organization; increases the level of integration with the organization; contributes to a better understanding and acceptance of the objectives, tasks, mission and vision; stimulates employees to act; boosts motivation; and encourages greater openness. It means that employees have to continuously develop, understand the main assumptions underlying the functioning of the organization, be open to changes and willing to take risks.

Employee participation is related to the level of decentralization, which is another element that has a significant impact on organizational culture management. Decentralization can be defined as "economically isolating the subsystems of an organization and making them responsible for the results to the extent adequate to the

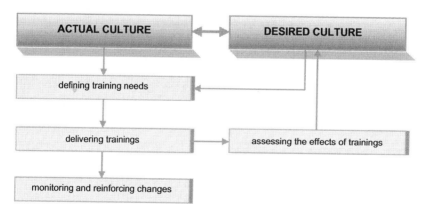

FIGURE 4.1 Relationships between organizational culture management and the organization of training. (Own work based on: Lauer T., *Change Management. Grundlagen und Erfolgsfaktoren*, Springer, Berlin, Heidelberg, 2014, pp. 13–27.)

decision-making autonomy granted to them. Such results must be presented in the form of appropriate measures" (Weber 2017, pp. 16–23). Decentralization enables the creation of smaller units with different degrees of structure decentralization. Decentralization is about the level of organization at which decisions are made. The bigger the number of employees who participate in the decision-making process or the broader their powers, the larger the decentralization. Decentralization boosts employees' motivation and productivity, allows them to focus on key activities, increases the quality of decisions, increases initiative and boosts morale among employees at the lower levels of the structure. In addition, decentralization also impacts employees' creativity and their openness to changes, increases acceptance of uncertainty, facilitates knowledge and experience sharing, teaches teamwork and motivates employees to develop professionally.

A very important role in organizational culture management is played by the management style of the managerial staff, which is defined as a set of methods designed to induce employees to take effective actions for the benefit of the organization. Management style can also be understood as a specific, individual approach characterized by specific methods of acting. The managerial staff's impact on employees' actions can be considered in terms of the following aspects (Bernd, Altobelli and Sander 2016, pp. 617–624):

- The form, which distinguishes between:
  - *Direct management*—the superior distributes the resources, assigns tasks and defines how they should be executed; this is a very detailed management of a specific group of recipients
  - *Indirect management*—regulations are general in character; employees have a large freedom of action
- The scope of the superior's interference in employees' work:
  - *Small*—an employee is free to decide about the type and manner of execution of his/her tasks; the superior only suggests which tasks he/she should set himself/herself
  - *Large*—the superior obligatorily imposes the tasks, deadlines and time frames, and thereby defines the procedures

The choice of the management style depends on (Pipus 2015, p. 21):

- *Managerial staff*—espoused values, propensity for risk-taking, trust in employees, task orientation
- *Employees*—their needs, willingness to take on responsibility, implement objectives, independence, identification with their organization, as well as the knowledge and expectations regarding participation in decision-making
- *Situation*—type of organization, type of problem, form of the group that is managed, time pressure

Creation and promotion of an organization's mission and vision is another aspect of organizational culture management. Vision is the picture of the future of an organization. It is described at various levels defining future desired outcomes of activity that can be achieved in the long run. Vision fulfills the following functions (Esch and Buchel 2014, pp. 149–157):

- It mobilizes and inspires people to take actions, and arouses emotions
- It directs and organizes defining the desirable direction of pursued objectives, systematizes values and objectives of an organization
- It integrates motivating members of an organization and boosting their engagement
- It supports the success of an organization

The vision expands on the content of the mission, whereas the mission expresses the "aspiration, defines the purpose for which the organization was set up and specifies the function it fulfills in its environment" (Brunner et al. 2013, pp. 45–57).

The mission should be comprehensible to the members of an organization, relatively constant and unchangeable, as well as original. The formulation of the mission enables adaptation to changes, ensures security and prestige to the organization and emphasizes the dimension of intellectual capital in the life of the organization. The mission shows the direction of actions, mobilizes and unites all employees as well as builds the identity of the organization. The mission and vision should be accepted by the members of an organization, and the employees should participate in their formulation. The mission and vision should also be widely communicated in an organization to enable penetration into deeper levels of organizational culture management by shaping the norms and values that are desirable in an organization.

In order for organizational culture management to be possible, all the members of an organization must be engaged and the managerial staff must apply various methods to modify the norms and values propagated in the organization. It is also necessary to impact all aspects of organizational culture, because only then it can be changed. Organizational culture management is a long-term, difficult and costly process, but necessary during decision-making. The benefits of managing organizational culture change usually exceed the costs that have to be incurred to implement the change. The most effective way of implementing this change is to impact both soft elements, such as norms and values, and employee beliefs, and hard ones, such as procedures, structures or physical artifacts.

4.3 INTENSIFICATION OF KNOWLEDGE GENERATION IN TERMS OF ORGANIZATIONAL CULTURE MANAGEMENT IN AN ORGANIZATION

The process of knowledge management also includes evaluation and measurement of the existing knowledge. Knowledge measurement is an area that functions almost independently, sometimes even separately from knowledge management, focusing on measuring the value of intellectual capital. There is a range of methods designed for that purpose, yet they still seem imperfect in terms of the objectives of knowledge management, especially creating competitive advantage (Shujahat et al. 2019, pp. 442–450).

The right way to proceed is to develop a procedure for evaluating what knowledge is key to the functioning of the organization, what are the key competencies of the organization and how they should be developed. Such evaluations are generally connected with organizational culture. The system of dominating values defines priorities regarding the types of knowledge and the vision of which competencies should be built. The ways of making such evaluations should also be accepted in the system of values.

The above-presented issues of knowledge management mainly concern the relationships between the different stages of this process and organizational culture. An important issue is also the improvement directions and problem-solving in knowledge management in organizations. One of the problems is the conversion of individual competencies to form part of the organizational structure. This is important because it creates the knowledge base of an organization that is available to all of its units. This conversion may also contribute to the improvement of both the use and generation of knowledge. The knowledge and experience embedded in operating practices and products provide a good basis for activities aimed at creating knowledge in the future and developing competencies that improve the ways in which the existing knowledge is used. This may lead to a variation in the characteristics of processes, sometimes greater than the variation in the key components of the knowledge base. Zaim, Muhammed and Tarim indicate two additional advantages. The first is standardization, which increases flexibility. They claim that standardization at a lower level creates flexibility at a higher level (at which features that are a "response" to consumer needs are designed). Thanks to saving time and costs, and reducing the difficulties in creating the foundations of a new project, more attention can be devoted to designing innovative features of a product. The second advantage is that discipline increases creativity. Innovations can be developed as a result of a disciplined application of well-defined principles followed in design processes. They may involve combining things in a new way while following a set of existing principles (it is improvisation within existing possibilities) and creating a new set of principles designed to combine things that create new possibilities (Zaim, Muhammed and Tarim 2019, pp. 24–38).

In general, a good use of an organization's knowledge resources means wide adoption of best practices, sharing of good ideas and participation of the whole organization in value creation. This requires possession of "the best intellectual capital." By creating a culture of perfect use of knowledge, an organization can compete at a higher level. When the intellectual capital of an organization is well motivated to think in an innovative way, it develops the possessed knowledge in the best possible way. When knowledge sharing occurs on a large scale, conditions are created for new ideas to emerge. When it can be seen that these ideas are converted into practical actions, there is willingness to participate in shaping the future. Conditions are created for a self-organizing cycle: A good use of knowledge leads to the development of new knowledge.

Dissemination of knowledge in an organization can be viewed in terms of two dimensions that set boundaries for this process: degree of knowledge organization (codification) and intensity of its dissemination.

Given the globalization, the second dimension seems particularly important to an organization, as it is about how quickly the whole internal structure of an organization becomes imbued with knowledge.

New knowledge is rarely created in an expected way. It is usually born in an inconspicuous way, somewhere in an organization when a specific problem is solved or originates from employees or individuals or institutions cooperating with the organization. Next, it spreads, reaching one by one other employees working in various units of the organization.

Best practices and actionable knowledge are usually systematized and codified, and as the resources become organized, the degree of their codification increases, which is an important parameter of the function of knowledge penetration in an organization. This is because codified knowledge spreads faster, and so the extent of its spread in an organization increases. Then, it is used in various parts of the organization, thus improving the competencies of both individual employees and the organization as a whole.

An organization that has acquired new competencies expands its area of activity, which is now made up of new solutions and new knowledge, which leads to the emergence of new chances for the organization's expansion and development. The intensity of the spread of knowledge is determined by a number of factors, both internal and external, that exist in an organization's environment (Figure 4.2).

It is strengthened (or weakened) by the character of knowledge exchange, which is essentially organized (formalized), although knowledge may also spread in an informal way. Both of these ways can take on different forms: written, oral or electronic; they can target different levels and departments in the organizational structure and vary in terms of the level of detail and importance. Thus, when assessing the issue of the intensity of knowledge diffusion in organizations, it seems particularly important to take into account the position of communication nodes, which exist where the pathways of the knowledge exchange network intersect, and which are an important construction of a kind of knowledge map and transmitters that enable even spread of knowledge within the whole organization.

Each component of an organization and an organization itself operates within certain boundaries of autonomy, which at the same time act as knowledge gateways. If such boundaries divide an organization into complementary areas—as is the case with well-designed and capable organizations—they may open, turning an organization into a networked organization, facilitating knowledge sharing and enabling access

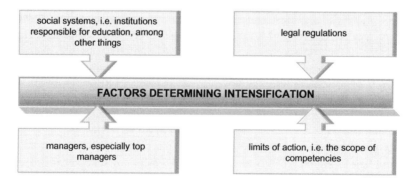

FIGURE 4.2 Factors determining the intensity of knowledge generation. (Own work based on: Salunke S., Weerawardena J., Mccoll-Kennedy J.R., The central role of knowledge integration capability in service innovation-based competitive strategy. *Industrial Marketing Management*, 2019, 76: 144–156.)

to knowledge to all employees. Otherwise, such boundaries may become barriers to the spread of knowledge.

The aim of rules, norms and legal regulations is to specify the principles governing the operation of an information system, ways of gaining access to knowledge resources and whatever is needed to make new decisions aimed at increasing knowledge and creating new solutions.

An instrument that facilitates the spread of knowledge in an organization is a well-functioning system of knowledge dissemination, without which knowledge cannot be gathered, capitalized on or transferred. This requires that an organization follows a "decalogue" of instructions, which it should have in place (Figure 4.3).

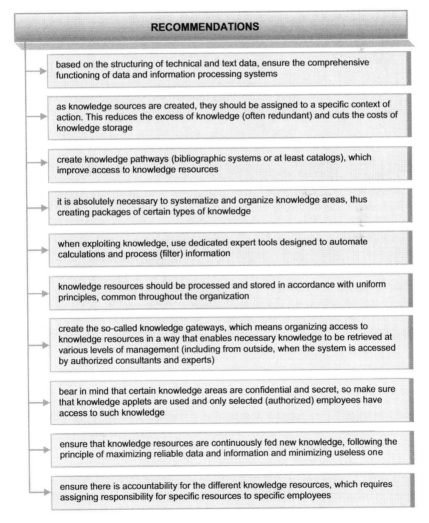

RECOMMENDATIONS

based on the structuring of technical and text data, ensure the comprehensive functioning of data and information processing systems

as knowledge sources are created, they should be assigned to a specific context of action. This reduces the excess of knowledge (often redundant) and cuts the costs of knowledge storage

create knowledge pathways (bibliographic systems or at least catalogs), which improve access to knowledge resources

it is absolutely necessary to systematize and organize knowledge areas, thus creating packages of certain types of knowledge

when exploiting knowledge, use dedicated expert tools designed to automate calculations and process (filter) information

knowledge resources should be processed and stored in accordance with uniform principles, common throughout the organization

create the so-called knowledge gateways, which means organizing access to knowledge resources in a way that enables necessary knowledge to be retrieved at various levels of management (including from outside, when the system is accessed by authorized consultants and experts)

bear in mind that certain knowledge areas are confidential and secret, so make sure that knowledge applets are used and only selected (authorized) employees have access to such knowledge

ensure that knowledge resources are continuously fed new knowledge, following the principle of maximizing reliable data and information and minimizing useless one

ensure there is accountability for the different knowledge resources, which requires assigning responsibility for specific resources to specific employees

FIGURE 4.3 Factors determining knowledge generation in an organization. (Own work based on: A.H. Gold, A. Malhotra, A.H. Segars, Knowledge management: An organizational capabilities perspective. *Journal of Management Information Systems*, 2001, 18.1: 185–214.)

The aforementioned requirements may seem beyond the capabilities of a single organization, especially one with low aspirations concerning knowledge management and small (technical, financial, organizational) potential. However, in the case of organizations with diversified activities, this problem appears marginal and insignificant. Indeed, new information technologies open up vast possibilities regarding knowledge collection, processing and exploitation, and as the use of such technologies becomes inevitable, knowledge life span gets shorter—so, access to knowledge must become easier and faster (Chang and Lin 2015, pp. 433–455).

A good illustration of a well-functioning information system is a description of steps to prepare cost estimate based on knowledge resources stored in electronic archives of a global organization.

Such a knowledge base, systematically updated with reliable and up-to-date information and processed as needed, is the central element of a knowledge management system. Knowledge management, understood as all the processes that enable acquisition, storage and use of knowledge for the purposes of accomplishing the goals of an organization, should by definition contribute to increased effectiveness of an organization: Higher productivity, better quality and increased efficiency, as a result of increasing the resources of knowledge that is useful, facilitate creative thinking and elevate an organization to a higher level of functioning.

This is because knowledge, combined with work processes and business processes at all levels of management of an organization, which is suited to the needs and character of the business of an organization, creates a new space for acting based on new quality of management. Therefore, more and more organizations do not want to compete in the market only based on products, especially those highly labor intensive, but build their success by drawing on employees' knowledge and the resources gathered in vast repositories created using state-of-the-art technologies.

The logic behind such approach is clearly connected with the character of the challenges faced in the global environment and the necessity of adopting the directions and mechanisms of adaptation derived from strategic management.

These, in turn, based on research, education and cooperation, create knowledge resources and instruments for knowledge use (especially in terms of the need to enhance the capabilities of using material resources) (Wright et al. 2019, pp. 50–58) as well as knowledge designed to improve the effectiveness of management. It should be stressed that knowledge resources are subject to both exploitation and exploration. The former type of knowledge is used in daily operations and enables an organization to adapt to the competitive environment through reactive activities using the mechanism of feedback loop. Exploration, in contrast, enables the anticipation of changes in the environment and formation of feedforward responses to them, and consequently taking actions aimed at gaining and sustaining strategic competitive advantage.

Both the processes provide a platform for identifying desirable directions of changes, implementing solutions that enable the implementation of adopted strategies (main and sub-strategies) and at the same time adapting an organization to the requirements of a turbulent environment. This means relying on sources of knowledge to find assets that will allow an organization to effectively compete in the market. For knowledge systems to be useful in managing an organization, especially on a global scale, priority should be given to research and activities aimed at self-development of an organization. Apart from the capability of financing this sphere of activity, an organization must properly understand the role it plays in the free market economy. An organization must gradually get free—without harming its business—from the message that the main goal is to survive, and the only desired value—gain. Instead, as a knowledge-based organization, it should promote a paradigm of management whose philosophy is based on a multitude of goals and areas of operation that drive the organization's dynamic and market position.

An organization, depending on its potential, current market position and strategic plans, creates and mobilizes knowledge resources, which vary in terms of how important they are to its functioning. If we acknowledge the view established in the literature and business practice stating that the condition of an effective operation of an organization is its ability to take actions that can be classified as survival, adaptation and development, and that the ability to identify the micro- and macroenvironments and shape activity according to their changing demands is the basis of the functioning of every organization and the main determinant of its successes, then organizations can and should tap different categories of knowledge (Figure 4.4).

The extent to which global organizations manage to make use of the knowledge they possess depends, on the one hand, on their ability to enrich the existing knowledge and acquire new one, and on the other hand, on their ability to create conditions for appropriate rationing and further transfer of knowledge. This requires both overcoming barriers to acknowledging the importance of knowledge management and creating conditions for improving the ability to close the gap between creation of knowledge resources and their use in an organization.

Luhn is right when he argues that the overwhelming majority of organizations are poor at learning. Using a metaphor, we can say that in this regard, they are similar to people, among whom only a small percentage of geniuses kindling the holy fire of

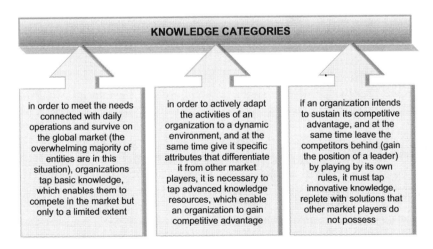

FIGURE 4.4 Categorization of knowledge from the differential perspective. (Own work based on: North K., Brandner A., Steininger T., Die Wissenstreppe: Information–Wissen–Kompetenz, [in:] *Wissensmanagement für Qualitätsmanager*, Springer Gabler, Wiesbaden, 2016, pp. 5–8.)

knowledge can be regarded as diamonds in terms of knowledge (Luhn 2016, pp. 1–13). In organizations, employees are still too attached to their functions and do not feel responsible for the outcomes of the collective effort. Consequently, targets are met to a limited extent as a result of failure to fully complete the tasks.

We can also observe the so-called false activity (Reinhardt 2017, pp. 197–220), where people are self-satisfied with the knowledge they possess and attribute the causes of their failure to increase knowledge to the organization's environment, blaming the so-called external enemies for the lack of inflow of knowledge. Real activity is a consequence of observations and a result of understanding to what extent the organization is responsible for the problems that it solves.

Moreover, problems do not tend to be solved in a systemic way. Rather than perceiving an organization as an open system linked with the environment, employees focus on solving current and isolated as well as minor issues, failing to notice future threats—especially if these threats emerge gradually (Weber et al. 2019, pp. 1–18)—which are much more important to the strategic existence of an organization. Often, they also show lack of skills needed to assess experiences and learn lessons from the most important activities and decisions, which often depend on a number of different elements that comprise a management system. Last but not least, there are still myths in organizations about cohesion of the management (Heisig et al. 2016, pp. 1169–1198), who in fact only think about their position—territory and influences. Thus, this cohesion is often superficial and only observed in a stable reality. When pressure is growing, the management in most organizations is unable to maintain cohesion.

The above-presented background of negative phenomena creates a context in which various groups of problems that are vital in knowledge management in a global organization emerge. Explications of these groups of problems are shown in Figure 4.5.

Organizations seeking a competitive position in the global economy strive to reduce the gap between thinking and acting, trying at the same time to reconcile conceptualization with operationalization. They attach great importance to the use of sophisticated technologies that support knowledge management processes, and at the same time foster an atmosphere that facilitates communication. Such an atmosphere enables employees to develop their competencies and—what is important—creates conditions for continuous, collective learning of an organization as a whole.

As was highlighted, knowledge-based organizations must create conditions for acquisition, accumulation, processing and creation of a broad range of categories of knowledge. At the same time, they should create areas of intensive cooperation. The aim is to ensure that the creators and co-creators of the strategy and policy of a global organization (within the organization and in its environment) can engage in an exchange across functions and processes with a view to increasing knowledge resources (Hislop, Bosua and Helms 2018, pp. 72–76). Flexible organizational structures, especially network structures, play a significant role in this process. Hierarchical functional structures facilitate acquisition, accumulation and use of knowledge, whereas open structures are better suited to the creation of new knowledge. Further, development of new knowledge in an organization facilitates the creation of the so-called knowledge maps that combine into a knowledge network. Although acquiring external knowledge, accumulating and processing it within an organization is necessary, it is not sufficient in terms of developing knowledge that can guarantee gaining competitive advantage. The ability to

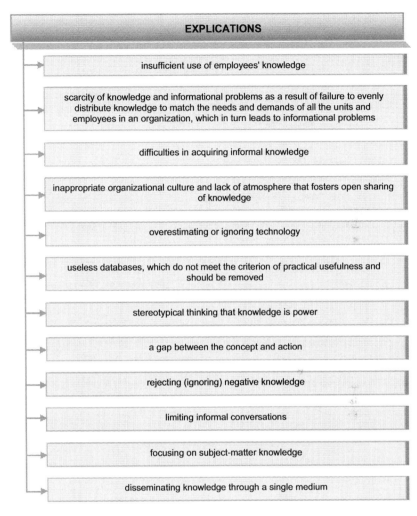

FIGURE 4.5 Exemplification of knowledge management in global organizations. (Own work based on: Kasemsap K., The roles of knowledge management and organizational innovation in global business, [in:] *Civil and Environmental Engineering: Concepts, Methodologies, Tools, and Applications*, IGI Global, 2016, pp. 1156–1180.)

manage knowledge translates into an effective implementation of strategies—converted from assumptions, plans and programs into a bundle of winning strategies—which, supported by key competencies, create conditions for gaining and sustaining competitive advantage (Girard and Girard 2015, pp. 1–20).

It is also necessary to mobilize tacit knowledge of various partners (customers, suppliers, banks, shareholders, institutions, social organizations, etc.), who may possess important knowledge in terms of shaping action programs that can contribute to the success of an organization. To meet these requirements, there are the factors stimulating the undertaking of actions in an organization, as shown in Figure 4.6.

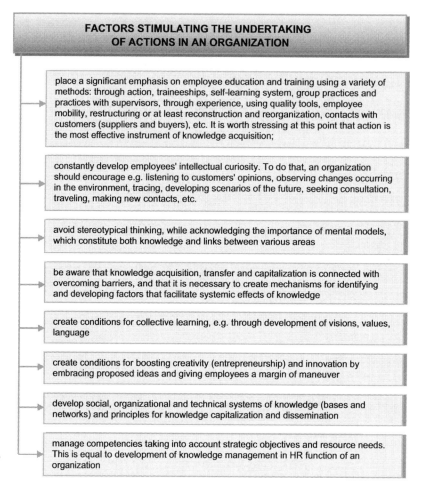

FACTORS STIMULATING THE UNDERTAKING OF ACTIONS IN AN ORGANIZATION

place a significant emphasis on employee education and training using a variety of methods: through action, traineeships, self-learning system, group practices and practices with supervisors, through experience, using quality tools, employee mobility, restructuring or at least reconstruction and reorganization, contacts with customers (suppliers and buyers), etc. It is worth stressing at this point that action is the most effective instrument of knowledge acquisition;

constantly develop employees' intellectual curiosity. To do that, an organization should encourage e.g. listening to customers' opinions, observing changes occurring in the environment, tracing, developing scenarios of the future, seeking consultation, traveling, making new contacts, etc.

avoid stereotypical thinking, while acknowledging the importance of mental models, which constitute both knowledge and links between various areas

be aware that knowledge acquisition, transfer and capitalization is connected with overcoming barriers, and that it is necessary to create mechanisms for identifying and developing factors that facilitate systemic effects of knowledge

create conditions for collective learning, e.g. through development of visions, values, language

create conditions for boosting creativity (entrepreneurship) and innovation by embracing proposed ideas and giving employees a margin of maneuver

develop social, organizational and technical systems of knowledge (bases and networks) and principles for knowledge capitalization and dissemination

manage competencies taking into account strategic objectives and resource needs. This is equal to development of knowledge management in HR function of an organization

FIGURE 4.6 Aspects of dynamizing activities in a global organization. (Own work based on: North K., Brandner A., Steininger T., Benötigtes Wissen bestimmen, [in:] *Wissensmanagement für Qualitätsmanager*, Springer Gabler, Wiesbaden, 2016, pp. 15–18.)

A good idea is to transfer best practices from established organizations to newly launched ones. By doing so, it is possible during designing a new organization to use the knowledge of employees and external experts on best practices formerly used in processes. Employees, knowing that they are creating a new organization for themselves, are motivated to work well and have an opportunity to acquire knowledge about processes that will allow them to be prepared to perform their tasks later, while the skills acquired during creating the new organization become a set of that organization's key competencies.

It should be noted that a common way of addressing the problem of uneven distribution of knowledge (Stehr 2017, pp. 299–322) is by exchanging knowledge resources across departments, i.e., by requiring each department to regularly inform the other departments about its results. Such results are then analyzed at meetings of department managers so that knowledge concerning best practices can be shared with other departments. Knowledge that is complicated and difficult to capture is passed with the assistance of employees (specialists) who are delegated to other departments so that along with the knowledge they can pass and reinforce mental patterns.

Every organization has its own way (system) of managing knowledge. It depends, among other things, on an organization's business profile. This means that knowledge management should be suited to the character and needs of an organization. In order for a knowledge management system to give positive effects, organizations focus on two main aspects: aligning it with their own interests determined by the strategic direction of the goals and working on developing an organizational culture that is focused on knowledge sharing and cooperation.

An example related to this part of discussion that illustrates a proper approach to creating systems for knowledge accumulation and dissemination designed to ensure easier access to knowledge resources and enable knowledge use is well-organized knowledge resources that can be commonly used by employees (Dneprovskaya et al. 2016, pp. 159–165). There is a variety of factors, mainly cultural ones, that facilitate collective learning, which include creating an atmosphere conducive to establishing close and direct contacts between employees, departure from a culture that is based on extreme individualism, rewarding employees who are willing to share knowledge with others and motivating not only individual employees but also entire teams.

Knowledge creation and diffusion within an organization and its nearest environment is an immanent feature of knowledge management, but insufficient for an organization to gain and sustain a competitive position. This applies in particular to organizations aspiring to operate in global markets. Such organizations must acquire and use knowledge residing in their environment. The main source of the supply of knowledge is stakeholders, with which an organization enters into various relations. However, apart from research and development facilities, customers and suppliers, an organization can tap knowledge possessed by its competitors or representatives of other industries. Strategic alliance is the most commonly used instrument for acquiring knowledge from the environment. It enables appropriation of skills that are tacit, difficult to imitate and strictly protected from competitors. An organization (party in the alliance) can significantly benefit from the possibility of learning and developing such skills with a view to using them outside of the coalition (Havakhor, Soror and Sabherwal 2018, pp. 104–141).

There are numerous instruments for knowledge exchange between organizations. Which one will be selected depends on how knowledge is interpreted, the type of knowledge and knowledge generation model. In other words, it depends on the adopted concept of knowledge management. Below is an approach to the concept of the flow of knowledge between partners in an alliance, derived from Foote and Halawi, which shows logical and sequential links between the stages of this process (Figure 4.7).

Figure 4.8 presents the process of knowledge exchange taking into account the situation resulting from two organizations forming alliance.

The process of knowledge exchange takes place in the above-specified stages and starts with the identification of the existing knowledge resources by each partner in the alliance. Such assets are then structured by characteristics, sources and types of knowledge, and classified as resources of explicit knowledge and/or tacit

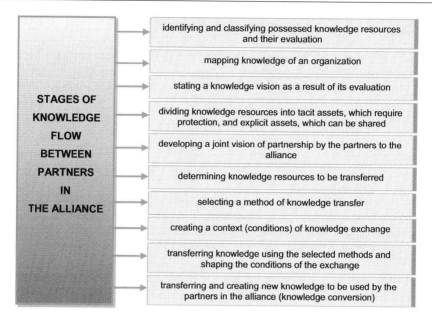

FIGURE 4.7 Concept of knowledge flow between partners in the alliance. (Own work based on: Foote A., Halawi L.A., Knowledge management models within information technology projects. *Journal of Computer Information Systems*, 2018, 58.1: 89–97.)

knowledge. This stage provides a useful foundation for mapping knowledge and helps in selecting the methods, means and people that will participate in the transfer and conversion of knowledge (Battistutti and Bork 2017, pp. 461–477). The vision statement stage involves specifying which types of knowledge should be developed. It also includes identifying knowledge gaps that should be filled and forming resources that underpin key competencies (usually strictly protected) and resources that can be shared.

The next stages are executed jointly by the partners in the alliance, usually by specially appointed teams. Their task is to determine which resources should be transferred and developed. During their work, some resources previously regarded as tacit knowledge may be reclassified as explicit knowledge, and vice versa—knowledge earmarked for transfer may be categorized by the team as protected. When knowledge assets to be transferred are finally determined, the stage that follows involves the selection of the methods for knowledge transfer.

The next stage involves creating conditions for the exchange of knowledge resources between the parties in the alliance and—based on the knowledge map—establishing appropriate relations between the locations where the individual knowledge resources reside. An important problem to be solved at this stage refers to agreeing contexts (cultural, historical, social, etc.) between the partners. This is to ensure proper coding and development of knowledge. A context mismatch may lead to misinterpretation of transferred knowledge, which means that such knowledge will be read and interpreted incorrectly, and knowledge transfer may even be abandoned.

The final stages involve launching and performing the processes of knowledge conversion. In practice, this means adaptation, externalization, combination and internalization of knowledge transferred between the partners. Although this process by definition refers to transfer of the existing knowledge, it is highly likely that combinations made within transferred resources will result in new knowledge. This is because during knowledge conversion the context of knowledge exchange also changes; i.e., change occurs in the conditions that depend on the type of relations and instruments used to transfer knowledge.

The execution of the stages (executed jointly by the partners in the alliance) should be overseen by a special team composed of top managers of the participants in the alliance and designated experts, such as IT specialists and electronic engineers, among others, whose main task is to make sure that the transfer of knowledge proceeds correctly.

The last stage presented in Figure 4.8 is implementation into the organizations' own practice of the knowledge acquired as a result of the transfer. The process of knowledge conversion occurs independently in the individual organizations, and the acquired knowledge permeates the resources of the existing knowledge. Thus, new knowledge resources appear that can fill gaps in the existing knowledge and develop the existing resources.

Moving on to a new situation means beginning another cycle and repeating the whole cycle, starting from the stage of identification of knowledge resources and their evaluation by the partners in the alliance. The concepts of intellectual capital estimation may prove useful at this point. The evaluation results of each cycle of transfer should be compared so as to indicate the benefits (losses) of the exchange of knowledge resources for each partner in the alliance.

Creating competitive potential, ability to use knowledge in decision-making processes and ability to learn are three basic competencies that should be developed through knowledge management. However, for an organization to be able to develop, an additional competence is needed. It is the ability to create and maintain relations that enable knowledge to be supplied to an organization from outside rather than only from inside, as well as relations through which an organization can supply its own knowledge to its environment to its benefit. Only appropriate interactions with the environment can make knowledge more valuable. Note that the advantage of knowledge as a factor in creating and sustaining competitive potential over physical and financial factors comes from the fact that knowledge creates much more possibilities of building and using such potential. For an organization to compete effectively, there must be an appropriate flow of knowledge from and to its environment. Knowledge is a special resource, as contrary to material resources, it can be common to most competitors, which means that it is less affected by supply constraints. It can be used by a number of competitors at the same time and is relatively easy to reproduce (Gloet and Samson 2020, pp. 1198–1218). The value of knowledge in terms of competition is highly changeable in longer time spans. Consequently, constant supply of knowledge to an organization from its environment may determine whether or not the organization will survive. This means that where knowledge is a basic source of value creation, effective competition strategies require a constant seeking of sources of external knowledge, absorbing it and using at least as effectively as the competitors do. As flow of knowledge between an organization and its environment is a two-way process (mainly due to relationships with consumers), an

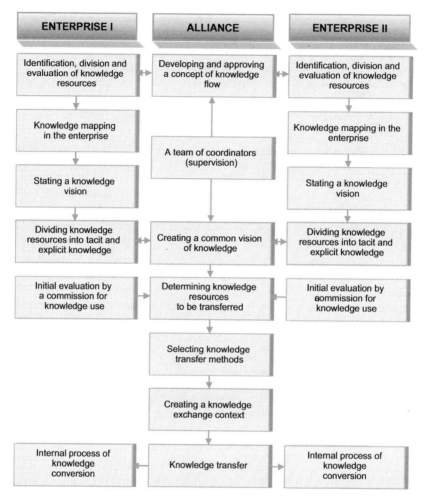

FIGURE 4.8 Diagram of knowledge exchange between the partners of an alliance. (Own work.)

organization must carefully consider what knowledge it can share with its environment so that it does not end up reducing its competitive potential but can actively cooperate with consumers in creating the value it delivers to them in its products and services. An important thing is how strongly the environment impacts an organization. If the external conditions change quickly, knowledge focused on the inside of an organization can at best correct what an organization does wrong. There are numerous examples showing that an approach like "only we know what we need to be successful" can lead to spectacular failures of companies that once were market leaders. Thus, understanding the sense and meaning of changes in an environment is a basis for understanding the necessity and direction of changes in possessed knowledge. This may also have an impact on the mission, vision and strategic goals. Thus, learning is becoming an important priority in organizations that are managed based on knowledge. This priority enables an organization to learn faster than its competitors do, leading to a faster return on investment in knowledge. Competitive advantage is gained by organizations that (Nisar, Prabhakar and Strakova 2019, pp. 264–272):

- Appropriately combine the necessary knowledge acquired from the environment with that part of their own knowledge that is and will be necessary for them to compete
- Selectively transfer their own knowledge to their environment, thereby impacting the changes occurring in that environment

Therefore, it is necessary for an organization to identify what knowledge it possesses and what knowledge that it needs resides outside of it (e.g., resides in competitors). If we define an organization as a structure of relations built for the purpose of knowledge creation, in which human experience is the beginning of processes executed in a knowledge cycle, then we must accept the fact that the boundaries of such an organization are not established by the formal organizational structure, or even by formal cross-organizational relations, as human experiences are diverse and constantly change. Knowledge in an organization is diffused and creates different values that depend on the context of its use. The boundaries of an organization seem artificial in light of the wealth of knowledge resources that can be acquired. Much of such knowledge is acquired through relationships, whether internal or with the environment. Knowledge-based strategies must take into account relations that generate the knowledge that an organization needs. This is because knowledge is a basis for designing a strategy. Competing in terms of the value of ideas, innovations and information differs from competing in terms of tangible assets. It is much less stable and less analyzable in terms of cause and effect. A huge role is played here by the unpredictable impact of knowledge on generation of economic values. Access to knowledge is not as limited as, e.g., access to money. In fact, the more widely knowledge is used, the more possibilities of its application exist. This is a problem of knowledge dynamic. At the level of a single business, the individual knowledge of every person constantly changes as a result of interactions with other people, i.e., sharing experiences gained in various conditions; therefore, the stable state of knowledge is never achieved, as it constantly fluctuates. Constant changes in the state of knowledge create infinite potential of knowledge. It is difficult to predict in advance or even evaluate post-factum how knowledge has impacted business performance. It is even more difficult to forecast the development of knowledge in the sector. One can only perceive the average level of knowledge of a sector as manifested in products and services. Only in some cases is it possible to estimate based on such products and services the actual knowledge possessed by individual companies in a sector. There are sectors where companies have a well-developed R&D function. However, it is strictly protected from the competitors. Predicting the future based on that is difficult. It is claimed, for instance, that only 10% of ideas are converted into profit-driven activities, many of which are abandoned before return on investment is achieved. The situation is uncertain. Sector-specific knowledge is a common, universal resource that apart from a positive impact may also negatively affect the sector if its quality is low. Knowledge does not always bring expected results when it is used. At the same time, knowledge resources do not shrink as they are used, and as with other resources, they can be a source of not only successes but also failures. Thus, an organization should be protected from the detrimental use of knowledge. Instead, the use of knowledge should strengthen its position.

The discussion leads to the conclusion that an organization can not ignore the activities undertaken outside of it. Significant strategic decisions concerning knowledge management must always be taken based on the big picture of sector-specific knowledge. We should bear in mind that a lot of our competitors may be way ahead of us. Ignoring what is happening in the competitors in the area of knowledge puts our organization at risk of being misaligned to the landscape of knowledge shaped by our competitors. They may show more flexibility in adapting to the conditions of competition. The above discussion shows that there are three main factors resulting from an organization's relationships with its environment: knowledge that enables achievement of the so-called increasing return on its flow into the environment, knowledge that is co-created at the level of the sector and increasing possibilities of knowledge absorption, whereby the more knowledge we possess, the bigger economic values we can generate.

Global Management of an Organizational Culture

5

Today, almost all organizations have to respond to the changes occurring in their environment. The stimuli that require response may have different character—market, technological, legislative or social; some of them are local, while others global. Depending on the specificity of a given organization, the impact of the different aspects of the environment varies. In a response to a change in their environment, modern organizations have to adapt to the new conditions of operation, which often involves the implementation of organizational changes, most broadly defined as any significant modifications of any element of the organization. The significance of organizational change in the functioning of modern organizations is evidenced by the attention given to this issue in management literature. In their works, management theoreticians more and more often use such categories as flexibility, agility, capacity for self-renewal, imperative of change and creative destruction, and describe modern organizations as balancing between order and chaos. All these processes can be described as an accelerating shift from Weber's ideal type (bureaucracy) to Toffler's ideal type (adhocracy).

5.1 IMPORTANCE OF ORGANIZATIONAL CULTURE IN TERMS OF ECONOMIC DEVELOPMENT

The process of organizational culture management requires looking at it through the prism of four characteristics, which is presented in Figure 5.1.

Due to the specificity of these characteristics, organizational culture takes time to be shaped. This is because it is largely connected with the nature and character of people—employees of an organization—the layer of personality that is least prone to changes. That is why consistency and persistence are key in the process of management.

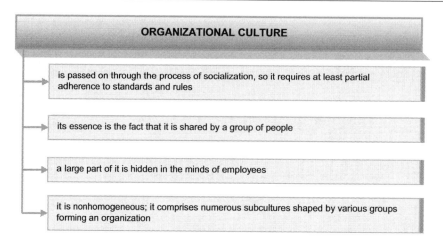

FIGURE 5.1   Shaping organizational culture in the management process. (Own work based on: Homma N., Bauschke R., *Unternehmenskultur und Führung: Den Wandel gestalten-Methoden, Prozesse, Tools*, Springer Verlag, Berlin, Heidelberg, 2015, p. 57.)

The process of organizational culture management involves impacting seven aspects of behaviors in an organization (Osterhold 2013, pp. 111–123):

1. *Innovation and risk-taking*—i.e., how much employees are motivated to be innovative and take risk
2. *Attention to details*—expectations regarding employees' precision, analytical approach and attention to detail
3. *Results orientation*—whether the managerial staff focus on results or the methods and processes that are used to achieve them
4. *People orientation*—whether and to what extent human capital is taken into account during decision-making
5. *Team orientation*—what are the preferences concerning the way of working, i.e., whether an organization promotes teamwork or individual work
6. *Aggressiveness*—whether and to what extent aggressive behaviors are accepted in an organization
7. *Stability*—whether an organization's activity demonstrates that it strives to maintain its current stable position or to develop

These characteristics are shaped by a great number of various factors. On terms of the quality of organizational culture, the most important of them is the role of the managerial staff, i.e., the attitude of the top management of an organization. In an organization with a high—consciously shaped—organizational culture, the aspect of leadership undergoes transformation, and the important thing is that it is not only the basis of governance but above all the role of the leader in an organization that changes. In an organization managed through the prism of organizational culture, management is perceived not as a sense of power, but conscious responsibility (Schmid 2013, pp. 35–47). Management mainly plays the role of an author of the vision of an organization's development, strategist and guide, coordinator, creator, mentor and coach. It is up to managerial staff's actions and attitude whether employees will support them in the implementation of an organization's objectives.

Other factors that impact organizational culture management include (Schönborn 2014, pp. 145–159):

- Specificity of the industry, in particular the formal and legal conditions regulating a given economic activity
- Region/country, i.e., the aspects of national culture
- Location, in terms of both geography and the character of the seat of an organization
- Structure of employees by age and sex

However, we must bear in mind that even if at a certain point organizational culture is optimally shaped, it will "age" more or less quickly depending on external conditions. It will cease to fulfill its positive role and become a barrier in the development of an organization. When this happens, the managerial staff should be able to make a decision about changing the culture, being aware that this process is difficult to execute and at the same time key to the future of every modern organization. Therefore, it is important that the following fundamental mistakes are avoided when changing the management of organizational culture (Warnecke 2013, pp. 34–46):

- Managing organizational culture based on external standards
- Managing organizational culture based on universal standards
- Managing organizational culture only in the area of its visible elements

The quality of organizational culture management is manifested in:

- *Its prevalence*—how many employees accept the values that prevail in the organization
- *Degree of implementation*—to what extent employees identify themselves with these values
- *Clearness of standards*—how clear are the ideas of what is desirable or prohibited
- *Scope of application*—in which spheres the behavior is regulated
- *Duration*—how long the values are espoused in an organization

In an organization with a strong organizational culture, the overwhelming majority of employees adhere to the norms in the organization. The norms and values are known and—more importantly—observed. Employees have a clear idea of what is desirable and what is prohibited, know how to behave in specific situations and are convinced of the rightness of the norms existing in an organization, often "transferring" them to their private life.

A strong organizational culture is also manifested in the psychology of employees, to whom it gives confidence; sense of security and conviction that they can rely on their organization; higher self-esteem; the sense that they can receive help, recognition and acceptance from the group; and professional pride and prestige. In an organization with a strong organizational culture, employees are loyal and identify themselves strongly with the organization's objectives. As a result, they show more commitment to the tasks assigned to them and there is no need for their behavior to be shaped through formalization. In a strong organizational culture, the managerial staff do not have to waste time on developing and controlling the compliance with instructions, rules or procedures, which means higher efficiency and effectiveness of operation.

However, once a critical point is passed, a strong organizational culture becomes the biggest barrier to the development of an organization. This is because an organizational culture that is too strong blocks the possibility of introducing changes and innovations, which is key to the survival of an organization in today's economy. There are several signs indicating that such a critical point has already been passed in organizational culture (Figure 5.2) (Nörr 2016, pp. 1–16):

- *Unwillingness to accept other views*—whatever is not rooted in an organization is regarded as a threat to the identity of the group and a destructive factor. Such an organization will struggle to develop and change, as no criticism will be carefully considered or prompt an objective discussion
- *Collective attitude of avoidance*—employees abandon self-reflection and are unable to rationally assess their conduct
- *Decreasing flexibility*—a strong organizational culture increases employees' inertia; as a result, they do not acknowledge the need for changes and for a long time ignore the signs of danger
- *Conformism*—some organizational cultures are so strong that they almost completely subordinate organizational members to themselves, often using deeply rooted beliefs, including irrational ones

The state of passing the critical point is called *cultural lock-in* (Wien and Franzke 2014, pp. 213–215). This state means that an organization is unable to change its organizational culture and adapt to its environment despite increasingly strong signals from it.

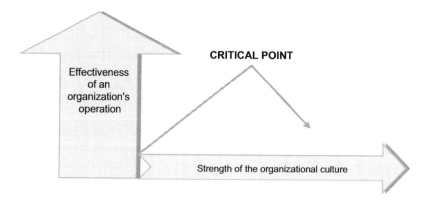

FIGURE 5.2   Relationship between the effectiveness of an organization's operation and its organizational culture. (Own work based on: Wien A., Franzke N., *Unternehmenskultur: zielorientierte Unternehmensethik als entscheidender Erfolgsfaktor*, Springer–Verlag, Berlin, Heidelberg, 2014, p. 45.)

The abovementioned aspects are reflected in the idea of Project GPTW (Von Hehn, Cornelissen, and Braun 2016, pp. 1–23), which aims to cause evolution in the global economy in the way of thinking about business, which today is only perceived through the prism of profit growth. According to the Project, the aim of economic activity should be profit but achieved with regard to human relations. It should be supported by appropriately shaped organizational culture, built on two pillars: trust and engagement.

For the assessment of the quality of organizational culture in the GPTW model, of key importance is the area of trust, which is analyzed based on the so-called Trust Index© (Bentele and Seidenglanz 2015, pp. 411–429). For an organization to be regarded as a great workplace and appear in the ranking, its Trust Index© must be at least 60%. Complementary to this index is Culture Audit© (Barrett 2016, pp. 35–49), which aims to gather numerical data about organizational culture.

The GPTW model looks at the quality of organizational culture in terms of five correlated areas of analysis (Figure 5.3).

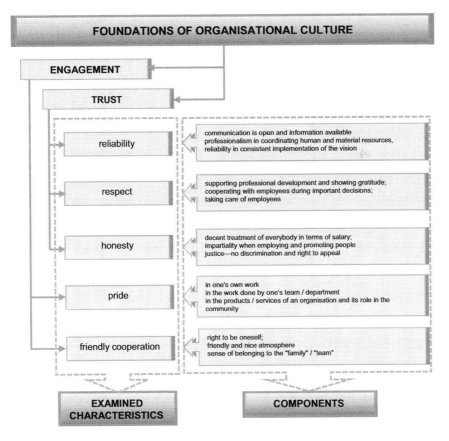

FIGURE 5.3 Areas of analysis in the GPTW model. (Own work based on: Hackl B., et al., New Work in der Praxis – Projekterfahrungen und Ideen, [in:] *New Work: Auf dem Weg zur neuen Arbeitswelt*, B. Hackl, M. Wagner, L. Attmer, D. Baumann (eds.), Springer Fachmedien, Wiesbaden, 2017, pp. 103–160.)

GPTW (Burchell and Robin 2011; Robin and Burchell 2013) reports show that organizations that were at least once regarded as a great workplace try to strengthen this position in the next years.

It is clear that in many organizations, this is often a result of implementing a comprehensive program of organizational culture management, as many of them improve their position in the rankings "exponentially." GPTW (Burchell and Robin 2011; Robin and Burchell 2013) reports also show that more and more international organizations try to adapt the organizational culture in their regional structures to the specificity of the local markets. Many organizations achieve the status of a great workplace in several countries, sometimes with very significant cultural and economic differences.

Assessment of organizational culture management is determined by a lot of demographic, environmental and professional factors. The largest disparities between assessments are due to (Burchell and Robin 2011; Robin and Burchell 2013):

> *The age of the person making assessment*—young people, up to the age of 35, are much more optimistic about their company, while people aged 35–40 are most critical.
>
> *Number of years worked in an organization*—like with age, those with the shortest length of service in a company rate their workplace best, and the longer an employee worked in one organization, the more unsatisfied he/she is, with employees with 10–20 years worked in a company giving the lowest rates.
>
> *Place in the organizational hierarchy*—this relationship is predictable; i.e., the higher the position, the better the assessment of organizational culture.
>
> *Type of executed tasks*—the best rates are given by HR (human resources) department, i.e., people directly responsible for shaping an organization; are slightly lower, but still higher compared to other departments, and are the assessments by employees of those units that due to their specificity involve creative, unconventional tasks, such as IT or R&D; the more routine the tasks, the lower the assessment of organizational culture.

The main idea of managing an organization in terms of its organizational culture is to create such conditions of operation that will allow an organization to develop effectively at a time of dynamic changes. In a knowledge-based economy, this means the creation of innovation capacity of an organization, which comprises the perception of innovation itself and the way of managing innovation processes.

An organization's innovation capacity can be assessed by analyzing its activity based on the so-called innovation chain (Banse and Reher 2015) comprising four components, which is presented in Figure 5.4.

Invention is a basic dimension of innovation which, perceived as traditional research and development activity, is based on own solutions, technologies and products. Organizations at this level of "innovation chain" (Banse and Reher 2015) regard themselves as innovative because they established an R&D department in their structures, have their own inventions and included the term "innovative" in their mission.

Business model innovation (Romanowska 2016, pp. 29–35) represents a more advanced level of innovation and facilitates the development of an organization in a

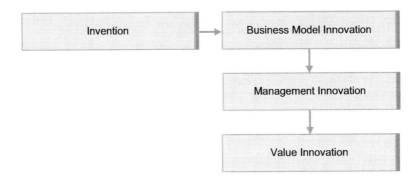

FIGURE 5.4 Innovation chain. (Own work based on: Banse G., Reher E.O., Technologiewandel in der Wissensgesellschaft – qualitative und quantitative Veränderungen, Sitzungsberichte der Leibniz–Sozietät zu Berlin, Bd. 122, Berlin, 2015.)

knowledge-based economy much more so than the first one. In business model innovation, the focus is on human capital, partnership as well as knowledge and information. Material resources of an organization—infrastructure and financial resources—are perceived as one of the tools to achieve business objectives rather than the basic condition.

Management innovation (Kraśnicka, Głod and Wronka 2014, pp. 333–349) is regarded as the basic distinguishing feature of a knowledge-based economy. Innovation is perceived here as a capacity for implementing the best practices, but with a clear shift of focus towards identifying practices that refer to new phenomena in the economy, such as information advantage, social networks or adaptive strategies.

Value innovation (Wicharz 2015, p. 121) is the highest level of an organization's innovation and refers to the next-generation economy. Innovation is understood here as a process of building relationships between an organization and its products on the one hand and the market on the other hand. In this component of "innovation chain," it is assumed that success will be achieved only by those organizations that will deliver "emotions and experiences" rather than "products and services." However, such approach to competitiveness requires the development of mechanisms in an organization that will permanently protect the unique character of its offer. This in turn requires managing organizational culture in terms of values impacting an organization's environment.

Innovation capacity can be based on one or all four components of "innovation chain." However, for the assessment of an organization's capacity for development in today's economy, it is important which of the components dominates in management and operational processes. During a period of economic upturn, when the demand is growing and organizations can generate relatively high financial surpluses, organizational culture may play a significant role provided that the managerial staff perceives this aspect of the functioning of an organization as important and undertakes deliberate actions in that area.

Whether organizational culture is really a permanent element of managing an organization or it is only a superficial behavior can be seen in times of a crisis. Appropriate organizational culture management should help an organization to overcome difficulties and transform the slowdown in economic situation into a springboard for further development. It is facilitated mainly by two features of organizational culture, which gain special importance in times of crisis (Szymańska 2015, pp. 35–45):

1. *Strong emotional connection* of employees with their organization, which allows them to sacrifice their individual interest for the interest of the organization
2. *Putting in place mechanisms of innovation* and creative search for solutions, so that in times of a crisis employees do not panic and take ill-considered and short-term actions, but are able to engage into a constructive discussion and together agree on changes that will help the organization to survive in the difficult period

A good test of the quality of organizational culture management for modern organizations is the financial crisis that started in mid-2008. Its mechanisms and development differ radically from previous periods of economic downturn. Observers of macroeconomic processes stress that the current crisis is a crisis of sales rather than a crisis of costs, as it is not about a lack of resources, but about decreased trust in practically all markets. This causes completely different relations between the buyer and the supplier than before. Thus, the crisis impacts the sphere of demand factors, irrevocably changing (Baschera and Gundrum 2013, pp. 33–36):

- Customers' attitudes, causing them to analyze the rationality of every expenditure more carefully than before
- Directions of previous globalization processes; the guarantee and stability of cooperation become more important than the price; therefore, the use of cheap but remote (e.g., in China) production capacities is no longer perceived as profitable

Simple activities focused exclusively on the cost sphere are insufficient for such trends. There are various studies that to a greater or lesser extent assess the effectiveness of the functioning of organizations in the modern economy, but the most objective test for the quality of their organizational culture is employees' loyalty. Management of the development of an organization in terms of its culture is about recruiting the best employees and—more importantly—retaining them. For organizational culture management, a particularly disturbing phenomenon is the increasing trend to change jobs among managers, i.e., the very group of employees that plays a key role in the process of building the values of an organization and a consistent system of behavior patterns both inside an organization and in contacts with partners from its environment.

One of the symptoms of the maturity of an organizational culture has to do with the way it is perceived in conflict situations. In interpersonal relations, conflicts have always occurred and will continue to occur. However, only in an organization with an established organizational culture, they become an instrument that facilitates its development rather than leading to crises. In times of dynamic changes, organizations functioning without conflict situations are doomed to failure. This is because full harmony and atmosphere of peace cause an organization to become static, passive and insensitive to the need for changes and innovations. A conflict, when skillfully managed, provides an organization with the necessary dose of dynamism, which by "stirring up a hornet's nest" can cause new directions of operation—better than the previous ones—to be set within a short period.

In a modern organization, conflict, as a controlled and consciously managed instrument, is a permanent element of organizational culture, fulfilling two essential roles (Schmidt 2013, pp. 253–271):

1. It guarantees objectivity in decision-making, not allowing any decision to be made based on insufficient data or proper consideration of significant alternative solutions.
2. It eliminates the so-called group-thinking syndrome, which means that after a certain time, the established thought patterns start to dominate in every team, narrowing down the scope of discussion.

This makes conflict a tool that boosts employees' activity, makes them more self-critical, undermines the established ways of doing things in an organization and stimulates creativity through inquisitiveness and alternative ways of viewing the same situation. This can only take place in an organization with mature organizational culture, which shapes an organization not only through the mechanisms of cooperation, but also through assertiveness in all the directions of the superior/subordinate relationship—including the most difficult assertiveness, i.e., the vertical relationship (Gregorczyk et al. 2016, p. 422).

In organizations where assertiveness becomes a permanent element of organizational culture, employees openly say that they cannot do something or that somebody else will do it better. They only engage in those projects that match their abilities and ambitions. At the same time, on their own initiative and unselfconsciously, they present their ideas and innovative solutions to their superiors. Assertive employees openly speak about the reasons for their satisfaction or dissatisfaction at work, and actively look for solutions in negative situations.

Thus, maturity in organizational culture management in terms of assertiveness is achieved by those organizations where employees maintain peace, common sense and ability to verbally express their thoughts towards their superiors as well as a deep self-respect and respect for the work done by themselves and others. In such organizations, assertiveness is perceived as a tool facilitating open and factual discussion irrespective of the position one occupies, without the side effects in the form of releasing strong emotions or—quite the contrary—suppressed frustration.

As was repeatedly stressed, the functioning of modern organizations is about changes—to successfully develop, organizations have to not only observe trends in their environment, but also effectively adapt the business model to these trends. This means that employees of modern organizations are and will increasingly be subjected to the pressure of changes. A natural characteristic of a human being is aversion to changes. This is because change requires rejecting the familiar and proven status quo and replacing it with a new, unknown one. This undermines one of the essential human needs—the need for security. Therefore, the overwhelming majority of people subjected to the pressure of changes tend to react with resistance. Sometimes, when a change does not impact a given employee directly, their reaction will be indifference. For organizations that want to dynamically grow in the present-day and future reality, both these attitudes lead to negative consequences. Employees' resistance that prevents or significantly prolongs the process of adapting an organization to its environment results in the elimination of the organization or its marginalization in the market. Indifference towards implemented changes only appears to be a better reaction than resistance. This is because indifference means a lack of engagement, which in the long run will generate the state of stagnation.

Therefore, for a modern organization, it is important to create such mechanisms that when the inevitable changes occur will stimulate employees to adopt the attitude of acceptance, and by extension cooperation. The most effective tool, and at the same time one that requires significant maturity from an organization, is social dialogue. Its aim is to create such communication conditions in an organization where different parties, representing different groups of interest, can present their positions, and these positions are listened to and taken into consideration by the other partners.

In addition to being a tool facilitating the implementation of changes, social dialogue is also treated in a modern organization as inspiration for changes (Hajdys 2015, p. 404). By creating a platform for free exchange of thoughts and views among different groups of interest, it is very often possible to develop unique solutions that enhance the competitiveness of an organization and are acceptable to all parties of the dialogue. For parties to engage in an effective social dialogue, they must have certain potential that comprises (Rhein 2016, pp. 25–37):

- *Analytical capabilities*—assessment of basic factors impacting stances in negotiations
- *Empathy*—ability to be put oneself in the shoes of another person
- *Planning capabilities*—developing and implementing negotiation strategy and tactic
- *Interactive capabilities*—maintaining good relationships with other people
- *Communication capabilities*—ability to present information and arguments in a clear, logical and positive way

The highest form of public dialogue is participative style of management, which, however, requires from an organization to develop conciliation attitudes instead of confrontation attitudes. This applies above all to the two main parties in an organization, i.e., the managerial staff and employees. For the former, this will mean limiting the use of power as an element of pressure, while for the latter assuming co-responsibility not only for the fate of the staff they represent but also for the fate of the whole organization, and often its environment as well.

For modern organizations, these trends mean that they have to be prepared to manage a team of people with very different, sometimes even opposing, views and behaviors. This requires that the process of organizational culture management applies a complex approach that allows for the coexistence of numerous subcultures, which in certain areas will require compromise-based relations with the main organizational culture. This will naturally increase the costs of managing organizational culture. However, taking into account the above aspects in the functioning of a modern organization, it may significantly strengthen its competitive position, as it will help it to win employees' loyalty, learn more about markets targeting minority groups and increase its creativity. Organizations that will implement the above instruments will certainly see them translated into actual economic benefits and as a result will improve their competitive potential.

5.2 PROFILE OF ORGANIZATIONAL CULTURE IN ACCELERATION OF ENTREPRENEURSHIP

Until relatively recently, organizations based their competitive advantage on material resources, to which they had to have a clear ownership title. The priority of every entity striving to secure a position among the leaders was possession of a well-developed production infrastructure, own distribution network and logistic infrastructure. It also had to have its own ancillary and administrative infrastructure.

In today's market realities, this traditional source of competitive advantage more and more turns out insufficient. The evolution of social behaviors, the globalization of markets and the increasing pace of changes in the business environment, due to technological progress, force organizations to resort to alternative immaterial attributes of competitiveness. Thus, in modern business models, the foundation of development is not machinery and buildings, but human capital with its knowledge, creativity and personality (Jelonek 2012, p. 37).

With competitiveness relying on immaterial foundations, organizations in the modern economy undergo a radical transformation in terms of the way they carry out operational activities. What is mainly changing is the source of inspiration in business. In the developing market economy, the natural business model of organizations was to imitate the best in the industry and adapt their solutions to organizations' own needs; it was the largest players in the industry that set business standards to be followed by smaller players. This led to a uniform development of industries based to a large extent on copying standardized solutions; this is because organizations operating in a given economic area behaved very similarly, which significantly narrowed down the field of competitive struggle. It resulted in markets becoming hermetic and the structure of their players becoming "frozen." Market leaders were almost always the largest organizations in terms of capital and resources, and transformation from the category of small to even medium-sized entities was practically unattainable due to limited possibilities of development.

With increasing competitiveness of markets, including the emergence of cutting-edge technologies, opposing this model of development was only a question of time. Owing to innovations—especially in the field of ICT—pioneer organizations emerged which succeeded thanks to following their own path of development built on breaking the previous conventions and going beyond the widely accepted behavior patterns in a given industry. That is why in today's world of business such characteristics as courage, creativity, innovation and flexibility are becoming more important for an organization than the ability to copy and adapt to the established standards in a given industry.

We also see a change in HR management. In today's economy, being an owner of certain resources not only does help in development, but also increasingly becomes a serious burden for an organization. "Ownership" of resources is increasingly replaced by "access" to them. Today, it becomes common in many industries that leaders are organizations that practically do not possess their own assets, and most of their operations are based on outsourcing and contract manufacture. In today's business, intellectual capital is more important than physical capital, and the key skill allowing an organization to succeed is not the consumption of resources but the ability to quickly identify them and ensure a flexible access to them (Antczak 2013, p. 117).

Transformation is also seen in access to capital. Just because an organization possesses large enough financial resources and invested them in what was at that time the most profitable business does not mean that it will be able to survive and grow. In today's market processes, financial resources are no guarantee of success anymore. Instead, the key to the business world is knowledge, creativity and perseverance. With such competencies, access to capital no longer represents a serious barrier for an organization today.

Such changes require from organizations a high degree of individualism in operation. But the essential question for a modern organization is: Where should this individualism be manifested?

Missions, visions and general strategies are usually formulated in a similar, sometimes even identical, way among competitors. Thus, the ability to be better must have to do not with how the strategy is called but with the tools applied to implement it. However, the solutions applied in today's business are usually widely available. Therefore, in practice, it turns out that "being competitive" actually means doing the same things as other market players, but better than them. This requires developing a combination of such attributes and competencies that are effective yet rare and difficult to copy by the competitors.

Still, the ability to develop unique competencies cannot be a basis for success—it brings short-term effects. This is because in an increasingly fast-changing environment, the characteristics that have been developed become obsolete very quickly. Thus, for building a long-term competitive advantage, it is important to be able to both create unique competencies and replace them quickly with others.

These conditions of today's economy represent a huge challenge and require a completely different approach to managing an organization (Brzozowska 2013, pp. 5–18). One of the leading concepts of succeeding in business, which falls under the so-called new wave, is the concept based on the idea of creating competitive advantages by building a conscious organizational culture (Deszczyński 2016, pp. 280–288). It is worth stressing that it is one of the few management concepts that were developed by theoreticians based on scientific research and appreciated by business practitioners.

Nowadays, the idea of managing an organization through shaping its organizational culture has become a determinant of the modernity of the economy and is wildly promoted worldwide. Its increasing importance is evidenced by the fact that more and more business processes are executed taking into account the quality of organizational culture. More and more, it becomes:

- An element of shaping an organization's image among its customers and cooperating parties
- A tool for attracting/retaining valuable employees

- An element that is taken into account in the assessment of an organization's value, along with measurable elements such as assets or financial results
- A key determinant in the success of merger and acquisition processes

There are no organizations without organizational culture. Every economic entity has its own organizational culture, but not every one is able to perceive it, let alone shape it consciously. Results of different studies (Serafin 2015, pp. 87–100) conducted among organizations indicate that the degree of awareness of the organizational culture directly results from the level of economic development and the business models applied in the economy, which is presented in Figure 5.5.

In the industrial economy, the competitiveness of an organization is perceived in terms of its resources. An organization is based on the prescriptive and controlling model and focuses mainly on building hierarchical relationships among employees and managing their behaviors through procedures and instructions. The organizational culture is not conscious and is created spontaneously and accidentally. This leads to huge alienation of people positioned in various functional areas of an organization, in both internal and external contacts. As a result, information flow and decision-making processes are longer, rigid and based on superficial premise. Consequently, an organization functions out of touch with the changes that take place in its environment, which is presented in Figure 5.6.

In the market economy, an organization's market position is built on intangible assets, such as mission, vision, strategy and reputation—these elements define how an organization operates. The prescriptive and controlling model is replaced by management through market position. An organization is based on business divisions (Kujawski 2017, p. 471), and employees' behaviors are controlled by processes and management systems. Organizational culture is perceived as an organization's strategy and its organizational model. As a result, an organization possesses a system of values and norms shaping the behavior of its employees, which can be defined as organizational culture, but it is usually only "on paper." This is due to the lack of tools for implementing this system in an organization and transferring it onto interpersonal relations.

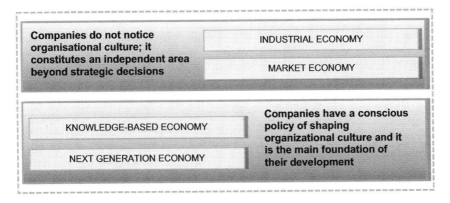

FIGURE 5.5 Economic development in the aspect of organizational culture. (Own work based on: Sackmann S., *Erfolgsfaktor Unternehmenskul- tur: Mit kulturbewusstem Management Unternehmensziele erreichen und Identifikation schaffen – 6 Best Practice-Beispiele*, Springer Verlag, Berlin, Heidelberg, 2013, p. 7.)

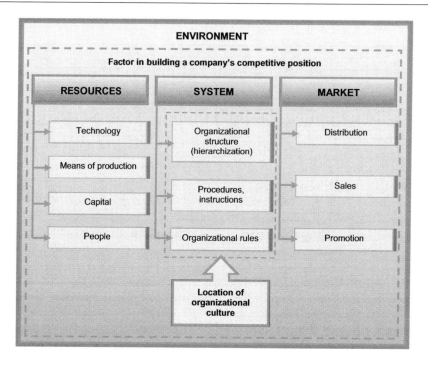

FIGURE 5.6 Perception of the organizational culture in the industrial economy. (Own work based on: Fehr U., Nutzinger H.G., Hans G., *Unterneh- menskultur und innerbetriebliche Kooperation: Anforderungen und praktische Erfahrungen*, Springer Verlag, Berlin, Heidelberg, 2013, pp. 57–59.)

Thus, organizational culture is to remain only declarative, and will have little impact on the actual functioning of an organization, which is presented in Figure 5.7.

It is only in a knowledge-based economy, where competitive edge is built on human capital and intellectual potential, that organizational culture is a conscious tool for creating development. It is perceived here as an instrument for shaping interpersonal relations within an organization and used for stimulating employees' activity, creativity and engagement. Here, organizational culture takes on the form of a "web" that covers all areas of an organization's activity. As a result, an organization is coherent, and its development objectives are understood by all its employees, which is presented in Figure 5.8.

But even today we can see trends where organizational culture is given even more importance than in a knowledge-based economy. It is more and more wildly assumed that in the near future, an organization's competitiveness will be built not only on "knowledge and innovations," but also on the "feelings and experiences" it will provide to its environment. Thus, the development of organizations will be determined by replacing business relations by emotional relations with the environment. Such relations will be built on a common system of values and norms, with organizational culture being the tool that ensures consistency. Thus, in the "next-generation economy," organizational culture will go beyond an organization and shape not only employees' attitudes, but also the attitudes of the entities from the organization's environment, which is presented in Figure 5.9.

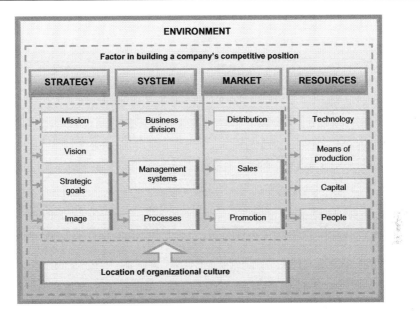

FIGURE 5.7 Perception of organizational culture in the market economy. (Own study based on: Fehr U., Nutzinger H.G., *Unternehmenskultur und innerbetriebliche Kooperation: Anforderungen und praktische Erfahrungen*, Springer Verlag, Berlin, Heidelberg, 2013, p. 112.)

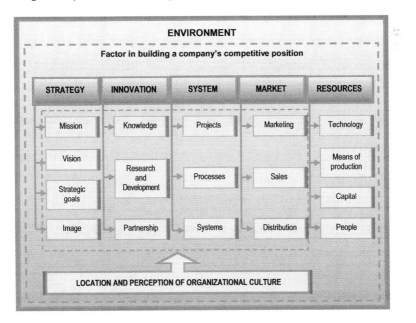

FIGURE 5.8 Perception of organizational culture in a knowledge-based economy. (Own study based on: Fehr U., Nutzinger H.G., *Unternehmenskultur und innerbetriebli-che Kooperation: Anforderungen und praktische Erfahrungen*, Springer Verlag, Berlin, Heidelberg, 2013, pp. 78–93.)

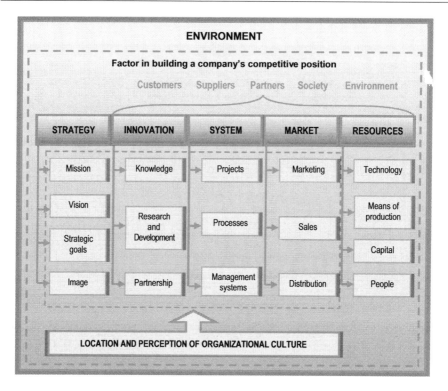

FIGURE 5.9 Perception of organizational culture in the "next-generation" economy. (Own study based on: Osterhold G., *Veränderungsmanagement: Visionen und Wege zu einer neuen Unternehmenskultur*, Springer Verlag, Berlin, Heidelberg, 2013, p. 93.)

In organizations where organizational culture is not shaped in a deliberate way, it takes less time to see negative symptoms in it such as (Lichtarski 2015, pp. 33–42):

- The attitude of the managerial staff, characterized by conviction of one's own infallibility and strength, and at the same time distrust of the environment and employees
- Display of aggressive, dismissive and depreciative behaviors towards others
- Domination of the so-called loyalty bonds over a realistic assessment, maintaining illusion at the cost of a careful diagnosis of the situation, work addiction, overload with work and tasks
- Increasing conflicts and misunderstandings, which leads to the cumulation of negative emotions and reinforcement of mutual prejudices
- Atmosphere of gossips and intrigues, which become the dominant channel of information flow within an organization
- Manipulation of information
- Workplace harassment
- Lack of motivation for teamwork
- Lack of clear principles

- Pursuing hidden self-interest; internal competition at the level of the managerial staff and operational employees, which does not benefit the global goals of an organization
- Learned helplessness syndrome
- Decreased work productivity, which does not result from the lack of employees' competencies but decreased work motivation; errors, being late, high staff rotation, mistakes, neglect
- Motivation system based on punishments and criticism
- Lack of positive reinforcement—rewards, praises, feedback
- Coalitions within an organization
- Finding a "scapegoat" as a mechanism of defusing tensions

The idea of organizational culture is of key importance in implementing social and economic objectives through (Szymańska 2015, pp. 35–45):

Transformation to a knowledge-based economy, including the development of information society, research and innovation, and teaching appropriate qualifications and skills.

Liberalization and integration of markets and sectors not covered by the common market.

Development of entrepreneurship—deregulation and removal of administrative and legal barriers, easier access to capital and technologies, reduction of public aid, creation of a level playing field.

Increase in employment and change in the social model—increased labor market participation, more flexible labor market, improvement in the level of education, modernization of the social insurance system, reduction of poverty and social exclusion.

Care for sustainable foundations of development and the natural environment—reduction of climate changes, preservation of natural resources.

The main idea behind the new trends is to strive to make a better use of the existing potential—labor, knowledge and capital. A potential defined in this way means perceiving competitiveness not in terms of resources or natural wealth, but in terms of intellectual capital. Thus, in terms of undertaken activities, priority is given to any instruments that can strengthen this capital—the idea of organizational culture is one of them.

In the simplest terms, organizational culture is defined as a system of behaviors and rules of conduct adopted in a given organization. From the perspective of the functioning of an organization, two functions of organizational culture are important (Kocoń 2015, pp. 47–52):

1. *External adaptation*—which is connected with defining an organization's identity, i.e., positioning it in the industry in which it operates and in the social environment; at this level, organizational culture enables understanding of the mission, objectives and strategies towards customers, competitors, cooperating parties, as well as the socioeconomic environment in the broad sense. The higher the quality of organizational culture, the better the understanding of an

organization's mission, objectives and strategies. The measure of the quality of organizational culture in the "external" aspect is economic efficiency and effectiveness of an organization's operation on the market.

2. *Internal adaptation*—at this level, organizational culture unites "the inside" of an organization into one coherent organism, fulfilling integration, perception and adaptation roles.

In organizations where organizational culture is not conscious, the priorities of development, which are formulated in the form of vision, mission and strategic objectives, usually remain empty marketing slogans. They can only gain meaning when employees understand them and become engaged in implementing them, which is impossible without having an established organizational culture in place. The quality of organizational culture is determined in this area by three indicators (Gołębiowski 2014, pp. 33–42):

- Employees' loyalty; the higher the culture, the better the atmosphere at work
- The fewer the conflicts, the less the stress, and consequently the more satisfaction with work and attachment to the organization
- The time it takes for new employees to assimilate in an organization; the more established the organizational culture, the faster a new employee learns how to navigate through it, how to communicate with other employees, what rules and values to follow and what can be the consequences of failing to follow them

In today's world, the characteristics of organizational culture are mostly affected by correlation of forces in two areas, which is presented in Figure 5.10.

These relationships are the basis for distinguishing four main types of organizational culture, which is presented in Figure 5.11.

In the hierarchy culture (Figure 5.12), the organization is highly formalized and hierarchical. As procedures and instructions govern their operation, such organizations tend to show high bureaucratization. Leaders in this model of culture are above all good organizers. The aim of an organization is permanence, predictability and effectiveness. The long-term focus is in stability, productivity and smooth operations. Regulations

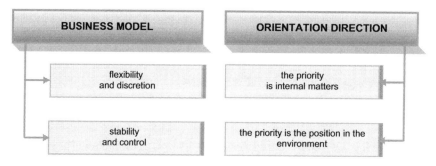

FIGURE 5.10   Correlation of forces in the aspect of the character of organizational culture. (Own work based on: Schmid C.H., *Planung von Unternehmenskultur*, Springer Verlag, Berlin, Heidelberg, 2013, p. 78.)

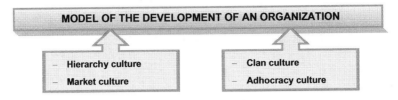

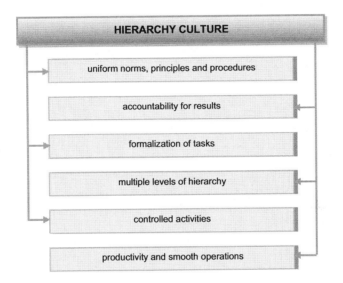

FIGURE 5.11   Types of organizational culture. (Own work based on: Homma N., Bauschke R., Konzeption der neuen Unternehmenskultur und des Roll-out, [in:] *Unternehmenskultur und Führung*, N. Homma, R. Bauschke (eds.), Springer Fachmedien, Wiesbaden, 2015, pp. 83–93.)

FIGURE 5.12   The hierarchy culture. (Own study based on: Homburg Ch., Marktorientierung der Unternehmenskultur und der Führungssysteme, [in:] *Marketing Management: Strategie – Instrumente – Umsetzung – Unternehmensführung*, Ch. Homburg (ed.), Springer Fachmedien, Wiesbaden, 2017, pp. 1287–1318.)

and principles hold the organization together. The measure of success is operational reliability, meeting deadlines and low costs.

As far as the market culture is concerned (Figure 5.13), the efficiency of an organization is determined by the costs of transactions. There is a predominant external focus, and the priority in development is to achieve a certain position in the business environment. Contrary to hierarchy, where control is based on regulations and centralized decisions, the market culture is driven by economic market mechanisms. The operation of an organization is determined by profitability, bottom line and market position. Competitiveness and productivity are the most important values. The underlying assumptions of the market culture are a lack of a friendly environment and a constant need for strengthening the market position. The leaders are demanding, and the style of management involves the promotion of aggressive competition. Success orientation holds the organization together. Success is measured by market share and profit.

FIGURE 5.13 The market culture. (Own work based on: Homburg Ch., Marktorientierung der Unter- nehmenskultur und der Führungssysteme, [in:] *Marketing Management: Strategie – Instru- mente – Umsetzung – Unternehmensführung*, Ch. Homburg (ed.), Springer Fachmedien, Wiesbaden, 2017, pp. 1287–1318.)

In the clan culture (Figure 5.14), shared values and goals, participation and the sense of belonging dominate. The team is more like a huge family than an organization. Instead of procedures (hierarchy) and competitiveness (market), the organization is managed through teamwork and employee development, customers are treated as partners, and there is a nice atmosphere at work.

The main tasks of the managerial staff include delegating responsibilities to employees and encouraging participation, engagement and loyalty. In the clan culture, an organization is a pleasant place to work. The leaders play the role of mentors and caregivers. The organization is held together by loyalty and attachment to tradition. The measure of success is a good atmosphere within the organization and care of HR. The clan culture is a model typical of Asian organizations, mainly Japanese ones.

The adhocracy culture (Figure 5.15) is the newest type of organizational culture. As its name suggests, it refers to dynamic entities that are set up on ad hoc basis. Teams are formed on ad hoc basis as needed, and dissolved once the task is completed. This culture supports the ability to be adaptive, flexible and creative in the situation of information overload, uncertainty and ambiguity. It is focused on innovation and quick response to emerging opportunities.

Contrary to the market or hierarchy cultures, in adhocracy there is no centralized center of power or a clear hierarchical dependence. Power is handed over by people or task groups depending on the task at hand. Unconventional solutions, risky proposals and prediction capabilities are expected. Entities showing characteristics of the adhocracy culture may exist within larger organizations where a different type of culture dominates.

FIGURE 5.14 The clan culture. (Own work based on: Homburg Ch., Marktorientierung der Unter- nehmenskultur und der Führungssysteme, [in:] *Marketing Management: Strategie – Instru- mente – Umsetzung – Unternehmensführung*, Ch. Homburg (ed.), Springer Fachmedien, Wiesbaden, 2017, pp. 1287–1318.)

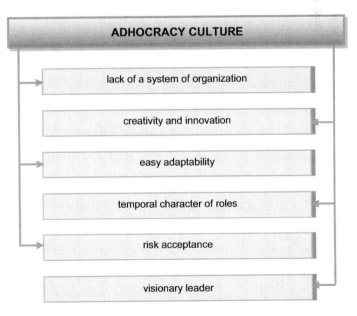

FIGURE 5.15 The adhocracy culture. (Own work based on: Homburg Ch., Marktorientierung der Unter- nehmenskultur und der Führungssysteme, [in:] *Marketing Management*, Springer Fachmedien, Wiesbaden, 2017, pp. 1287–1318.)

In the adhocracy culture, people are willing to take risk, and the leader is a visionary and innovator who is not afraid of risk. The organization encourages freedom and initiative. The organization is held together by innovation and experimentation. The emphasis is on fast growth and acquiring new resources. The success is equated with producing unique, even disruptive products.

5.3 ORGANIZATIONAL CULTURE IN A GLOBALIZED WORLD

An organization's compliance with ethical norms in its activity undoubtedly facilitates the strengthening of appropriate relationships with its environment, winning of customer loyalty and establishment of appropriate ties with cooperating partners, thereby leading to the organization's economic growth resulting from economies of scales due to, among other things, repeated purchases of goods and services, and—as stressed by Crane, Kawashima and Kawasaki—improved employee motivation caused by increased job satisfaction, decreased production costs due to the scale of production and staff's experience (Crane, Kawashima and Kawasaki 2016, pp. 11–36). Nowadays, we can see a clear shift towards formulation of missions that include not only pursuit of economic interests, but also social and environmental ones, and specify the scope of responsibility of managers and supervisory boards arising from social commitments made by enterprises.

The economy and ethics may be governed by their own, separate principles, but there are strong relationships between them. It is not irrelevant what impacts, in terms of benefits and damages, the activity of an organization will have on its micro- and macroenvironment—especially if the organization operates on a global scale. Therefore, as was strongly stressed, ethical norms should be part of any activity, and actions of an organization should be assessed not only in terms of economic criteria, which are about own gains, but also in terms of moral behaviors and ethical attitudes, manifested in an organization's concern for social issues (Schreyögg 2012, pp. 171–194).

Looking at today's business practice, clear changes can be seen in the global economy in terms of balancing economic and ethical considerations in favor of harmonizing these domains, and opposing human and environmental degradation and serving the public good through the formulation of appropriate principles and recommendations regarding the creation of a framework for the development of quality of business.

In other words, principles generating progress in economic and environmental spheres are promoted, corporate social responsibility becomes a sign of a new economic governance, and profit is not the only raison d'etre, but equally important is long-term survival of a company which also fulfills certain social commitments having regard for social responsibility—both internal and external (Frank 2018, pp. 1–13). Seufert Sabine understood that very well, recognizing the need to show moderation in seeking gains, the need to create utility, the need for recognition of and respect for another human being, concern for a common good and diligence in acting and thinking (Seufert et al. 2016, pp. 112–120).

The issue of putting one's interest first and adopting egotistical attitude still seems relevant. Resulting from conformism, this attitude is difficult to reconcile with moral principles, but it seems acceptable and reasonable from the social point of view. The problem is how to reconcile the demands of the environment, which necessarily drives an organization to achieve short-term gains, with the expectations of social life, which are manifested in moral order, ethical behaviors and the need to ensure order and security. For business practice, this means that an organization's business operations should be perceived through the prism of the social context of the economy; otherwise, the conditions facilitating the achievement of objectives at the level of the whole economy may be put at risk. Thus, the organizers of economic life—politicians and creators of economic developments on a macro scale as well as managers running global organizations—should be required to be able to reconcile the needs of their own economic institutions with the expectations of social life, i.e., finding a way to achieve balance between material values and humanistic and environmental ones.

This requires evolution in the approach to economic processes, starting from promotion of the government's political involvement in that area to compliance with the principles of social responsibility at the level of an individual organization. Thus, global managers must perceive their activity not only in terms of pragmatism and efficiency in the narrow sense, but also in terms of ethics and culture, because—as Awan writes—conventional economic thought has lost touch with the fast-changing reality (Awan 2018, pp. 113–118).

Such approach requires a sort of compromise—an instrument combining the criteria of economic efficiency with ethical demands and social expectations, especially that corporate social responsibility seems to gain importance, and organizations that do not make ethical principles part of their business activity will be rejected by society as maladapted (not friendly), even if their performance is satisfactory and products and services are of the highest quality.

For organizations, this means that, on the one hand, they will be forced to listen to the market needs, while on the other hand, they will be required to monitor and meet the expectations and demands of their environment in the broad sense (social, institutional, cultural, etc.). Seeking the right solution, an organization may adopt a number of attitudes that increase its capability to consider the issues of social responsibility, four of which seem characteristic of global economy: adaptive (legalistic) attitude, meaning that an organization adheres to legal regulations being convinced that they will work to the benefit of its business; conformist (market) attitude, meaning that an organization acts on all the signals coming from the environment (market) that refer to the preferences of its participants (customers). In this way, an organization meets, as a sort of side effect, the demands raised by society, doing so in a selective way that suits its own needs and interests: business attitude, which is an extension of the conformist attitude, as it additionally takes into account the interests and demands of various entities in the environment. As a rule, activities as part of this type of attitude are coherent and encompass a bundle of various measures resulting from demands of pressure groups. For instance, an organization that undertakes initiatives that promote environmental protection builds its reputation and at the same time establishes its image by maintaining appropriate relations with the institutions interested: orthodox attitude, which manifests in ultra-rigorous compliance with legal regulations and declaration of behaviors and attitudes, through actions, that are based on the respect for moral and ethical values (health, culture, politics, philanthropy, etc.) in the broadest sense. This inspires a reflection that it is necessary to make sure that organizations in the global economy can drink, breathe and excrete in a way that enables them to function in an ecosystem (Kagermann et al. 2016, pp. 37–40).

When examining the issues of organizational culture in the globalized world, it is necessary to address mutual interactions between different cultures all over the world. The economy has always had less regard to national borders than politics. Already in the ancient times, and later in the Middle Ages, merchants and businessmen crossed the officially established borders between countries to supply, sell and acquire goods and technologies. Sometimes, they did so legally; other times, they broke the law and acted as smugglers or spies. It was primarily materials and ideas that were transferred between countries, specialists—less so. Naturally, there were cases when some brilliant inventor changed his country of residence, but they were rather sporadic. This picture started to change in the second half of the 20th century. The rise of global organizations, which first appeared one at a time and then sprang up in all industries, completely changed how technologies and ideas are transferred and how work is organized.

Today every organization has hundreds if not thousands of employees referred to as expats—managers working on a contract basis who go away for a few years to a foreign country so that in the local office of their corporation, they can promote the ways of thinking and doing things typical of the country where their organization is headquartered. Since global organizations are by definition present in most countries of the world, their expats also go everywhere. As a result, every country hosts representatives of other cultures, who have sufficient power guaranteed by their organization to effectively pass on and inculcate in their subordinates their own culture.

The factor of power is key here. Immigrants have always existed—moving from country to country, fleeing political turmoil, wars, oppression or religious persecutions. Upon arrival in their new home countries, they had the lowest possible status and had to struggle to achieve everything on their own, slowly creating a space for living and chances for success. The new species of immigrants is in a completely different situation. Expats are provided with everything they need for daily life—accommodation, insurance, schools for children and a high-ranking job. Interestingly, compared to the locals working at the same positions, expats, as representatives of their organization, tend to be much higher in the symbolic hierarchy, which translates into greater power.

Through their actions, expats shape the organizational culture, because that is what their most important task is. Organizations invest huge amounts of money in their salaries, travel costs and all the comforts in their new places of residence, but in return expect them to constantly make sure that the organizational culture is coherent throughout the organization. Expats have always been treated as the most important channel of transmission of organizational culture. Interestingly, shaping the way of thinking and promoting culture often does not seem to be a conscious or intentional aim of expats. Consultants working with expats often perceive them as individuals who above all wish to generate maximum performance within the short period of their stay in a foreign country. As they live there for only a few years—usually two to four—they do not see any personal interest in deep restructuring of mentality that will bring visible effects when their term ends. Consequently, they are performance-driven and act in ways that they deem most effective. By doing so, they manifest the basic assumptions of their cultures. In this way, they act as channels through which other cultures are transmitted.

In addition to that, organizations have a lot of other tools that can be used to transmit their culture. One such tool is the Internet, which enables the creation of unified software or shared internal networks (intranet). It allows the same solutions to be used in different continents and facilitates direct contacts with employees from other countries through such means as e-mail, teleconferences and video conferences. As a result, we can see cultural islands within a country which are inhabited by people following norms and values of a completely different society.

The situation would be relatively simple to analyze if—as in the 19th century—there were a few colonizing countries and all the rest were colonized countries. However, contrary to the past, in today's business colonizers and those colonized are the same countries. This leads to a complicated mix of various conflicting influences observed in the world. In every country, there are hundreds of islands whose inhabitants function by slightly different rules.

In such organizations, we will find expats, who naturally have their home country's culture instilled in them deeply. There are also top managers, who are frequently in touch with IT solution and have been thoroughly trained and regularly travel to the country where their organization has its headquarters. As a result, they have absorbed the culture of that country to a significant degree. The closer to the bottom, to line workers, the weaker the cultural influences are, but there will always be some. Such an island will not be homogeneous culturally, but all of its inhabitants will to some extent respect the values of the country where the concern is headquartered.

Each of such inhabitants—employees—has a family, friends and acquaintances from other companies. The culture of his/her company and values that are important to him/her will accompany him/her not only in the professional but also in private life. In conversations about work, when organizing a party or engaging in other activities, he/she will to a some extent spread the culture of his/her company, including in the place where he/she lives.

Looking at the issue from a broader perspective, we can state that the same thing happens in every relatively developed country. Hundreds of organizations with various cultural background transfer their values to a new place. When this is a multilateral process, we can say that everyone changes everyone. A huge melting pot of different cultures is created.

Cultures converge, as every change made in a given country merges with its culture over time. With everyone changing everyone, a slow process of cultural integration takes place. However, this phenomenon is not strong enough to unify the culture of the entire world making it one coherent whole in all aspects; especially that in many countries, there are mechanisms that block such integration at the level of entire communities. Still, this globalization of cultures is increasingly seen in business. No matter how sharp the differences between individual countries are, they seem insignificant against the growing number of similarities that result from the process of continuous, mutual transformation of all countries.

Having presented the global scale, we can narrow down the perspective and look at a single country. This simplification will allow us to understand another important piece of the puzzle of today's mixing cultures. In one country, there are several thousand local offices of different international organizations. In each of them, there are managers at different levels who are responsible for the functioning of their organizations. This means that they need to have a deep understanding of and implement the culture of the organization for which they work—spreading it among their subordinates. At the same time, managers have absorbed the culture of their former organizations. They cannot avoid promoting in their current organizations those elements of culture that they accepted in their previous job.

Consequently, every manager who changes job to some extent also changes the organization he/she subsequently joins. Before he/she learns the way of thinking and the system of values in the new organization, he/she will transform them so that they match his/her beliefs developed earlier during his/her professional career. Naturally, organizations attempt to prevent negative effects of introducing individuals from other cultures. The most common practice is to select managers that are likely to fit in, because they come from an environment in which similar values are espoused. However, no two organizations are the same, so the transfer of a manager leads to a change in the organization. Sometimes, such a change is desired—there are organizations that at some point deliberately look for a new CEO from a completely different line of business of culture.

But how big is the scale of such changes? Do managers really change organizations so often? The answer is: Rather yes. Not definitely yes, because there are certainly organizations and people that are connected with each other for decades. But young, dynamic executives or CEOs stay less and less time in a company before they actively search for an opportunity to move to a new job with a more senior position. It is easy to explain—when an organization has an established position in the market—it is unlikely to grow rapidly. Therefore, it may take a long time before a person in a more senior position leaves it. It is much safer to look for a better job in a different company.

The transfer market is supported by headhunting firms. Headhunters are well-informed specialists who know hundreds of managers from different lines of business and regularly offer them transfer from one organization to another. Thanks to them, even if a manager does not know that interesting opportunities emerged on the market, he/she will immediately learn about them. In this sense, headhunting agencies and firms encourage cultural integration.

Thus, at the highest level, we have national cultures, transmitted by major organizations, which transform each other. Cultures also intermingle and shape each other within a single country, transforming the melting pot of cultures into an even more "colorful" place.

Among many different lines of business, organizations providing advisory, auditing and training services play the biggest role in transforming organizational cultures. The aim of their activity is to change or assess the functioning of the organizations to which they provide services. Each of these types of services impacts a different area, but all of them cause organizations to change their structure or how they operate, and by extension their culture.

Consultants are the most diverse of these groups. The aim of consulting organizations is usually to propose modifications to an organization's operation. The range of their services encompasses such disparate areas as IT systems, methods for production quality assurance, accounting systems or designing principles of interim evaluations. Consultants providing such services usually stay at a company for a certain period of time, propose, design and then help to implement new solutions. In some cases, they provide maintenance services for the next few months or even years.

An example of the activity of consultants is implementation of the *kaizen* philosophy, which aims to eliminate waste in daily operations. *Kaizen* is a process of continuous improvement, which involves, among other things, changing the physical work environment so that it is easy to identify what is located where, who is responsible for the state of a given area and which elements are unnecessary in it (Koch 2015, pp. 47–114). Introducing such changes in an organization requires not only presenting the general concept or reading about it in a handbook, but also an organized campaign lasting for a certain period of time and run by consultants, who help to transform all available spaces in the organization. It also requires changing the way of thinking, and thus organizational culture. Another example is deploying computer systems to manage accounting in an organization. Like *kaizen*, SAP (*Systems, Applications and Products in Data Processing*) systems are commonly used in various lines of business and countries. Their implementation requires many months of work by consultants, who conduct an in-depth analysis of the functioning of an organization to match solutions to its needs. During hundreds of hours of the cooperation, a soft transfer of cultural values takes place from the consultants to the organization's employees. By soft transfer, we mean one that is unaffected, based on conversations, sharing experiences and best practices. At the same time, "hard" solutions, such as new procedures, are implemented, organizational structures are changed, new computer software is installed, etc. All that also changes the mindset of the people working in that environment. This is because work conditions shape the way of thinking, norms, values and even basic assumptions about how business should be done (Koch 2015, pp. 47–114).

Consultants implement the solutions they promote all over the world. They can be roughly divided into two categories: solutions created in one organization and then propagated in others and solutions developed from scratch for the purpose of offering advisory services. The latter case is simple: Somebody had a good idea for business which involved offering some professional services to others. The former case is, however, more interesting: One solution worked well in one specific organization, bringing results that were so phenomenal that everybody wants to copy them.

A good example of that is Six Sigma or Lean Manufacturing (Koch 2015, pp. 47–114). Both of these methodologies have been taking the world by storm in the past two decades, revolutionizing manufacturing systems and all kinds of mass scale activity. In addition to manufacturing, such systems are also implemented in mass services provided by banks or logistics companies. Both are based on maximizing quality by eliminating waste, unnecessary procedures and quality errors. The name "Six Sigma" comes from the symbol σ (sigma), which signifies standard deviation in a normal distribution. Six Sigma programs aim to achieve a situation when standard deviation from the production quality is 6σ, i.e., around 2–3 errors per billion manufactured products. This aim as well as visible excellent outcomes of quality programs motivated hundreds of organizations worldwide to adopt, from the late 1980s, the modes of operation created in Motorola (Six Sigma) and Toyota (Lean) (Koch 2015, pp. 47–114).

These solutions were developed in specific organizations and in a specific cultural context. Their fundamental assumptions were originally deeply rooted in American and Japanese organizational cultures, respectively. Six Sigma is highly consistent with

American universalism and analytical approach—belief that accurately (preferably statistically) measuring a problem and proposing appropriate solutions is key to success. Lean, like the Japanese culture, is more holistic, concentrated on process, understanding and contemplating the essence of every organization, i.e., creation of value to a customer. Each of these systems can work in other organizations. However, when implemented, in addition to purely technical solutions, they also bring an element of foreign organizational culture (Mason, Nicolay and Darzi 2015, pp. 91–100).

The most interesting aspect of the propagation of such systems is the fact that their key promoters are advisory companies, which send their consultants to organizations interested in implementing the methodology. Consultants do not have to be in any way connected with the original culture in which a given method was created, but, consciously or not, they are transmitters of organizational culture and bring completely new content to the organizations to which they provide their services. This is very consistent with the idea of memes, created by British scholar Richard Dawkins (Al-Shawaf and Zreik 2018, pp. 1–5), who proposed a theory of cultural changes, in which the most important role is played by memes: the smallest cultural units, such as beliefs, values or even single artifacts. According to Dawkins, memes that are better adapted to the cultural conditions replace those that are ill-adapted, thus making the evolution of cultures a natural extension of biological evolution. Taking this concept even further, we can say that consultants are *de facto* transmitters of the virus of another culture. Naturally, such a virus does not have to be hostile, but if it proves strong, it may replicate in a given organization and cause its lasting transformation (Waddell et al. 2019, pp. 435–440). Consultants are not the only group that carry out such cultural transmissions. An equally important and influential caste is trainers and coaches who run workshops, training courses, development programs and coaching sessions. No matter how we name such activity or people who engage in it, they involve changing human behaviors by means of a group work or, sometimes, individual one (in the case of coaches). Trainers run workshops covering a variety of topics. Most of them are associated with strictly technical skills or knowledge. Such training courses have a certain impact on organizational culture, sometimes compared to that of consultants. But organizational cultures are shaped most by the activities of interpersonal or soft skill trainers. Interpersonal skills encompass such competences as communication, assertiveness, management and motivation.

Trainers teach skills, pass knowledge, but above all change the attitudes of people. They differ in that from lecturers whose task is only to provide knowledge, preferably in the form of presentation. Training courses in interpersonal competencies usually require a high level of commitment and are very engaging, which causes their participants to remember the content covered in them for many years. This does not seem to have much to do with shaping culture. However, we have to ask ourselves the question: From where do the trainers take the knowledge and skills necessary for running their training courses and what criteria do they use to select those attitudes that are to be changed? They do not make up them themselves or derive from research studies. Most often, the source of the content of training courses is other training courses. Their official aim is to teach skills and shape appropriate attitudes, but the criteria of appropriateness usually have their source in other culture.

Most training courses in interpersonal competencies originate from the American culture. An excellent example of that is assertiveness—a skill that only makes sense in a highly individualized cultural context. Being assertive is the ability to respond to the actions of others in a way that, on the one hand, does not demonstrate aggression, while on the other hand does not allow others to impose their will. There are cultures where assertiveness is highly valued—all those where an individual and his/her rights and obligations are much more important than group rights, obligations and relations. These are mostly the countries of the so-called Western Euro-Atlantic cultures. However, an attempt to be assertive in countries where community is most important would not make any sense. Such countries include most countries of the Far East and a large group of African countries. Knowledge passed by consultants or trainers is not culturally neutral. Every skill treated as "appropriate," or desirable in business, carries with it, in addition to technical competencies, a deeper, hidden message. Thus, by transferring know-how, values and fundamental assumptions can also be transferred.

A special element that shapes the cultural map is technological development. Introducing computers has not made a big difference. But the Internet and mobile telephones have massively transformed the way people communicate, build relationships and cooperate. It has increased the scope of freedom and completely changed how cooperation is perceived. One might think that technology is bound to significantly change many cultures, opening them up and bringing closer the moment when people all over the world will think in the same way. But is this assumption correct?

It turns out that the technological development does not essentially change the values or basic assumptions adopted in organizations. Still, it has some impacts on them. The emergence of the latest technological solutions usually preserves and reinforces those cultural values that prevail in a given organization.

The use of technology rarely changes culture. Rather, it reinforces the existing assumptions and values, causing the existing artifacts to be replaced by new ones, better suited to the current conditions. There are, however, cases when the implementation of a new technology may lead to cultural changes. This usually happens not because of the technology itself, but because the technology changes work organization. An example is computerization of an increasing number of the areas of life, combined with automation of production and transport and the rise of increasingly intelligent robots, which are able to perform more than the simplest tasks. As a result, HR can be moved from basic manual work to administrative, office and creative work. When technology enables humans to be replaced by machines in the most routine activities, people turn to areas such as solving complex problems, developing ideas and other domains where automated systems still have a long way to go. This causes a global change in what is required from people. As the work of humans becomes more "mental," requires creativity and openness, organizations that are able to create cultures fostering the development of such characteristics are in a better position. This results in a global shift towards greater openness in work culture. Naturally, there are still organizations that could be called "labor camps" without too much exaggeration. These are predominantly plants that are located in developing countries and employ local people, who work in the worst possible conditions. However, although such organizations still exist, the development of technology gradually causes the culture of physical work to be replaced by the culture of intellectual work. This process is naturally very slow and difficult to notice from the perspective of a single worker or even a single organization. But it is visible on the global scale and will probably transform organizational cultures of most companies worldwide in the near future.

Positive thinking and approach to criticism is hardly an important aspect of organizational culture. Yet, in the work environment, it becomes the key cultural difference, which causes many tools for effective interpersonal communication to produce astonishment, laughter or reluctance when presented in organizations.

Before an organization implements solutions developed by others, it must check what effects it will have. In order to develop, every organization needs to absorb innovations, created in many cases by others. But it should use only those solutions that best suit its organizational culture and the direction in which it should evolve.

It also should be stressed that although how organizational culture is shaped depends largely on managers, no organization exists in void. Organizations are not isolated islands. Every organization, including its employees, managers, technology and procedures, is part of the culture of a region, country or planet. We can guide an organization in a certain direction and to some extent determine how it functions. But we cannot eliminate all the impacts of global changes, which shape the culture of a country and cultures of specific industries and professions.

Global Dimension of Organizational Culture Management

Functionalist and Metaphorical Approaches

6

6.1 CRITICAL VIEW IN THE CONTEXT OF THE FUNCTIONALIST ORIENTATION IN ORGANIZATIONAL CULTURE MANAGEMENT

The model of organizational culture and the resulting typology of organizational cultures predominantly constitute a theoretical concept and require a more in-depth verification in empirical studies in the future. We need investigation into the value systems of organizational members and analysis of the type of human resources (HR) management, strategies, power and structure of organizations.

It can be noted, as a result of the discussion, that organizational culture fulfills the following five functions: (1) integration, (2) perception, (3) adaptation, (4) giving identity and (5) stimulating organizational changes. According to P. Bate, it serves as social "glue" that holds the organization together. This "glue" is essentially participation in an organization, which manifests in acceptance of shared goals, values, norms and views. The second function (perception) is associated with the way organizational members perceive the reality, environment, organization and themselves. A.M. Pettigrew defines organizational culture, referring to this function, as a system of collectively accepted meanings that can be understood by a group in a given time. P. Bate sees it as meanings that people collectively share and define as the organizational reality (Heinze and Heinze 2018, pp. 1–26). The perception function of organizational culture may manifest in perceiving the organization's reality and environment through the prism of cognitive filters and stereotypes shared by organizational members.

The third function of organizational culture (adaptation) is connected with the development of patterns of acting in specific situations thanks to perceiving the organization's reality and environment as relatively stable. Thus, organizational culture reduces uncertainty, gives meaning to the reality and provides patterns of behavior in specific situations. E.H. Schein sees it in terms of the adaptation function, which enables a group to adapt to the conditions of the environment, which is connected with the integration function—holding a group of employees together. The integration function of organizational culture involves group members reaching a consensus on their attitude to the organization itself. Schein lists the factors that help to evaluate the degree of cultural integration of a group of employees (Figure 6.1).

Culture also allows employees to identify with their organization. This happens through consensus building. According to E.H. Schein, the elements that constitute negotiable components of that consensus are as follows: (1) vision, mission and strategy;

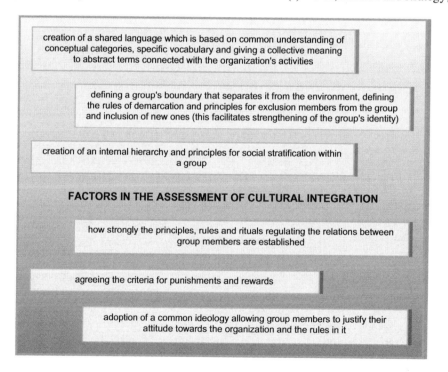

FIGURE 6.1 Factors in the assessment of the extent of cultural integration of a group of employees according to Schein. (Own work based on: Turner J.H., Functionalism. *The Wiley-Blackwell Encyclopedia of Social Theory*, 2017, pp. 1–9.)

(2) goals of an organization, which, on the one hand, allow it to achieve its mission and, on the other hand, take into account the interests of the subgroups functioning within the group of employees; (3) means that enable the accomplishment of goals, such as management system, decision-making procedure, work distribution, and technology; (4) criteria for the evaluation of an organization's operation and assumed strategies and methods for correcting actions in unforeseen situations. Giving identity to an organization involves creating a shared, consistent image of the organization and a sense of community among its participants. Different images of the organization confront each other and then converge. This leads to the creation of a coherent image of the organization that is intelligible to both its employees and environment.

Bormann and Rowold point out that the functions of organizational culture were usually seen in the literature in terms of stabilizing the social relations in an organization. This static view of culture was based on the functionalist concept of culture of stability, harmony and status quo. It also resulted from the preferred view of organizations as focused on reduction of uncertainty. However, in the postindustrial age, which is characterized by rapid changes, such conservative functions of culture become irrelevant and are replaced by new ones that facilitate functioning in the conditions of uncertainty. Culture becomes a catalyst and tool for organizational changes (Bormann and Rowold 2015, pp. 51–57).

The role of organizational culture depends on an organization's stage of development. E. Schein distinguishes the following stages: birth, early growth, middle age and maturity (Schein 2010, pp. 390–401). At the birth and early-growth stages, organizational culture is shaped by the values and personality of the founder. It mainly fulfills the function of integrating the organization. The middle-age stage usually sees diversification of culture. Employees who are not family members or members of the original founding group dominate in an organization. New values, subcultures and sometimes countercultures are created. An organization may undergo identity crises and changes. Culture becomes a source of organizational rules, and the following functions gain importance: perception, adaptation and identity building. At the maturity stage, the most desirable function of culture is catalyzing changes; otherwise, an organization risks becoming dominated by the stabilizing functions, which may lead to fossilization of organizational culture. A fossilized culture constrains flexibility and competitiveness of an organization. Naturally, culture may to a varying degree catalyze changes at each stage of an organization's development. Attempts to develop a classification of cultural values and patterns that differentiate organizations should acknowledge the importance of the functions of stabilizing and holding together an organization as well as change facilitation. Functionalism and neopositivism have been much criticized in social sciences, with the negation of the dominant paradigm leading to the emergence of alternative paradigms (Westwood and Jack 2007, pp. 246–265). It is worth addressing a few points in this criticism, especially the problem of integration, stability, homogeneity, reification and inadequateness of methodology.

Functionalism tends to describe a stable state and equilibrium, making it difficult to study such a dynamic process as organizational culture. Focus on integration results in culture being perceived as a relatively cohesive and homogeneous value system, which contradicts the view of an organization and culture as consisting of often conflicted and opposing subcultures and countercultures. The assumption that a functioning organization must have at least a minimum degree of integration should not be understood as meaning that all the elements of an organization serve its cohesion and that harmony and unity underlie its operation. Given fast changes in the environment, the radical, integration-focused and functionalist approach cannot be sustained. Conflict, lack of cohesion and contradiction may accelerate change and development of minimum degree of cohesion in an organization, which allows it, despite cyclical internal conflicts, to remain a whole. There are two issues connected with the integration of an organization that should be addressed: First, organizational management should also seek to strengthen the cohesion of the organization, as a perfectly integrated organization is hermetic and ill-adapted to changes—both internal and in the environment. Second, sources of integration are complex, which means that a lasting increase or reduction of an organization's cohesion requires taking into account the impact of strategic, structural and cultural factors at the level of individuals, social groups and organizations in the environment (Bührmann 2016, pp. 1–12). As the criticism of the integration-focused approach increased, functionalists developed a concept aimed at defending their equilibrium-based view. T. Parsons proposed a concept of "punctuated equilibrium," which allows for change and at the same time indicates a system's tendency to re-establish equilibrium in the process of transformation (Beyer, Breunig and Radojevic 2017, pp. 42–51).

Representatives of CMS (critical management studies) accuse functionalists of creating a false conciliatory and cooperative vision of organizational culture, while in reality it is ideological and covertly promotes the interests and power of the dominant groups. Thus, functionalism preserves the unjust status quo through indoctrinating and manipulative organizational culture (Wickert and Schaefer 2015, pp. 107–130). Functionalism, due to reification of culture, struggles with capturing the processual character of culture, which is transformation, flow rather than a thing that can be studied. Applying the neopositivist cause-and-effect framework to explaining cultures is, according to representatives of alternative paradigms, problematic. They argue that in cultural discourse, we deal with meanings that are part of a complex network of relationships and thus require interpretation in terms of interrelationships rather than a causal analysis of variables, which is derived from the scientific method of natural sciences. Interpretivists raise methodological objections to functionalism. By using objectivistic and statistical methods applied mainly to studying large-scale phenomena, it is not possible, according to representatives of interpretive and symbolic paradigm, to understand the essence and sense of an organization, which resides in deeply internalized meanings.

What is also criticized is the fundamental assumption of functionalism, which refers to the use of function, and thereby utility, to explain the existence of a given phenomenon in culture. Indeed, it seems that a lot of cultural phenomena are nonfunctional, or even dysfunctional. For instance, it is hard to find any benefits of certain destructive countercultures forming in organizations (Chandler 2017, pp. 49–65). The functionalist vision of culture, according to critics, is too over-rationalized, close to the concept of homo economicus and thereby false. Interpretivists also argue that the functionalist explanations provide a vision of a human being and culture that is too deterministic, where people behave according to a model. There is not much space for free will, and people are not cultural puppets according to interpretivists. Another problem is overly optimistic stance on both getting to know and improving culture. Studies have showed (Chandler 2017, pp. 49–65) that a lot of methods for getting to know and improving organizational culture are unreliable.

This means that the directions of cultural changes are unpredictable in the long run, and so we should avoid forecasting and focus on diagnosing. The local approach to cultural change assumes that generalizing models are pointless, because they cause the peculiarity of a given culture to become lost. That is why interpretivists study individual cases in detail.

The most important concepts in managing cultural change in the interpretive and symbolic paradigm include sensemaking, enactment, management of the identity of organization and management of meaning. Since the concept of organizational identity has been addressed in the chapter dedicated to the interpretive understanding of culture, I will focus here in sensemaking and management of meaning (Combe and Carrington 2015, pp. 307–322).

The concept of sensemaking was proposed by Sandberg and Tsoukas and became a subject of interest among other interpretivist researchers (Sandberg and Tsoukas 2015, pp. S6–S32). It seems to be the most popular management concept within the interpretive and symbolic paradigm. It is based on the assumption that the organizational reality is socially constructed through interpretations, perceptions, intentions and emotions of social actors. Thus, an organization is a network of meanings that make up the collective identity, but at the same time consists of multitude of individual and group identities (subcultures) (Sandberg and Tsoukas 2015, pp. S6–S32). Such a vision of an organization places culture understood interpretively as a root metaphor, at the center of the discourse of management. An organization, which is equated with organizational culture, is created and stays within social macrostructures, but is located at mezzo level in relations between social actors. In fact, interpretivists treat organizational culture as a root metaphor, equating it to an organization itself (Sandberg and Tsoukas 2015, pp. S6–S32). Therefore, in contrast to functionalism, there is no point within this paradigm in separating culture from other subsystems (strategy, organizational structure). An organization is by definition permanently cultural. Thus, organizational change and change of organizational culture are essentially the same in the interpretive and symbolic paradigm.

Interpretivists are skeptical about the possibility of managing organizational culture. Most authors stress that culture develops in a spontaneous way and is not subject to control, as it is embedded in complex interactions. These interactions involve numerous social actors and various processes related to communication, negotiations, status building and power relations. Most of them occur intuitively and are not fully controlled on a conscious level. Based on these arguments, a large group of interpretivists rejected cognitive and pragmatic optimism, so characteristic of functionalists. According to most interpretivists, it is possible to get to know culture, but controlling it is practically impossible.

Interpretivists, just as representatives of alternative paradigms (based on social constructivism), also oppose the instrumentalization of the issues of culture in management. Culture should not be predominantly treated as a tool for manipulating employees. From the perspective of interpretivists, the instrumentalization of the approach to organizational culture, so characteristic of many functionalist concepts, is not only unethical, but also ineffective in exploratory, methodological and pragmatic terms. Deterministic and universalistic understanding of cultural change is embedded in the fundamental assumptions of NFS paradigm (Zamorano 2016, pp. 165–186). This means that culture can be subjected to analysis by being placed within a causal framework, which not only provides diagnostic possibilities, but also is characterized by predictive strength. The interpretive approach to cultural change is the opposite of functionalism, and as such, it is based on the indeterministic and local view.

An emancipatory project is in turn a methodological element connected with demystification of instrumentalism and organizational culture. The criticism that it formulates aims to introduce changes; it is essentially about changing the unfair order rather than increasing the effectiveness or efficiency of an organization, although these aspects have also to be taken into account when modifications are made. The objectives are to indicate and analyze dehumanizing and empowerment-limiting behaviors and conflicting interests. Another objective of an emancipatory project is bigger participation of disadvantaged groups in decision-making and governance, i.e., increasing employees' presence in the managerial structures and organizational democracy. The division in an organization must also take into account disadvantaged groups. This involves changing the system of human capital management in an organization, as well as changing the ways of employee motivation and development. Organizational justice cannot be achieved without mentality change among both employees and managers.

Emancipatory changes should be accompanied by the creation of a completely new organizational culture, which should be concentrated on empowerment and equality of individuals. In order for a new culture to be created, structural and strategic changes must be made, i.e., changes to the goals, mission, organizational structure, espoused values, existing norms and functioning management systems. As there is an informal culture functioning along the formal one, a total control over the change of culture is not possible. For a change of culture to be completed, it must be rooted. The effect is adoption of emancipatory values as vital for the organizational identity and culture. The task of employees is to strengthen and maintain their participation in the organization. It is in their interest to look critically at the organization in order to prevent "the iron law of oligarchy" as put by R. Michels, i.e., handing over the power to the organizational bureaucracy (Scott and Davis 2015, pp. 234–250).

The above concept of the implementation of cultural changes also applies to the views propagated by representatives of CMS, who consider culture as a root metaphor for management or "metaphor for organizing" (Schoeneborn, Kuhn and Kärreman 2019, pp. 475–496). Thus, cultural change refers to the whole organization and entails modifications of the strategy and organizational structure, management system and management styles.

Table 6.1 illustrates analysis of culture and implementation of an emancipatory change in eight stages. The aspects of critical analysis (stages 1–4) are connected here with an emancipatory project (stages 5–8).

It should be borne in mind that each change is accompanied by resistance. An emancipatory project is particularly vulnerable to this phenomenon, because it may involve radical changes affecting the interests of those who have power. Thus, progressive, evolutionary changes are easier to implement. A gradual change occurs, e.g., when criticism of organizational culture results in reduced exploitation of employees

TABLE 6.1   Modification of organizational culture in the CMS perspective

UNDERTAKEN ACTION	STAGES, METHODS OF CHANGES	OUTCOMES
Denaturalization of organizational culture	Critical stage	Reduced sense of organizational justice and naturalness among employees
Identifying cultural patterns that preserve status quo	Critical stage	Developing greater awareness, discovering power reinforcing myths
Exposing the ideology, indoctrination and false consciousness		Access to knowledge about the social engineering and manipulations used against the employees and customers of an organization
Demystification of symbolic violence	Critical stage Discourse analysis, observations, interviews	Increasing employees' awareness of the mechanisms of organizational control
Increased employee participation, organizational democracy	Emancipation stage Modification of the mission and strategy as well as management patterns and styles Education and training	Implementation of a new strategy reflecting humanization and emancipation
Modification of human capital management and organizational structures	Emancipatory stage Change of the HRM system and organizational structures Education and training courses	Functioning of a new structure that reflects humanization, employee participation and emancipation
Creation of emancipatory culture	Emancipatory stage Change of cultural patterns and values Education and training courses	Implementation of a culture with such values as employee empowerment, justice
Rooting of the emancipatory culture	Emancipatory stage Management of meaning and management of an organization Education and training	Employee participation in further development of the emancipatory culture

Source: Own work based on: Schoeneborn D., Kuhn T.R., Kärreman D., The communicative constitution of organization, organizing, and organizationality. *Organization Studies*, 2019, 4.40: 475–496.

and increased work humanization. However, it is vital that critical studies do not only address descriptive aspects, but also strive to implement actual emancipatory changes in an organization.

CMS representatives seek to propagate patterns of an emancipatory organizational culture that would develop as a result of criticism of the existing oppressive managerial practices and increased awareness among employees. The main techniques of change management include critical education of managers and communication tools. Thanks to an emancipation project, the currently predominant patterns of instrumentalism-based culture would evolve towards greater humanization. However, the barrier that needs to be overcome is the interest of groups that are in power and derive the biggest benefits from the functioning of an organization, i.e., managers, owners and entrepreneurs (Ziek and Anderson 2015, pp. 788–803).

The methods of implementing cultural changes that are based on alternative paradigms and the methods of shaping organizational culture are rooted in adopted fundamental cognitive assumptions, referred to as paradigms. Depending on education, knowledge and professional experiences, researchers studying organizations and managers prefer and use different models and methods for improving organizational culture. It seems that there is no definite answer to the question about which way of understanding organizational culture, and by extension which methods for shaping organizational culture, should be preferred. Thus, there exists ambiguity, which can be turned into value, if it leads to increasing reflectiveness and criticism of organizations. Both researchers studying organizations and management practitioners should be familiar with various paradigms of culture and related methodologies. There is a gap in such knowledge, because the functionalist approach obviously dominates today. However, attempts should be made to better explore and propagate interpretive and critical methods of culture management.

6.2 METAPHORICAL METHOD IN THE IDENTIFICATION OF THE PARADIGMS OF ORGANIZATIONAL CULTURE IN MANAGEMENT

The concept of change varies depending on which management paradigm has been adopted. Naturally, there is no consensus among scholars about which classification of paradigms to apply. Some opt for linking change management with schools of or approaches to organizational thinking, thus enriching the theories and methods developed over the last century. Other scholars seek paradigms that are more specific to change management, an example of which is the dichotomy: evolutionary (continuous) change versus revolutionary (radical) change. There are also attempts at an integrated approach to change management that would include various cognitive perspectives (Lindlof and Taylor 2017, pp. 411–417). Another approach is to point to the links of change management with paradigms of social sciences, i.e., looking for the broadest possible point of reference.

Irrespective of the adopted paradigm of social sciences, different types of organizational changes can be distinguished, depending on the criterion. The basic type is naturally evolutionary changes. The functionalist understanding of change refers to an increase in the effectiveness or efficiency of the operation of an organization. Thus, a positive change means a progress and improvement in organizations and their members, which allows them to operate more effectively. A negative change means regress, i.e., decrease in the effectiveness or efficiency of an organization's activities. Functionalists seek a full control over the process of changes understood as transformation of the organizational system and subsystems, which leads to a better use of resources and adaptation to the environment. The most important subjects of changes are organizations themselves, but also their subsystems (e.g., strategy, culture) and employees. An evolutionary and continuous change is preferred, mainly due to the need to maintain the integrity of an organization in the process of changes. Therefore, the methods designed to improve organizations rather than radically to reconstruct them, such as TQM, organizational development and lean management, dominate among methods for change implementation. Yet, the functionalist instruments also include the methods that seek profound changes (or at least that is the intention), for instance, reengineering. The functionalist paradigm draws on neopositivism, which translates into the postulate of axiological neutrality, which posits that the assessment of organizational change should avoid assigning moral or ethical values, and concentrate on the pragmatic aspect of outcomes. Among metaphors that could describe the functionalist change, evolution seems particularly apt.

Propagated meanings can reinforce the perception of organizational change as evolutionary or other. Therefore, the process of meaning management, which is often unconscious, is key to the implementation of changes. Meaning management can introduce the dominant type of interpretation which will spread among organizational members obscuring other ways of understanding the change. Established stereotypes and consensus around an organization also lead to difficulties in implementing projects of controlled changes. This is because the planning and implementation of change is enmeshed in the processes of social communication game and sensemaking, which are spontaneous, uncontrolled, but often key to an organization. Change management is permanently valuative in the interpretive paradigm, which means that every decision and action carries with it a context of moral and ethical values. Even language, narrative and mental images are not neutral axiologically. An apt metaphor would be acting or flow in the Heraclitean sense (pantarei) (Mciver, Fitzsimmons and Flanagan 2016, pp. 47–75). Interpretive approach to cultural change is proposed by numerous authors, such as M.J. Hatch, G. Morgan, L. Smirich, J. van Maanen and M. Pacanovsky (Myers 2019, pp. 112–119).

Representatives of CMS adopt valuative axiological orientation. A positive change leads to emancipation of disadvantaged social groups, reduction of organizational inequality and oppressiveness and blurring of "false consciousness" (Gabel 2018, pp. 61–70). The assumptions of CMS are radical, so the change must be deep, revolutionary. Many CMS (Gabel 2018. pp. 61–70) scholars also hold a pessimistic view that the present direction of organizational changes often promotes a negative change, i.e., one that increases inequality and dominance of the groups that are in power and false consciousness. This trend is evidenced by growth of neo-imperialist practices as a result of increasing globalization, preference of management methods that instrumentalize people and increasing importance of the manipulative propaganda of the media and marketing. Proposed methods for changing organizational governance involve denaturalization of the managerial discourse and deconstruction of the concepts and structures of power. Applied techniques of change include empowerment, quotas, changes in language and discourse (towards political correctness) and critical text analyses. Positive changes, according to CMS representatives, encounter resistance mainly from the groups in power, which face loss of influences. Thus, barriers to change can be conscious and controlled by the elites of the economic and political power, but they can also appear spontaneously and escape conscious control. Managers rationalize their instrumentalism and manipulativeness by referring to the naturalness of the capitalist and organizational order, impossibility of reducing inequalities and their responsibility for the growth of an organization towards the owners. Change of the oppressive managerial culture has been addressed by H. Willmott, M. Alvesson, D. Knights and J. Brewis, among others (Romani, Mahadevan and Primecz 2018, pp. 403–418).

Postmodernists argue that change is subjective and permanent in character, because it is connected with spontaneous, uncontrolled and unconscious flows of interpretations, narratives, senses and power between various intersecting narratives. A good metaphor for shapeless change proposed by Deleuze and Guattari is rhizome, which can be crossed unpredictably and grow anywhere. In this sense, change cannot be managed in any way, as it is completely beyond control. Thus, any methods for managing changes are merely narratives and rationalizations, which may impact discourse, but cannot control it. Change, according to postmodernists, occurs through discourse and culture, within multiplicity of senses and identities of the different participants of the linguistic and social game (Taylor and Harris-Evan 2018, pp. 1254–1267). The ephemeral deconstruction method proposed by J. Derrida would lead to changing and rejecting the dominant way of interpreting a work or the reality in favor of multiplicity of interpretations. Several scholars refer to the postmodernist thought in their analyses, although they often do not call themselves postmodernists (Patrick 2018, pp. 76–81).

Thus, the concepts of change management vary depending on which paradigm has been adopted. The dominant paradigm is the neopositivist-functionalist-systemic approach (Basalingappa and Kumar 2018, pp. 149–160), within which most contemporary works on change management are located. Interpretivism negated the neopositivist illusion of early functionalists that the processes of change management can be studied using purely objectivistic methods, and instead pointed at social creation of change (Ryan 2018, pp. 41–49). Postmodernism sees change as unforced, spontaneous and uncontrolled, and thereby, it is impossible to manage. In this sense, postmodernism can supplement the skepticism towards change management so characteristic of CMS.

Drawing on the elementary epistemological division in social sciences, which differentiates neopositivist paradigm from social constructionism paradigms, we can indicate specific understanding of change in alternative perspectives. The broad term "social constructionism" encompasses here paradigms that assume that the organizational reality is constructed by active actors participating in the social game. These are symbolic interactionism, radical structuralism and radical humanism (postmodernism) within the meaning by G. Burrell and G. Morgan (Frederickson and Walling 2019, pp. 63–84).

Within the constructivist paradigms, change is not an objectively existing state, but a process constructed by perceptions, interpretations and actions of the participants of organizational processes. This means that the understanding of change is closely connected with meaning and sensemaking (Kelly, Dowling and Millar 2018, pp. 9–13). L. Smircich describes the concept of leadership and implementation of changes as meaning management, i.e., creation and imposition of the leader's own organizational vision (Calás and Smircich 2019, pp. 327–331). Likewise, Smircich points out that an effective implementation of a strategy of organizational changes requires a process of constructing, interpreting a sequence of events, implementing meanings and acting in accordance with them in an organizational group (Calás and Smircich 2019, pp. 327–331).

Deriving inspiration from various paradigms, complementary models for changing organizational culture can be proposed, accompanied by various organizational methods and techniques.

The multiplicity of the meanings of culture and the complexity of its interpretations within a variety of paradigms lead to the adoption of epistemological and methodological pluralism. This means that a model of cultural management will use concepts of culture that were created based on different paradigms, and the set of methods of cultural study will combine the methods established in different perspectives and methodologies.

Change management is predominantly based on systemic and functionalist assumptions. This is due to the pragmatic character of this area of management, which is concerned with developing a set of methods for implementing changes to improve organizations, mainly in terms of their economic efficiency. Culture change, especially in the case of organizations with a strong organizational culture, is a difficult, long-term process that cannot be fully controlled.

When looking for a general reference point for managing cultural change, it is worth drawing on the works of one of the most distinguished functionalists. R.K. Merton proposed a deviance matrix (Mongardini 2018, pp. 214–219), which, adapted to management, seems to aptly describe the types of reactions of social actors to cultural changes. Merton's matrix describes a functionalist concept of the consistency of cultural goals, with applied institutional means understood in sociological terms. Applying it to management, we can propose an analysis of the compliance of the basic assumptions of organizational culture with the intended goals of change. Social actors, stakeholders, members of subcultures or even all employees (if the change is imposed from outside) choose from among five variants of potential actions. The choice depends, on the one hand, on the extent to which the goals of change are accepted, while on the other hand, on acceptance of the new values and cultural norms that the change entails (Mongardini 2018, pp. 214–219) (Table 6.2).

Conformity is the correct reaction from the point of view of those planning the change. It means acceptance of the goals of changes as well as new values, which are gradually internalized. Innovation means engagement on the part of social actors (stakeholders) that manifests in rejecting the goals of change and proposing new ones. At the same time, the stakeholders are aware of the need to change the values of the organizational culture and accept cultural change. It is a case of social actors putting pressure on decision-makers to significantly correct the adopted goals of change while acknowledging that changes are necessary and positive. Ritualism means that social actors accept the goals of change and at the same time stick to the "old" values. Here, strong attachment to the norms and values from before the change and impact of fossilized organizational culture are at play. Since the old values and norms will be inconsistent with the new goals when the change is implemented, this leads to ritualism; i.e., organizational habits are detached from their rational (functional) foundation. In practice, this means that certain collective behaviors will be practiced ritually, but they will be no longer connected with the real goals of an organization. The consequence will be

TABLE 6.2   Cultural change models in different paradigms

MODEL OF CHANGES	TECHNIQUES OF CHANGES	PARADIGM
1. Cultural audit 2. Ideal model of culture 3. Identification of a gap 4. Planned change, controlling 1. Model of an effective culture 2. Evolutionary or revolutionary change	Surveys and questionnaires, interviews, focuses, expert panels, observation, analyses of documentation, case studies, planned and controlled activities of leaders and change agents in the area of strategy, HRM, reorganization of the structure, training	Neopositivist-functionalist-systemic
1. Creation and rooting of meanings 2. Enactment Incremental change of the triad: vision–culture–organizational identity	In-depth interviews, focuses, discourse and text analyses, anthropological case studies, spontaneous activities of leaders and change agents in the area of changing identity and practices which are based on intuition and ad hoc actions	Interpretive symbolic
1. Deconstruction 2. Denaturalization Implementation of emancipatory culture	In-depth interviews, critical and reflective text analyses Empowerment, quotas, action research, sociology of intervention, activities of leaders and change agents in the area of strategy, HRM, reorganization of the structure, training	Critical approach
Increasing reflectiveness, distance and irony	Glossing, metaphorical and paradoxical references to an organization	Postmodernism

Source: Own work.

a lack of coherence of the organizational system in the cultural and strategic spheres. The last two reactions involve the rejection of change, in the sphere of both goals and values. This rejection may take on a passive form, i.e., withdrawal from the activities and from engagement in the life of the organization, or active one, i.e., rebellion that means defiance and organizing a resistance movement against the changes. This brief analysis enables the application of the matrix to specific cases of changes, which should take into account different reaction to changes, not only from stakeholders, but also from individual significant organizational actors (Mongardini 2018, pp. 214–219).

An important functionalist problem concerning change management is its relation to the concept of equilibrium. An organizational system is stable when it is in equilibrium. Every change by definition disturbs such equilibrium, so the challenge is to create models of equilibrium re-establishment by an organizational system. An example of such a concept is punctuated equilibrium (Radojevic, Breunig and Beyer 2017, pp. 64–74).

The systemic character of change management through culture can be seen in most concepts of organizational learning and development perceived as an activity of creating and reinforcing positive values and patterns of culture. In his systemic concept of change, P. Senge notices the existence of cultural barriers to changes, rooted in organizational values and norms, which may inhibit organizational development. Overcoming such barriers requires research, reflection and insight into the functioning of the organization (Senge, Hamilton and Kania 2015, pp. 27–33). It is necessary to combine traditional tools for managing a whole organization with methods for shaping organizational culture. Organizational culture should be subject to changes that adapt it to emerging key changes in the environment, especially in a competitive sector. E. Schein lists several potential negative effects of the lack of cultural change, which also affect other elements of an organization (Schein and Schein 2018, pp. 215–121):

1. *Limiting the possibility of implementing new strategies*—the values of the "old" culture are in conflict with the assumptions of the new strategy
2. *Problems in case of fusions and alliances between businesses*—inadequacy of the cultures
3. *Difficulties in implementing new forms of organization, new technologies and structural changes*—mismatch between the existing values and planned changes in the activity
4. *Emergence of inter-group conflicts in organizations*—excessive reinforcement of subcultures and countercultures
5. *Problems with the communication system*—distinct cultural perspectives of the subcultures in an organization (lack of the convergence of perceptions)
6. *Difficulties with employees' secondary socialization*—in a hermetic culture, new organizational members have a limited possibility of assimilation
7. *Reduced work effectiveness*—cultural norms result in the decrease in the efficiency and effectiveness of employees' activities

As regards the possibility of shaping organizational culture, we should adopt a cautious stance. Changes in culture are difficult to predict in the long run. But it is possible to see the signs of changes as they occur or a new orientation as it is created. It is also possible to carry out intervention, which may result in a change of the orientation or correction of the values and cultural patterns. However, such intervention does not guarantee that the intended cultural configuration will be achieved.

The following stages of the development of organizational culture can be proposed (Nerdinger 2019, pp. 163–177):

- Diagnosing the culture (map of values, norms and cultural patterns)
- Examining the links between the culture and the strategy, structure and power
- Preparing cultural intervention: desired values, norms and patterns
- Cultural intervention: propagating, promoting, informing, inculcating values, norms and patterns, readapting other elements of the system to the culture
- Monitoring the outcomes of the cultural intervention
- Reinforcing the cultural configuration

Shaping organizational culture fulfills a particularly important function when organizations have to make changes quickly. In a globalized economy, there is a growing need for organizational changes in more and more economic sectors. Culture should not be a barrier to changes, but their catalyst. R.H. Kilmann distinguishes the following stages of managing cultural change (Nerdinger 2019, pp. 163–177):

- Extracting the existing norms
- Defining new directions of development
- Establishing new norms
- Identifying the cultural gap
- Closing the cultural gap

This is a rather instrumental approach to organizational culture, which assumes that it is possible to identify the characteristics of both the existing culture and the "ideal" one facilitating greater effectiveness of the organization in given conditions. Cultural changes can be stimulated but they cannot be fully controlled, and defining the "ideal" culture in a highly changeable and heterogeneous environment may be highly risky. T.G. Cummings and C.G. Worley formulate six principles (Waddell et al. 2019, pp. 136–148):

1. Formulating a clear strategic vision that includes organizational values
2. Displaying management commitment, especially top management, to the process of changes
3. Implementing change at the highest level of the hierarchy and appointing change agents
4. Adjusting all organizational elements to the new culture and strategy, i.e., systemic transformations in the structural sphere and HR policy
5. Socializing employees according to the new principles, which means that new employees are selected and trained accordingly, and the existing organizational members are provided with appropriate conditions and time to adapt to the changes
6. Developing ethical and legal sensitivity, because cultural change always upsets the status quo and usually creates beneficiaries and losers. At this stage, it is particularly important to identify barrier to changes

The techniques that can be used to shape organizational change, including reinforcing, correcting, developing and changing, include (1) redefining organizational values; (2) creating new normative rules; (3) changing elements of culture (myths, stories, heroes, models, rituals, symbols, taboo, language); (4) adapting the artifacts to the changing core of values; (5) composing and decomposing the mission; (6) designing systems of communication and power; (7) changing the content of job descriptions; (8) employee meetings, discussions and training; (9) shaping the roles of leaders in an organization (e.g., as agents of changes, role models, heroes, innovators); (10) shaping motivation systems; and (11) changing selection criteria. These are different techniques (individual or group) that shape the sphere of organizational culture directly (points 1–4) or indirectly (points 5–11). In the first place, it is necessary to redefine earlier values and "cautiously" adopt the target configuration of values. Then, all the other elements of culture should be adapted to the changing values. At the same time, changes in culture should be aligned with potential changes in the strategy, structure and HR. The method of cultural intervention assumes that changes can be made in a revolutionary or evolutionary way. A revolutionary change occurs quickly, focuses on negating and destroying the existing configuration of culture, and usually entails a profound transformation of an organization that involves significant changes in all subsystems and replacement of the core staff. An evolutionary change is a modification of the existing culture, occurs more slowly and does not negate or break its continuity.

In conclusion, according to the assumptions of functionalism, organizational culture can be shaped, although this process cannot be controlled. Actions by management and employees may cause changes in the culture. But culture is a very complex variable, and the directions of its changes can be difficult to predict or plan. In addition, the process of changing organizational culture is complicated by other organizational processes connected with culture, i.e., power structure, strategy or impact of changes in the environment.

An important issue in the perception of cultural change is retrospection and creation of collective memory (Edy 2019, pp. 1–5). Organizational identity, in accordance with the criteria by S. Albert and D.A. Whetten, crystallizes through the sense of time continuity. This has to do with an intersubjective process of the creation of collective memory, which is a kind of narrative about the establishment and development of the organization created by its members, and often also stakeholders. Thus, cultural change occurs in two ways. The first type is an incremental, evolutionary and slow change, which is not perceived by organizational members as a change. The second type of change involves transformation of culture, which is visible to organizational actors and often also stimulated by them. Naturally, the directions of such a change cannot be controlled, because it occurs spontaneously. The changes of culture are reflected in the emerging and changing narratives, which, although they do not appear in and of themselves, should constitute a sort of projection of the ongoing transformations (Besharov and Brickson 2016, pp. 396–414).

The interpretive methodology for studying cultural change is qualitative in character, although not orthodox. It focuses on methods of individual, in-depth and nonrepresentative studies, which enable the understanding of cultural change but do not allow for an open, multi-paradigm approach. The methodology of the interpretive studies of cultural change in management has a few features characteristic of this paradigm, since it is (Klein 2016, pp. 277–301):

1. *Qualitative*—concentrates on hermeneutic, in-depth, nonrepresentative studies in which no measurement can be made
2. *Idiographic*—describes individual cases without the possibility of generalization
3. *Emic*—conducts individual, local studies that rely on "dense description" and colloquial categories of the subjects of the study

Methods for analyzing cultural change in the field of management from the interpretive and symbolic perspective are varied. Most important are the methods of organizational anthropology (organizational ethnology), i.e., field methods, which are based on the assumption that subjects should be studied in their natural environment.

The classic anthropological method, i.e., observation in all of its variations, i.e., both participant observation and nonparticipant observation, and explicit and implicit observation, is commonly applied. Specific anthropological methods have also been developed. An example is shadowing, which is used in studying cultural change-ability in the field of management. This method involves observation and passive participation in the work of the subject of the study for a longer period of time (days of weeks) (Graham 2016, pp. 183–194). Second most common interpretive method is an interview, which is always an in-depth and open interview. Organizational anthropology draws here on cultural anthropology, conducting studies in the form of in-depth and biographical interviews. In addition to individual interviews, there are also focus group interviews, which derive from functionalism, but were also adopted by interpretivists. The aim of focus group interviews is to understand actions in the social context, where they gain an intersubjective aspect and the impact of a group manifests (Yanow and Schwartz-Shea 2015, pp. 490–493). The third group of interpretive methods draws on linguistic studies (of speech or text) and encompasses conversational analyses, narrative analyses, metaphorical analyses, discourse analyses, as well as other qualitative analyses of text. The aim of a conversational analysis, which derives from ethnomethodology, is the interpretation of natural interactions that occur in a daily life. It is a perspective of culture that changes on a microscale, i.e., communication and interactions between individuals, which is expressed, e.g., through the sequence of utterances, preferred types of utterances and ways of resuming conversation. Today, it is a relatively common method that uses dedicated software (Yanow and Schwartz-Shea 2015, pp. 490–493). Narrative inquiry deals with interpreting the ways in which people give sense to the social reality by creating narratives. Storytelling is a research and pragmatic technique used in the narrative approach that enables a better understanding of organizational culture or more effective management (Mandl 2017, pp. 11–28). D.A. Jameson described how storytelling can be used by managers to interpret the world of the organization, solve conflicts and boost creative thinking. Other authors recognize the role of storytelling in building an organization's identity and image. Similar to narrative inquiry is metaphorical analysis, which was developed by G. Morgan and G. Burrell. It is based on the assumption that metaphors are fundamental categories of the human mind's interpretation of the world (Burrell and Morgan 2017). By comparing organizational culture and its change to other, more comprehensible processes or objects, we could better understand its complexity. For instance, organizational culture is compared, by both functionalists and interpretivists, to such objects as glue, glasses, temple, dance, text, language, religion and many more. What is interesting is the fact that a lot of studies conducted in the neo-evolutionary perspective also confirm that the human cognitive apparatus is particularly well prepared for processing and remembering narratives and metaphorical thinking.

The methods of linguistic studies also include text analyses, which are nonhomogeneous and encompass qualitative techniques often supported by quantitative ones. Qualitative text analyses can take the form of (Schmitt, Schröder and Pfaller 2018, pp. 29–41):

- Conversational analysis, which is inspired by ethnomethodology
- Content analysis, i.e., critical and reflective reading connected with the critical paradigm, which has both interpretive and functionalist contexts

Interpretive content analyses draw on hermeneutics, which is a philosophical method for getting to the sense of a text. They sometimes rely on the assumptions of phenomenology, seeking the sense of a text "in itself" (eidetic). The critical and postmodernist approaches to text analysis are often akin to interpretivism, but are placed within different paradigms. Although the classification of paradigms with regard to text analysis is not clear-cut, M.A. Janson proposes distinction of three paradigms: positivist, linguistic and interpretive. The interpretive approach to text analysis in organizational discourse always refers to a description of culture, which is usually perceived from a micro-perspective, i.e., social actions that are reflected in a polysemic network of meanings and symbols (Lacity and Janson 1994, pp. 137–155). Text analyses are widely used both as a research method and as a research technique, which is an element of a broader method, e.g., case study. The problems of studies connected with culture and change management include leadership through culture, textual interpretation of the cult of the theory of structuration and agency, relationships between text and conversation, and even textual approach to accounting (Lacity and Janson 1994, pp. 137–155).

Case study is not only a technique, but also a complex research methodology that can be located within different paradigms of social sciences. However, it is worth noting that its increasing popularity is connected with the development of the interpretive and symbolic paradigm and it is a very common method in management studies. The widespread use of case studies in management results from the practical orientation of the studies. Interpretive case studies are a subject of analyses of the anthropology of organizations, ethnomethodology, dramaturgical approach and other qualitative approaches to examining a broad spectrum of management issues, starting from identity and culture, through organizational strategy and change to accounting, managing SMEs, marketing and information systems. In organizational anthropology, cultural studies of organizations are the dominant research method. Very often, they are concerned with a dynamic approach to organizational culture, i.e., planned or spontaneous cultural change. The most common subjects of case studies are whole organizations, although some studies focus on people (employees, managers, leaders), smaller structural units (departments, cells, teams), and interactions (organizational situations, events). The selection of cases is naturally purposive and can be based on three frames of reference: key cases, outlier cases and local knowledge cases. Key cases involve selecting the most important entity, e.g., enterprise that dominates in a given sector. Outlier cases involve selecting a case that varies significantly from typical cases, e.g., a private enterprise in a sector dominated by public organizations. Local knowledge cases involve selecting a case or cases (in comparative analysis) that are more familiar to the researcher or for which in-depth studies can be conducted (Burrell and Morgan 2017, pp. 65–72).

Interpretive case studies have a few characteristics that differentiate them from case studies located within the neopositivist-functionalist-systemic paradigm. A case study is an interpretive method designed to understand individual, elusive, hidden and often unique aspects of organizing, which cannot be a basis for developing a pattern for generalization purpose. It is a qualitative method, although it can be based on quantitative data analysis, and even take the form of quantitative research (Blatter, Langer and Wagemann 2018, pp. 31–166). It is worth noting that attempts to combine case studies with other research methods, including quantitative ones, are also promising. The subject of such studies is usually a whole organization with its culture, identity, practices and interactions. It is most often perceived as a process, transformation, i.e., incremental change. A case study is the most important method for examining both culture and changes. Organizational culture, as well as its impact on organizations, is perceived predominantly at the microlevel through social practices (interactions, discourse, social game). Therefore, very often cultural studies concentrate on organizational identities, both collective and individual. Interpretivism-inspired studies seek to take a dynamic approach, i.e., capturing the sense of the changes and transformations that occur. This predominantly refers to spontaneous organizational changes, but also those planned, which, however, from the perspective of symbolic interactionism, are never controlled. Research methodology can even be based on methodological eclecticism (bricolage) (Mayer 2019, pp. 69–99), which entails the need for multiple research techniques, which may produce contradictory or disproportionate descriptions. The researcher should strive to have a position of an insider who is embedded in the culture and understands it intuitively. Assigning values and engagement are highly valued. Subjectivism does not represent a problem. By definition, studies usually focus on one case, which is analyzed in an in-depth, exploratory way. They mainly use qualitative, descriptive, subjective or intersubjective data, which is derived from communication with the subjects of the study, obtained by means of anthropological techniques: unstructured interviews, focus group interviews, participant and nonparticipant observation, discourse and text analysis.

As with most other interpretive methods, self-analysis and describing cases from personal experience are permitted. Subjectivity and involvement are supplemented here by an in-depth knowledge of the case, e.g., organization for which the researcher worked.

Other methods characteristic of various approaches to understanding culture include intervention sociology, frame analysis and breaching experiment, which in practice is hardly applied within management. They are used in analyzing change in cultural processes, but so far their application in studies within the field of management is very limited. The intervention method is based on the constructivist assumption regarding the formation of social movements, institutions, organizations and the entire society. This methodology, designed predominantly to study social movements, assumes that a team of researchers participates in the process of group identity formation (Kleineberg 2016, pp. 27–29). Observations, interviews, shadowing and meetings are meant to extract the essence of the community, but also impact the process of its formation and crystallization. Thus, the researcher is immersed in the social group he/she studied, he/she is engaged and he/she is someone between an outsider and an insider.

Grounded theory is applied in management studies mainly to investigate organizational culture, organizational change and the work process. The methodology is qualitative, i.e., concentrated on an in-depth, individual, nonquantifiable and unorthodox process of knowledge acquisition, mainly through a direct contact with the subject of the study. The emergence of theories and hypotheses assumes that the researcher understands the local categories, uses the language and conceptual framework of the subject of the study, i.e., to say he/she does not impose his/her own perspective, but discovers the one actually adopted by the subject. The following are postulated in the research process: cognitive openness, local approach, pluralism with regard to choosing data selection techniques and triangulation. The researcher should not have too many pre-conceptualizations, which means that he/she should try to begin the study with a clear mind, without prior reading or theoretical constructs. It is vital to understand the colloquial and local categories used by the subject of the study, which can be achieved by getting to the practices, social interactions and incidents. Studies of the processes of cultural changes focus on the processual approach and use the category of organizational identity or refer to the sphere of organizational behaviors. The research process in grounded theory basically consists of four stages, but it is flexible and enables return to individual phases of the study if needed. The first stage, which is called coding, aims to identify anchors for the understanding of the social processes in which the subjects of the study engage. For that purpose, it is desirable to use any available data collection techniques, i.e., interviews and observations and any available primary and then secondary written and documentation materials as well as expert panels, focus group interviews, consultations and more. Open, selective coding or cross-coding is postulated here in order to identify the relations between the primary categories derived directly from data. The second stage, which is called conceptualization, aims to group those codes extracted from the empirical material that share recurring pattern into broader categories. The third phase is categorization, i.e., going from inductive approach to inductive and deductive approach, in which generalizations and relationships between variables appear. The fourth, last, stage is theorizing, which constitutes synthesis of the study allowing an explanatory theory to be formulated (Hopf 2016, pp. 13–45).

Important issues of the interpretive management of organizational cultural change include (Urbach and Ahlemann 2016, pp. 16–28):

- Dynamic presentation of organizational culture in the process of its manifestation and permanent transformation
- Managing change through sensemaking and management of meaning
- Organizational learning understood as change
- Links with the efficiency of an organization
- Links with strategic management
- Reorganization and restructuring of an organization
- The problem of time in change management
- Longitudinal change
- Specificity of cultural change in different types of an organization
- Using archetypes in managing cultural change

Summing up, the interpretive approach to cultural change in an organization is a fundamental problem of symbolic interactionism. Therefore, a lot of concepts of an organization and management exploiting this approach emerged. The application of interpretivism is wide, and the importance of this paradigm is constantly growing.

Emancipation project is a methodological element that is integrally connected with criticism of the instrumentalism and oppressiveness of organizational culture (Sułkowski 2013, pp. 5–11). Critical evaluation should lead to change. The aim of an emancipation project is to change the unjust order rather than to increase economic efficiency or effectiveness of an organization. Of course, the aspects of efficiency and organizational effectiveness also need to be taken into account when changes are implemented. Identified conflicts of interests, limited empowerment and dehumanizing aspects of management should be exposed and analyzed, resulting in a decreased impact of false consciousness. An emancipation project leads to greater participation of disadvantaged groups in the power structures and decision-making. Thus, a project of changes should aim to increase employee participation in managerial structures and to develop organizational democracy. It is equally important to guarantee a fairer, more balanced distribution that will include disadvantaged groups. This requires changing the principles of rewarding, motivating and developing employees, i.e., the whole system of managing HR in organizations. The key directions of such a change will be greater equality and justice in organizations and change in mentality among managers and other employees. The process of implementing emancipatory changes should result in a new organizational culture focused on employee empowerment, justice and equality. Creation of such a new culture must involve key structural and strategic changes aimed at humanization and emancipation of disadvantaged groups. It is necessary to change mission, strategic goals, organizational structure, values, norms and management systems. However, it important to bear in mind that the control over cultural change is limited, because apart from the formal culture that is controlled by an organization, there also exists an informal culture. Therefore, the last stage of cultural change is its rooting, which corresponds to the stage of "freezing" in the model of social changes proposed by K. Lewin (Hussain et al. 2018, pp. 123–127). Rooting should mean that the emancipatory values are considered as key to organizational culture and identity.

The concept of cultural changes proposed here stems from the assumption, which is also adopted by CMS representatives, that culture is a root metaphor for management. Thus, cultural change is change of the entire organization, including its strategy, organizational structure, management patterns and styles, as well as management systems.

6.3 MODERN INNOVATIVE TRENDS IN ORGANIZATIONAL CULTURE MANAGEMENT IN TERMS OF CHANGES IN THE ENVIRONMENT

Nowadays, it becomes vital to answer the questions: How to shape innovative organizational culture, and what should be the characteristics and dimensions of an innovative culture that enables an organization to sustain competitive advantage? Thus, innovations are perceived today as a potential source of the success of an organization. However, innovation does not mean merely creating new, useful ideas, but also implementing such ideas in order to develop products, services, processes or new ways of performing work. Organizational culture will certainly facilitate creation and maintenance of such environment in an organization.

Organizational culture gains significance in today's conditions of the functioning of organizations, in which innovations mean an effort that is taken to make a planned organizational change. The changing environment forces change in the hierarchy of organizational values. The top of this hierarchy is occupied by fast pace of reactions to changes in the environment, which replaced stabilization as a condition of organizational efficiency. Thus, the conditions in which enterprises function, force them to create programs of continuous change of organizational culture, which means shaping organizational culture that initiates changes, shaping innovative culture.

However, making changes to the value system of employees is a long-term and difficult process; therefore, management should continuously take efforts to shape attitudes among employees that facilitate such changes. So, the question arises: How to shape innovative organizational culture, and what should be the characteristics and dimensions of an innovative culture that enables an organization to sustain competitive advantage?

The cultural patterns supporting the traditional organizational systems were conducive to a low tolerance of uncertainty. Currently, the prevalent view is that due to the intensity of changes, there seems to be chaos in which everything is possible (Augsten, Brodbeck and Birkenmeier 2017, pp. 143–152). Using forms of management that are suitable to the new situation requires a fundamental cultural change that involves a shift towards a culture that initiates changes in an organization.

The characteristics of an innovative culture should be regarded as an ideal model, as organizations implementing innovations will certainly vary in terms of the degree of such characteristics. This is due to the nature of organizational culture itself, as every organization has a distinct, unique system of values. On the other hand, it highlights the importance and links between innovative organizational culture and modern concepts of management, especially the concept of a learning organization.

Shaping organizational culture involves appropriate selection of management tools. This is because it is not enough to impose new symbols or other visible manifestations of culture. A change will not be lasting, unless deeper layers of organizational culture can be affected. Shaping organizational culture will not bring expected benefits, until the new system of norms, values and behavior patterns is commonly understood and accepted.

They have to be consistently promoted and followed by a manager, who can and should actively determine the shape of culture through a variety of actions. Success in creating an innovative culture depends on the competencies of management, how the organizational strategy and goals are perceived and what management techniques are applied.

The literature often lists activities that allow management to actively impact the shape of an organizational culture that facilitates innovation and implementation of changes. It is mainly recommended to harmoniously combine activities that address the issues shown in Figure 6.2.

By developing and accepting appropriate assumptions of the HR management strategy, it will be possible to inform individual organizational units and employees what is the subject of changes and how these changes will be implemented. The presented tools for shaping organizational culture indicate that it is necessary to combine all tools for shaping organizational culture, because, as can be seen, the different groups of tools are not fully separable and do not work in isolation from each other.

It is worth having a look at the activities that contribute to the development of innovative organizational culture. The theoretical and practical activities aimed at shaping organizational culture that facilitates innovation define the way to go for managers who

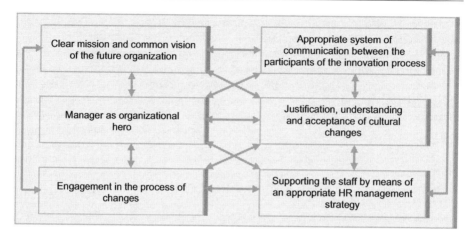

FIGURE 6.2   Relations determining the dimension of organizational culture. (Own work based on: Larcher S.B., et al. Fallstudien, Führung, organisationaler Wandel und Innovation, [in:] *Führung lernen*, Springer Gabler, Berlin, Heidelberg, 2018, pp. 157–208.)

perceive the significance of implementing innovations in an enterprise. Shaping innovative organizational culture can be considered as the basic condition of effective innovative activity in an enterprise in the area of organizational, technological, technical and product-related changes. Identification of the dimensions and characteristics of an innovative culture as well as activities facilitating such culture helps to create, maintain and develop innovative organizational culture.

Organizational culture stimulates innovative activity in dynamic organizations that are socially oriented, externally oriented, performance-oriented, process-oriented and frequently communication-oriented. Innovative organizational culture is one in which the main values are acceptance of uncertain conditions of operation, cooperation, creativity, independence, achievement drive and self-worth. Identification, diagnosis and analysis of these dimensions and characteristics of innovative organizational culture is the basic condition of proper development of such culture. An important role in this process is played by management whose task is to design a policy and strategy of action as well as management procedures. Organizational culture becomes a tool in the hands of management, who, through HR policy, can exert an influence on employees in order to ensure that the organizational goals are achieved. Moreover, managers' actions and statements shape the picture of the organizational world in the minds of their subordinates, which in turn impacts the behaviors and actions within the organization as a whole. This is vital in the dynamically changing world of business, where effective innovative activities determine competitive advantage.

However, organizational culture, treated as an analytical concept, raises significant ethical, methodological and pragmatical problems. It has been postulated that organizational culture should be treated as a sensitizing concept rather than a strictly defined one. This involves implementing into the debate on the theory of organizations a set of new categories, which originated from anthropological postcolonial criticism (Helpap, Bekmeier-Feuerhahn and Pinkernelle 2018, pp. 209–241).

The point of reference is the concept of culture itself, and more specifically its criticism within cultural anthropology. Modern anthropologists gave up attempts to create a universal definition of culture in favor of developing other categories used for culture-sensitive description. The distrust of what would seem to be the fundamental analytical category is grounded in methodological, ethical and pragmatic issues. In light of the discussion undertaken by representatives of postcolonial criticism (Dirlik 2018, pp. 172–179), it is reasonable to state that the concept of culture, understood as an analytical tool, generates more problems than actual benefits.

The vision of culture, *some* culture and our culture as a consensus about the fundamentals—accepted concepts, shared feelings and values—seems impossible to sustain in the face of such dispersion and breakup; landscapes of collective personality are full of flaws and rifts (Simon 2019, pp. 79–97).

Criticism of culture shows that the fundamental ideas and meanings shared by members of a given culture are merely one of many discourses, controlled by part of that specific community. That discourse is elevated to the position of the established and authoritative one and supersedes continuously emerging contradicting discourses. If we look at it through the prism of methodology, it can be seen that criticized concepts of culture make it more difficult for the researcher to understand the variety characterizing the modern world.

The new ways of understanding culture break with the consensus. What is also characteristic of the representatives of this approach is that while suspending the need to define culture, they go deeper and focus on examining rituals, myths, narratives, discourse, cultural gender, power relations, identity and other categories from the dictionary of cultural description. Culture comes to resemble "a sensitizing concept," which "only suggests directions in which to look" (Lauer 2019, pp. 231–263).

In the mainstream studies of organizational culture, theoretical considerations focus on defining this concept. However, as stressed by those who have undertaken this task, multiplicity of approaches makes it very difficult. Thus, suspension of defining culture is methodologically and pragmatically justified. Anthropological studies are inductive—scholars construct theoretical generalizations starting with an ethnographic detail. This opening up to different theories of cultural studies is a pragmatic aspect of the strategy to bracket the theoretical works within the studies of organizational culture.

With regard to the trends in organizational culture management in terms of changes in the environment, it is also worth mentioning the issue of mutual relationships between cultural factors and the process of a positive transfer of tacit knowledge. A constant challenge facing today's organizations, which may differ in terms of specificity of their activity but are similarly subjected to the impact of a turbulent environment, is to cope with changeable conditions in a way that allows them to survive and at the same time enjoy a stable development. To achieve that, organizations must base their activity on possessed and improved resources and skills. Strategic advantage is gained through a configuration of key competencies that are difficult to imitate. These are the qualities of intangible assets of an organization's potential, among which a special role is played by organizational culture and knowledge. Combining these two attributes has an impact on the acquisition and use of knowledge, as well as the development of experiences that are necessary in organizational efficiency and identity.

Cultural phenomena contribute to the deepening of the understanding of organizational behaviors and discovering of new capacities of organizations. Every organization has unique characteristics of operation that differentiate it from others, and impact, among other things, the character of the relatic nships between its members, leadership style, work organization techniques, material visualization and methods for implementing organizational changes. They both influence the contacts of an organization with its environment and cause certain, sometimes desirable, transformations within an organization. Since its emergence, the concept of organizational culture has remained an issue that is multifaceted and difficult to describe and identify.

An integrated approach to the subject addressed herein allows culture to be separated from an organization, and mutual relationships between them and the environment to be examined. It also enables objective description of organizational culture, which is subject to the processes of managing and shaping employee behaviors and takes into account the elements of subjectivity, symbols, metaphor and narrative. This requires the identification of the content of cultural phenomena through their symptoms, configuration and constituents.

Knowledge is created in the context of human mental processes of interpreting various information, verifying personal beliefs and taking advantage of experiences. Because it can be used in a variety of forms and implemented in multiple processes, and has unique qualities (dominance, inexhaustibility, simultaneity, nonlinearity), knowledge qualifies as a strategic resource. It is the main source of innovation, creativity and creative problem-solving of an organization. Therefore, it is vital to identify the existing knowledge accumulated in the heads of employees, understand the process of its creation and use it at the level of task teams within the organization. Thus, acquisition, generation, transfer and distribution of knowledge becomes one of the main tasks of the modern organization.

Knowledge is a key resource that allows an organization to effectively and flexibly adapt to the changes occurring in its environment and develop innovations. Therefore, the task of organizations that want to effectively use this resource is to create conditions facilitating the flow, renewal and utility of knowledge.

Transfer of knowledge is of vital importance among processes involving this resource. It should be continuous and uninterrupted, and allow knowledge to be distributed within a certain time frame to places and people in an organization where it is most needed. Knowledge that is not applied or used becomes useless. Thus, knowledge use is not possible without knowledge transfer. In order for this process to be successful, an organization uses appropriate tools, methods and other measures that facilitate it. Transfer of knowledge means its movement (flow) from the source of knowledge (people, organizations that possess it) to its destination, i.e., employees and units that implement and develop knowledge. The ability to share knowledge relates to the aspects of communication of an organization with its environment, and its internal relationships, and depends on the types of shared knowledge. Therefore, the execution of the transfer process is of particular importance for extracting tacit knowledge, which is intangible, based on individual skills and qualifications, and often specialized and expert. For a complete process of the flow of tacit knowledge to occur, its two coherent components must be present: transmission (sending or presentation) and absorption (receipt) (Mandel 2016, pp. 85–104). Thus, dissemination of tacit knowledge will be preceded by its identification; it requires translation and interpretation. This, in turn, leads to filtration and discarding of useless and outdated knowledge and creation of new knowledge resources. They gain current value by being reflected in various types of knowledge, i.e., products, competencies, concepts, data platforms, procedures, innovations, documents, inventions and patents.

A recognizable category of tacit knowledge is technical knowledge, which is transferred at three levels (Figure 6.3).

The following benefits of a successful transfer of knowledge are presented with regard to a business organization (although they are so universal that they can apply to other entities as well) (Figure 6.4).

Transfer of tacit knowledge is connected with human cognition, experience, intuition, openness, acting and communication, and as such, it refers to employee behaviors—culturally conditioned manifestations. Thus, organizational culture becomes a bridge in

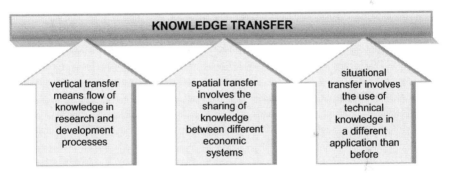

FIGURE 6.3 Levels of the transfer of technical knowledge. (Own work based on: Kuckertz A., Corporate Entrepreneurship und Unternehmenskultur, [in:] *Management: Corporate Entrepreneurship*, Springer Gabler, Wiesbaden, 2017, pp. 47–70.)

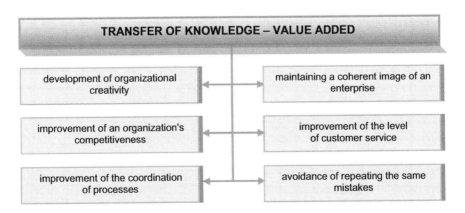

FIGURE 6.4 Universal positives of an effective transfer of knowledge. (Own work based on: Wiener M., Förderliche Organisationskultur für Open Foresight, [in:] *Open Foresight und Unternehmenskultur*, Springer Gabler, Wiesbaden, 2018, pp. 129–144.)

the process of the flow of tacit knowledge, containing at the same time an element of the vision of the functioning and development of an organization that is shared by organizational members. In such conditions, informal (spontaneous) transfer is regarded as the most appropriate form of sharing subjective knowledge. Realized through the processes of socialization, it usually occurs in small organizations. The main barrier in the development of the willingness to share tacit knowledge is the lack of appropriate communication skills. The instruments facilitating the acquisition of tacit knowledge include interpersonal (teamwork) training, creative thinking techniques, psychological workshops, decision-making training, delivering speeches during symposiums, mentorship, coaching, quality circles, and communities of practice.

Knowledge-oriented culture (focused on creation and transfer of knowledge) exists in an organization that promotes acceptance of failures, diversity, mutual support, learning and teamwork, among other things (Kühl 2018, pp. 7–35). It has clearly defined requirements for employees and is based on trust in mutual relations. Transfer of tacit knowledge can be stimulated by the system for managing the whole organization. It facilitates personalization and codification of this type of knowledge and assignment of utility value to it. The aim of the transfer of tacit knowledge is to provide appropriate information that will allow the right decision to be made, to create new knowledge and to use knowledge that leads to innovation. Transfer of knowledge is an indispensable bridge between the processes of its creation and acquisition on the one hand and application and storage on the other hand.

Organizational culture that facilitates innovative activities is a fundamental contributor to the creation of innovative solutions. They take the form of projects, new products and/or services, processes, systems and technologies. At the core of innovation is individual and organizational creativity. The latter is characterized by the following qualities (Petry 2018, pp. 91–100):

- Creativity always requires creative thinking or activity
- All creative endeavors are purposeful; i.e., they aim to achieve a specific goal
- Creative endeavors must produce something original
- The outcome must be valuable in terms of a given goal

The distinction between creativity and innovation indicates that the former involves creation and development of ideas and new concepts, while the latter is a result of their successful implementation in practice. Innovative applications vary in terms of the degree of novelty compared to the previous applications, and are implemented in a given environment to improve its functioning. Innovativeness refers to the generation of knowledge and ideas, search for the possibilities of their implementation and introduction to the market (Kastner 2017, pp. 507–534). Cultural phenomena, associated with the unique and varied collectivity of every organization, impact its internal changes and integration with its environment. The process of organizational learning helps to shape a culture that facilitates innovation and at the same time to maintain continuity. The technologies of its components, which enable people to constantly increase their capabilities to achieve desirable results, encompass five disciplines (Figure 6.5).

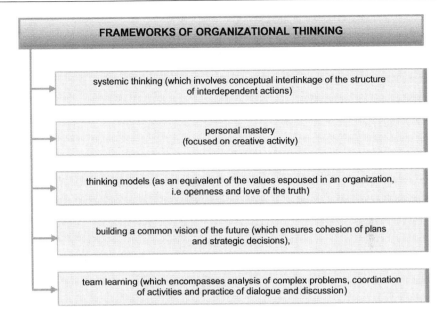

FIGURE 6.5 Aspects of the process of organizational thinking. (Own work based on: Fieseler Ch., Hoffmann Ch.P., Meckel M., Eine Kultur der Innovation: Die Bedeutung von Innovationsnetzwerken, [in:] *Business Innovation: Das St. Galler Modell*, Springer Gabler, Wiesbaden, 2016, pp. 313–337.)

Apart from self-improvement of an organization, the other factors forming a pro-innovation culture include (Jetzke 2015, pp, 32–55):

- Employee attitudes focused on entrepreneurship, inspiring changes and risk-taking
- Trust in the actions taken by the management
- Support for initiatives and promotion of achievements
- Flexibility and adaptive capabilities of an organization
- Identifying organizational values with the staff's standards of conduct and thinking patterns
- Selection of appropriate tools for transformation of culture
- Creation of an organizational climate that facilitates changes

Table 6.3 presents a list of ways of developing a culture that facilitates creativity, innovation and flexibility of an organization.

A constant rebuilding of a desirable innovation-oriented culture results in reinforcement of the behaviors of organizational members who show individual initiative, creativity, risk tolerance, exploratory passion, and tolerance of errors; accept changes; and are at the same time open to knowledge absorption and sharing. An additional role is played by the attitudes and norms shared by the managerial staff, who should create such physical and social conditions where employees are motivated and rewarded for acquiring new knowledge within and outside of the organization and want to cooperate

TABLE 6.3   Ways of modeling organizational culture

FACILITATING ACTIVITIES	IMPLICATIONS
Selection of innovative employees	Selecting employees who are open to changes and generate and implement ideas in a novel way Acceptance of the diversity of organizational population
Creativity and innovation training	Encouraging development training and innovation assessment Organizing training courses that facilitate innovation development
Development of a learning organizational culture	Supporting a culture of continuous learning During education, encouraging greater creativity, independent thinking and learning
Employee empowerment	Supporting the practices that increase participation in decision-making and responsibility Employee participation in governance
Taking account of employees' ideas in plans	Taking account of best practices in innovation plans Initiatives supporting the implementation of innovative activities
Management supporting employees' innovative activities	Manager who is a role model of desirable innovative activities, open to challenges and changes Creating opportunities for employees for innovative activities by giving them autonomy and necessary resources
Creativity as a requirement and work standard	Ensuring that innovation is required Making innovation part of career development and performance assessment
Appropriate system of rewards	Salary and non-salary incentives for showing innovative attitudes
Risk-taking permission	Focus on risk, experiment, challenges Use of risk evaluation techniques
Investment in research and development	Engaging the R&D department in the innovation process Focus on quality, implementation of new ideas

Source: Own work based on Jetzke T., Zukunftsforschung und Organisationskultur–Organisationskulturelle Zukunftskonzepte als Voraussetzung für die Zukunftsfähigkeit von Organisationen. *Zeitschrift für Zukunftsforschung*, 2015, 1.4: 32–55.

in a creative and effective way. Employees' individual inclinations and predispositions as well as engagement in building cooperation ties will facilitate identification with the direction of the organization's development and its ambitious, competitive plans. Creation of a culture that facilitates the flow of knowledge is a long-term activity, and its aim is not only to provide knowledge that is necessary in the functioning of an organization but also to focus on the process of its transfer in a way that ensures a significant shortening of the distance between the source of knowledge and innovation.

Conclusion

The issue of culture in the processes of managing organizations is an important element of the functioning of economic entities, especially in the context of explorations connected with the use of noneconomic factors of shaping their competitive position in the market. Thus, it reflects the humanist approach to managing organizations, which is mainly concerned with various phenomena and patterns from the perspective of a human being and his/her place in organizations. Interest in organizational culture is reflection of the research currently connected with social conditions of the process of work, which means that it should not be treated only in terms of the functioning of an organization, but more broadly in the context of cultural diversity of societies, i.e., cultural processes, occurring in the environment of an organization.

The authors of this publication stress that organizational culture is not a fixed phenomenon. Its shaping takes place in stages, and currently, it is essential to take into account such stages in the process of implementing the strategy of an enterprise. This is because organizational culture may support or hinder development projects. Therefore, it should be diagnosed and also changed if needed. In assessment of the phenomena of organizational culture and its impact on the competitiveness of economic entities, of fundamental importance is the model of competing values, and especially, the element of this model is referred to as market. In this case, culture should be externally oriented, i.e., focusing on shaping the position in the environment. But organizational culture also impacts how an organization looks and how its staff behave, allowing its values to be shaped, which directly translates into competitiveness of the organization. Therefore, the authors of this publication are convinced that analysis of a company's values must take into account organizational culture.

Organizational culture can also affect knowledge management in an enterprise, which also determines its competitiveness. This is because knowledge management should take into account both the factor of power distance and collectivism of a given employee community (teams of employees), which impact the relationships in an organization between superiors and subordinates. The employee behaviors indicated by the authors of this publication are certainly manifestation of the existence of a specific type of organizational culture in organizations. Therefore, the authors maintain that the way of managing knowledge is to a large extent the product of the organizational culture in an organization.

Shaping an organizational culture facilitating changes is possible. Organizational culture is by definition a living entity, which constantly undergoes transformations and modifications as the organization learns how to cope with the problems connected with adapting to a highly turbulent environment. Thus, change is inscribed in organizational culture and constitutes its integral element, which often determines the position of an organization in the market. The authors of this publication admit that changing organizational culture is a long-term process, which essentially should encompass only some elements of an organization. They note that we should talk about a fragmentary shaping of organizational culture rather than a revolutionary change, which in most cases is basically impossible to implement. The shaping of culture focuses on modifying values, norms and cultural patterns in accordance with the assumptions of managers. However, culture is a very complex variable, and as such, the directions of its change can be difficult to predict or plan.

In terms of organizational culture, the authors of this publication argue that the ability and possibility to both create and use knowledge is a source of gaining and sustaining competitive advantage. This requires conversion and transfer of knowledge between three types of knowledge sources, namely, competencies of organizational members, experience in organizing and coordinating activities aimed at delivering products and providing services, and relations with the external world. Knowledge may have a positive impact on the development of an organization when it enables it to find new ways of accomplishing its goals and at the same time use it for what has so far been done well. Creation of new knowledge requires the development of appropriate conditions by formulating clear, comprehensible plans of an organization; giving people and teams a relatively broad autonomy; creating conditions for a creative chaos; organizing buffer resources and a sufficient variety of approaches, activities and solutions for stimulating changes; proper assessment of new knowledge rather than the value of organizational factors; creating conditions for fast implementation of new product concepts, HR (human resources) management that promotes creativity and risk-taking.

Appropriate creation and use of knowledge is difficult, as these two aspects of the activity of an organization do not support each other. Quite the contrary, they may cause tensions and contradictions. Knowledge that is deeply rooted in an organization, more specifically in its products and processes, may create barriers to changes. According to the authors of this publication, optimization of the use of possessed knowledge and creation of new knowledge require the best possible transformation of individual knowledge into structures, processes, products and systems, which enable the use of values, which can be achieved thanks to the new knowledge. Therefore, the authors of this publication maintain that it is necessary to inspire people, create the principles of participation, increase the flexibility of organizational structures and create new jobs in order to cause changes in organizational culture.

References

Abecker A., et al. (eds.), *Geschäftsprozessorientiertes Wissensmanagement: Effektive Wissen-snutzung bei der Planung und Umsetzung von Geschäftsprozessen*, Springer Verlag, Berlin, Heidelberg, 2013.

Achouri C., *Human Resources Management*, Gabler Verlag, Wiesbaden, 2015.

Ackermann A., Wechselwirkung–Komplexität: Einleitende Bemerkungen zum Kulturbegriff von Pluralismus und Multikulturalismus, [in:] *Patchwork, Dimensionen multikultureller Gesellschaf- ten Geschichte, Problematik und Chancen*, A. Ackermann, K.E. Müller (eds.), transcript Verlag, Bielefeld, 2015.

Agrawal A.N., Patgaonkar Y., Building HR Competencies in RPG Group-Laying Foundation for a Strong Business Partnership. *NHRD Network Journal*, 2010, 3: 17–22.

Al Ahbabi S.A., et al. Employee perception of impact of knowledge management processes on public sector performance. *Journal of Knowledge Management*, 2019, 23.2: 351–373.

Al Saifi S.A., Toward a theoretical model of learning organization and knowledge management processes. *International Journal of Knowledge Management (IJKM)*, 2019, 15.2: 55–80.

Al–Laham A., *Organisationales Wissensmanagement: Eine strategische Perspektive*, Vahlen, München, 2016.

Al-Shawaf L., Zreik K., Richard Dawkins on constraints on natural selection, [in:] *Encyclopedia of Evolutionary Psychological Science*, T.K. Shackelford, V.A. Weekes - Shackelford (eds.), Springer, New York, 2018.

Antczak Z., *Kapitał intelektualny i kapitał ludzki w ewoluującej przestrzeni organizacyjnej (w optyce badawczej knowledge management)*, Wydawnictwo Uniwersytetu Ekonomicznego we Wrocławiu, Wrocław, 2013.

Arnold R., Von der interkulturellen Kompetenz zur Diversitätskompetenz, [in:] *Kultur - Interdisziplinäre Zugänge*, H. Busche, T. Heinze, F. Hillebrandt, F. Schäfer (eds.), Springer VS, Wiesbaden, 2018.

Ashikali T., Groeneveld S., Diversity management in public organizations and its effect on employ-ees' affective commitment: The role of transformational leadership and the inclusiveness of the organizational culture. *Review of Public Personnel Administration*, 2015, 35.2.

Asrar-Ul-Haq M., Anwar S., A systematic review of knowledge management and knowledge sharing: Trends, issues, and challenges. *Cogent Business & Management*, 2016.

Asree S., Zain M., Rizal M.R., Influence of leadership competency and organizational culture on responsiveness and performance of firms. *International Journal of Contemporary Hospitality Management*, 2010, 22.4: 500–516.

Augsten T., Innovation und Unternehmenskultur, [in:] *Strategie and Innovation*, T. Augsten, H. Brodbeck, B. Birkenmeier (eds.), Springer Gabler, Wiesbaden, 2017.

Awan A.G., Shifting Global Economic Paradigm. *Asian Business Review*, 2018, 4.3: 35–40.

Banse G., Reher E.O., Technologiewandel in der Wissensgesellschaft-qualitative und quantitative Veränderungen, Sitzungsberichte der Leibniz–Sozietät zu Berlin, Bd. 122, Berlin, 2015.

Barmeyer Ch., Romani L., Pilhofer K., Welche Impulse liefert interkulturelles Management für diversity management? [in:] *Handbuch Diversity Kompetenz. Perspektiven und Anwendungs-felder*, P. Genkova, T. Ringeisen (eds.), Springer Fachmedien, Wiesbaden, 2016.

Barmeyer Ch., Eberhardt J., Interkulturelle Kompetenz von Drittkultur-Managern in Schnitt-stellenpositionen multinationaler Unternehmen. *Interculture journal: Online Zeitschrift für interkulturelle Studien*, 2019, 18: 31–50.

Barrett R., Wie sich Werte auf Leistung auswirken, [in:] *Werteorientierte Unternehmensfuhrung*, R. Barrett (ed.), Springer, Berlin, Heidelberg, 2016.

Basalingappa A., Kumar K., Marketing, communication and democracy: Towards a dialogue between the disciplines of marketing and communication. *The Marketing Review*, 2018, 18.2: 149–160.

Baschera P., Gundrum E., Unternehmenskultur als Treiber des langfristigen Geschaftserfolgs–Personlichkeitsentwicklung als Basis der Unternehmensentwicklung, [in:] *Unternehmenskultur aktiv gestalten*, P. Baschera (ed.), Springer, Berlin, Heidelberg, 2013.

Battistutti O.C., Bork D., Tacit to explicit knowledge conversion. *Cognitive Processing*, 2017, 18.4: 461–477.

Becker J.H., Pastoors S., Persönliche Kompetenzen, [in:] *Praxishandbuch berufliche Schlüsselkompetenzen*, Springer, Berlin, Heidelberg, 2018.

Benhabib S., *Kulturelle Vielfalt und demokratische Gleichheit, Politische Partizipation im Zeitalter der Globalisierung*, S. Fischer Verlag, 2015.

Bentele G., Seidenglanz R., *Vertrauen und Glaubwurdigkeit: Begriffe, Ansatze, Forschungsubersicht und praktische Relevanz, Handbuch der Public Relations: Wissenschaftliche Grundlagen und berufliches Handeln, Mit Lexikon*, Springen Verlag, Berlin, Heidelberg, 2015.

Bernd R., Altobelli C.F., Sander M., Personalführung in international tätigen Unternehmen, [in:] *Internationales Marketing-Management*, R. Bernd, C.F. Altobelli, M. Sander (eds.), Springer, Berlin, Heidelberg, 2016.

Berndt R. (ed.), *Unternehmen im Wandel – Change Management*, Springer Verlag, Berlin, Heidelberg, 2013.

Besharov M.L., Brickson S.L., Organizational identity and institutional forces, [in:] *The Oxford Handbook of Organizational Identity*, Oxford University Press, New York, 2016.

Beyer D., Breunig Ch., Radojevic M., Punctuated equilibrium theory, [in:] *The Routledge Handbook of European Public Policy*, 2017.

Blatter J., Langer P.C., Wagemann C., Interpretative Ansätze und Methoden, [in:] *Qualitative Methoden in der Politikwissenschaft*, Springer VS, Wiesbaden, 2018.

Bormann K.C., Rowold J., Organisationskultur, [in:] *Human Resource Management*, Springer Gabler, Berlin, Heidelberg, 2015.

Broser Ch., *Vertrauen für föderiertes Identitätsmanagement*, BoD–Books on Demand, Norderstedt, 2016.

Bruhn M., Meffert H., Hadwich K., Internationales Dienstleistungsmarketing, [in:] *Handbuch Dienstleistungsmarketing*, Springer Gabler, Wiesbaden, 2019.

Brunner J. et al., *Value–based performance management: Wertsteigernde Unternehmen sführung: Strategien – Instrumente – Praxisbeispiele*, Springer Verlag, Berlin, Heidelberg, 2013.

Brzeziński S., Bubel D., Asymilacja standardów funkcjonowania organizacji inteligentnych w procesach zarządzania na przykładzie niemieckich przedsiębiorstw. *Studia i Prace Kolegium Zarządzania i Finansów/Szkoła Główna Handlowa*, 2016, 148.

Brzozowska A., Nowe perspektywy interpretacji zarządzania w świetle organizacji niegospodarczych. *Organizacja i Zarządzanie – Kwartalnik naukowy*, 2013, 3.

Bubel D., Konstatacja nad sekwencją podejmowania decyzji w praktyce i teorii zarządzania, Zeszyty Naukowe Politechniki Śląskiej 2015, seria: Organizacja i Zarządzanie, 2015.

Bubel D., Zarządzanie procesem zmian w aspekcie doskonalenia działalności przedsiębiorstw na przykładzie sieci dealerskich, Zeszyty Naukowe Politechniki Śląskiej 2016, seria: Organizacja i Zarządzanie, 2016.

Buche A., et al., Diversität und Erfolg von Organisationen/Diversity and organizational performance. *Zeitschrift für Soziologie*, 2013.

Buchner D., Hofmann U., Magnus S., *Prozess-Power: Durch Change Management den Prozesserfolgsichern*, Gabler Verlag, Wiesbaden, 2013.

Bührmann A.D., Diversitätsmanagementkonzepte im sozialwissenschaftlichen Diskurs: Befunde, Diskussionen und Perspektiven einer reflexiven Diversitätsforschung. *Handbuch Diversity Kompetenz: Perspektiven und Anwendungsfelder*, 2016.

Burchell M., Robin J., *The Great Workplace: How to Build It, How to Keep It, and Why It Matters*, John Wiley & Sons, 2011.

Burke W. W., *Organization Change: Theory and Practice*, Sage Publications, 2017.

Burrell G., Morgan G., *Sociological Paradigms and Organisational Analysis: Elements of the Sociology of Corporate Life*, Routledge, Abingdon, 2017.

Calás M.B., Smircich L. (eds.), *Postmodern Management Theory*, Routledge, London, 2019.

Camphausen B., *Strategisches Management: Planung, Entscheidung, Controlling*, Walter de Gruyter, Oldenbourg, 2013.

Cerchione R., Esposito E., Using knowledge management systems: A taxonomy of SME strategies. *International Journal of Information Management*, 2017, 37.1.

Chandler N.G., Cultural complexity in large organisations, [in:] *Managing Organizational Diversity*, Springer, Cham, 2017.

Chang Ch.L., Lin, The role of organizational culture in the knowledge management process. *Journal of Knowledge Management*, 2015, 19.3.

Combe I.A., Carrington D.J., Leaders' sensemaking under crises: Emerging cognitive consensus over time within management teams. *The Leadership Quarterly*, 2015, 26.3.

Crane D., Kawashima N., Kawasaki K., Culture and globalization theoretical models and emerging trends, [in:] *Global Culture*, Routledge, New York, 2016.

Deszczyński B., Upodmiotowienie pracowników jako element przewagi konkurencyjnej w organizacjach ukierunkowanych na zarządzanie relacjami, *Studia Ekonomiczne*, 2016, 255.

Dicle M.F., Increasing return response to changes in risk. *Review of Financial Economics*, 2019, 37.1.

Diebig M., Teamdiversity und innovation, [in:] *Innovationsförderndes Human Resource Management*, J. Rowold, K.C. Bormann (eds.), Springer, Berlin, Heidelberg, 2015.

Dirlik A., *The Postcolonial Aura: Third World Criticism in the Age of Global Capitalism*, Routledge, New York, 2018.

Dneprovskaya N., et al. Knowledge management methods in online course development, [in:] *Proceedings of the 15th European Conference on e-Learning-ECEL*. 2016.

Döbler T., Wissensmanagement: Open access, social networks, E-collaboration, [in:] *Handbuch Online-Kommunikation*, 2018, pp. 1–30.

Donate M.J., De Pablo J.D.S., The role of knowledge-oriented leadership in knowledge management practices and innovation. *Journal of Business Research*, 2015, 68.2.

Eberhardt D., Majkovic A.L., Zukunft der Führung: Veränderung in Sicht oder bleibt alles beim Alten? [in:] *Die Zukunft der Führung*, Springer, Wiesbaden, 2015.

Eberhardt D., Streuli E., Zukunft der Führung bedeutet Vielfalt führen, [in:] *Führung von Vielfalt*, Springer, Berlin, Heidelberg, 2016.

Ebert H., Pastoors S., Kulturelle Identität, [in:] *Praxishandbuch berufliche Schlüsselkompetenzen*, Springer, Berlin, Heidelberg, 2018.

Edy J.A., Collective memory, [in:] *The International Encyclopedia of Journalism Studies*, 2019.

El Elmary Ibrahiem M.M., Brzozowska A., *Shaping the Future of ICT: Trends in Information Technology, Communications Engineering, and Management*, CRC Press, Boca Raton, 2018.

Elsner A., *Werte als Governance-Mechanismus in transnationalen Unternehmen: eine empirische Analyse der Wirkung von Werten in grenzüberschreitenden Kooperationen*, Springer-Verlag, 2018.

Engelen A., Tholen E., *Interkulturelles Management*, Schäffer-Poeschel Verlag für Wirtschaft Steuern Recht GmbH, Stuttgart, 2014.

Esch F.R., Buchel D., Fallstudie: Mission, Vision und Unternehmensgrundsatze als Erfolgsfaktoren der REWE Group, [in:] *Corporate Brand Management*, F.R. Esch, T. Tomczak, J. Kernstock, T. Langner, J. Redler (eds.), Springer Fachmedien, Wiesbaden, 2014.

Fajen A., *Erfolgreiche Führung multikultureller virtueller Teams: wie Führungskräfte neuartige Herausforderungen meistern*, Springer-Verlag, 2018.

Fandel G., *Optimale Entscheidungen in Organisationen*, Springer Verlag, Berlin, Heidelberg, New York, 2013.

Fieseler Ch., Hoffmann Ch.P., Meckel M., Eine Kultur der Innovation: Die Bedeutung von Innovationsnetzwerken, [in:] *Business Innovation: Das St. Galler Modell*, Springer Gabler, Wiesbaden, 2016.

Fischer H., Organisation von Wissen. *ZWF Zeitschrift für wirtschaftlichen Fabrikbetrieb*, 2015, 110.6.

Foote A., Halawi L.A., Knowledge management models within information technology projects. *Journal of Computer Information Systems*, 2018.

Frank S., Internationale Unternehmenskultur, [in:] *International Business To Go*, Springer Gabler, Wiesbaden, 2018.

Franken S., Unternehmen, Unternehmenskultur und Unternehmensethik, [in:] *Verhaltensorientierte Führung*, Springer Gabler, Wiesbaden, 2019a.

Franken S., Vielfalt und Diversity Management in Unternehmen, [in:] *Verhaltensorientierte Führung*, Springer Gabler, Wiesbaden, 2019b.

Frederickson H.G., Walling J.D., Research and knowledge in administrative ethics, [in:] *Handbook of Administrative Ethics*, Routledge, New York, 2019.

Gabel J., Utopian consciousness and false consciousness, [in:] *Ideologies and the Corruption of Thought*, Routledge, New York, 2018.

García A.B., et al. The tower of power: Building innovative organizations through social dialogue, [in:] *Promoting Social Dialogue in European Organizations*, Springer, Cham, 2015.

Genkova P., Diversity und diversity management, [in:] *Interkulturelle Wirtschaftspsychologie*, Springer, Berlin, Heidelberg, 2019.

Gergs H.J., Neue Herausforderungen an das change management, [in:] *Führen in ungewissen Zeiten, Impulse, Konzepte und Praxisbeispiele*, O. Geramanis, K. Hermann (eds.), Springer Fachmedien, Wiesbaden, 2016.

Girard J., Girard J., Defining knowledge management: Toward an applied compendium. *Online Journal of Applied Knowledge Management*, 2015, 3.1.

Gloet M., Samson D., Knowledge management and systematic innovation capability, [in:] *Disruptive Technology: Concepts, Methodologies, Tools, and Applications*, IGI Global, 2020.

Gold A.H., Malhotra A., Segars A.H., Knowledge management: An organizational capabilities perspective. *Journal of Management Information Systems*, 2001, 18.1.

Gołębiowski M., Elementy kultury jakości w organizacji. *Zeszyty Naukowe Uniwersytetu Szczecińskiego, Studia i Prace Wydziału Nauk Ekonomicznych i Zarządzania*, 2014, 38, T. 1 Zarządzanie: 33–42.

Graham M., Method matters: Ethnography and materiality, [in:] *Queer Methods and Methodologies (Open Access)*, C.J. Nash (ed.), Routledge, London, 2016.

Graumann M., *Organisationstheoretische Untersuchung der Rückversicherungsunternehmung*, Duncker & Humblot, Berlin, 2015.

Gregorczyk S., et al., Paradoksy zachowań przedsiębiorstw w czasie kryzysu gospodarczego, Research Papers of the Wroclaw University of Economics, Prace Naukowe Uniwersytetu Ekonomicznego we Wrocławiu, 2016.

Güldenberg S., *Wissensmanagement und Wissenscontrolling in lernenden Organisationen: ein systemtheoretischer Ansatz*, Springer Verlag, Berlin, Heidelberg, 2013.

Gümüsa Y, Ali Aslan, Gesellschaftliche Herausforderungen und die Rolle von Religion in Unternehmertum und Führung, [in:] *Die Arbeit der Zivilgesellschaft*, Velbrück Wissenschaft, Weilerswist-Metternich, 2019.

Gutting D., Diversity management: in der Realität angekommen, [in:] *Führung im Zeitalter von Veränderung und Diversity*, Springer, Wiesbaden, 2017.

Hajdys D., Konsultacje społeczne jako jedna z determinant współpracy sektora publicznego z partnerem prywatnym w formule partnerstwa publiczno–prywatnego, Research Papers of the Wroclaw University of Economics, Prace Naukowe Uniwersytetu Ekonomicznego we Wrocławiu, 2015.

Hänel T., Felden C., Operational business intelligence im zukunftsszenario der industrie 4.0, [in:] *Analytische Informationssysteme*, Springer Gabler, Berlin, Heidelberg, 2016.

Havakhor T., Soror A.A., Sabherwal R., Diffusion of knowledge in social media networks: Effects of reputation mechanisms and distribution of knowledge roles. *Information Systems Journal*, 2018, 28.1: 104–141.

Heinze K.L., Heinze J.E., Individual innovation adoption and the role of organizational culture. *Review of Managerial Science*, 2018.

Heisig P., et al. Knowledge management and business performance: Global experts' views on future research needs. *Journal of Knowledge Management*, 2016, 20.6.

Helpap S., Bekmeier-Feuerhahn S., Pinkernelle L., Ambivalenzen in organisationalen Veränderungen. *Schmalenbachs Zeitschrift für betriebswirtschaftliche Forschung*, 2018, 70.3.

Hermann A., Erten Ch., Diversity Management in der Teamarbeit in multikulturellen Organisationen, [in:] *Personalmanagement*, Springer Gabler, Wiesbaden, 2018.

Herzfeldt E., Sackmann S., Interkulturelle Kompetenz – eine Schlüsselqualifikation von morgen, [in:] *Führung und ihre Herausforderungen*, Springer Gabler, Wiesbaden, 2019.

Hislop D., Bosua R., Helms R., *Knowledge Management in Organizations: A Critical Introduction*, Oxford University Press, Oxford, 2018.

Hofstede G., Cultural constraints in management theories, [in:] *Readings and Cases in International Management, A Cross-cultural Perspective*, Sage Publications, Thousand Oaks, 2003.

Hofstede G., *Interkulturelle Zusammenarbeit: kulturen-organisationen-management*, Springer-Verlag, 2013.

Hogan S.J., Coote L.V., Organizational culture, innovation, and performance: A test of Schein's model. *Journal of Business Research*, 2014, 67.8.

Hopf Ch., Soziologie und qualitative Sozialforschung, [in:] *Schriften zu Methodologie und Methoden qualitativer Sozialforschung*, Springer VS, Wiesbaden, 2016.

Hussain S.T., et al. Kurt Lewin's change model: A critical review of the role of leadership and employee involvement in organizational change. *Journal of Innovation & Knowledge*, 2018, 3.3.

Inkinen H., Review of empirical research on knowledge management practices and firm performance. *Journal of Knowledge Management*, 2016, 20.2.

Jedynak T., Kontrowersje wokół efektywności inwestycji społecznie odpowiedzialnych. *Zeszyty Naukowe/Polskie Towarzystwo Ekonomiczne*, 2011, 11.

Jelonek D., *Wybrane problemy zarządzania wiedzą i kapitałem intelektualnym w organizacji*, Sekcja Wydawnictw Wydziału Zarządzania Politechniki Częstochowskiej, Częstochowa, 2012.

Jetzke T., Zukunftsforschung und Organisationskultur–Organisationskulturelle Zukunftskonzepte als Voraussetzung für die Zukunftsfähigkeit von Organisationen. *Zeitschrift für Zukunftsforschung*, 2015, 4.1.

Kagermann H., et al. (eds.). *Industrie 4.0 im globalen Kontext: Strategien der Zusammenarbeit mit internationalen Partnern*, Herbert Utz Verlag, 2016.

Kasemsap K., The roles of knowledge management and organizational innovation in global business, [in:] *Civil and Environmental Engineering: Concepts, Methodologies, Tools, and Applications*, IGI Global, 2016.

Kastner M., Zusammenhänge zwischen Organisationskultur, Führung, Leistung und Gesundheit, [in:] *Handbuch Polizeimanagement*, Springer Gabler, Wiesbaden, 2017.

Kelly M., Dowling M., Millar M., The search for understanding: The role of paradigms. *Nurse Researcher*, 2018, 25.4.

Kiełtyka L., Wykorzystanie systemów eksperckich w zarządzaniu wiedzą, Zeszyty Naukowe Politechniki Łódzkiej 2013, Organizacja i Zarządzanie, z. 53.

Kirch J., Interkulturell besetzte Teams in der Pflege – eine konflikttheoretische Analyse, [in:] *Digitale Transformation von Dienstleistungen im Gesundheitswesen III*, Springer Gabler, Wiesbaden, 2017.

Klaus H., Schneider H.J., Mitarbeiterführung im Wandel–Vorbereitung auf „Führung 4.0", [in:] *Personalperspektiven*, Springer Gabler, Wiesbaden, 2016.

Klein G., Kultur, [in:] *Einführung in Hauptbegriffe der Soziologie*, Springer VS, Wiesbaden, 2016.

Kleineberg M., Integral methodological pluralism: An organizing principle for method classification, [in:] *Knowledge Organization for a Sustainable World: Challenges and Perspectives for Cultural, Scientific, and Technological Sharing in a Connected Society Proceedings of the Fourteenth International ISKO Conference*, 2016.

Kleingarn H., *Change Management: Instrumentarium zur Gestaltung und Lenkung einer lernenden Organisation*, Springer Verlag, Berlin, 2013, pp. 288–295.

Koch S., *Einführung in das Management von Geschäftsprozessen: Six Sigma, Kaizen und TQM*, Springer-Verlag, 2015.

Kocoń P., Funkcje i elementy kultury organizacyjnej, *Prace Naukowe Uniwersytetu Ekonomicznego w Katowicach*, 2015.

Kościelniak H., Analiza przedsiębiorstw w sieci – wybrane problemy, *Prace Naukowe Wałbrzyskiej Wyższej Szkoły Zarządzania i Przedsiębiorczości*, 2015, 32.

Kraśnicka T., Głod W., Wronka M., Pojęcie, determinanty i znaczenie innowacji zarządczych (management innovation) – stan badań nad zjawiskiem, Zeszyty Naukowe Politechniki Śląskiej 2014, seria: Organizacja i Zarządzanie.

Krause K.T., *Change Management: Vom sinnvollen Umgang mit Veränderungen*, BoD-Books on Demand, Norderstedt, 2015, pp. 57–59.

Krell G., Ortlieb R., Sieben B., Diversitybezogene Management-Konzepte, [in:] *Gender und Diversity in Organisationen*, Springer Gabler, Wiesbaden, 2018.

Kriegesmann B., Kley T., Gesund durch Veränderungsprozesse?! Belastung und Erschöpfung von Führungskräften in Change–Management–Prozessen. *Arbeit*, 2016, 23(2): 105–118.

Kuckertz A., Corporate Entrepreneurship und Unternehmenskultur, [in:] *Management: Corporate Entrepreneurship*, Springer Gabler, Wiesbaden, 2017.

Kühl S., Organisationskultur. *Managementforschung*, 2018, 28.1.

Kühne C., Knowledge management in legal operations, [in:] *Praxishandbuch Legal Operations Management*, Springer, Berlin, Heidelberg, 2017.

Kujawski J., Potrojna cena transferowa i jej sprawozdawcze konsekwencje. *Research Papers of the Wroclaw University of Economics, Prace Naukowe Uniwersytetu Ekonomicznego we Wrocławiu*, 2017.

Laßmann A., *Organisatorische Koordination: Konzepte und Prinzipien zur Einordnung von Teilaufgaben*, Springer Verlag, Berlin, Heidelberg, 2013.

Lacity M.C., Janson M.A., Understanding qualitative data: A framework of text analysis methods. *Journal of Management Information Systems*, 1994.

Lang M., Scherber S., *Der Weg zum agilen Unternehmen–Wissen für Entscheider: Strategien, Potenziale, Lösungen*, Carl Hanser Verlag GmbH Co KG, 2019.

Lang R., Baldauf N., Begriffliche Grundlagen: Vom Kulturellen zum Interkulturellen Management, [in:] *Interkulturelles Management*, R. Lang, N. Baldauf (eds.), Springer Gabler, Wiesbaden, 2016a.

Lang R., Baldauf N., *Interkulturelles Management*, Springer Gabler, Wiesbaden, 2016b, pp. 40–47.

Lang R., Baldauf N., Begriffliche Grundlagen: Vom Kulturellen zum Interkulturellen Management, [in:] *Interkulturelles Management*, Springer Gabler, Wiesbaden, 2016c.

Larcher S.B., et al. Fallstudien „Führung, organisationaler Wandel und Innovation", [in:] *Führung lernen*, Springer Gabler, Berlin, Heidelberg, 2018.

Lauer T., *Change Management. Grundlagen und Erfolgsfaktoren*, Springer, Berlin, Heidelberg, 2014.

Lauer T., Erfolgsfaktor Evolution–Permanenten Wandel initiieren, [in:] *Change Management*, Springer Gabler, Berlin, Heidelberg, 2019.

Laux H., Liermann F., *Grundlagen der Organisation: Die Steuerung von Entscheidungen als Grundproblem der Betriebswirtschaftslehre*, Springer Verlag, Berlin, Heidelberg, 2013.

Lichtarski J., O złożoności i zawodności decyzji menedżerskich w procesie przygotowania a zmiany organizacyjnej, *Przedsiębiorczość i Zarządzanie*, 2015, 16.3, cz. 2, Praktyczny wymiar dorobku nauk o zarządzaniu. Nauka dla praktyki gospodarczej i samorządowej.

Lindlof T.R., Taylor B.C., *Qualitative Communication Research Methods*, Sage Publications, Thousand Oaks, 2017.

Linnenluecke M.K., Griffiths A., Corporate sustainability and organizational culture. *Journal of World Business*, 2010, 45.4.

Luhn A., The learning organization. *Creative and Knowledge Society*, 2016, 6.1.

Mahringer C.A., Rost M., Renzl B., How individuals perform customer knowledge absorption practices-a contextual approach to open innovation. *International Journal of Technology Management*, 2019, 79.3–4.

Mandel B., Kulturmanagement in internationalen und interkulturellen Kontexten. *Jahrbuch für Kulturmanagement, transcript Verlag, Bielefeld*, 2016.

Mandl Ch., *Vom Fehler zum Erfolg: Effektives Failure Management für Innovation und Corporate Entrepreneurship*, Springer-Verlag, 2017.

Mäntymäki M., Riemer K., Enterprise social networking: A knowledge management perspective. *International Journal of Information Management*, 2016, 36.6.

Marques J.M.R., et al. The relationship between organizational commitment, knowledge transfer and knowledge management maturity. *Journal of Knowledge Management*, 2019, 23.3.

Mason S.E., Nicolay C.R., Darzi A., The use of Lean and Six Sigma methodologies in surgery: A systematic review. *The Surgeon*, 2015, 13.2.

Matschke Ch., Lug und Betrug beim Wissensaustausch. *Journal of Personality and Social Psychology*, 2014, 86: 419–434.

Mayer C., Methode und Design der Untersuchung, [in:] *Zum algebraischen Gleichheitsverständnis von Grundschulkindern*, Springer Spektrum, Wiesbaden, 2019.

Mciver D., Fitzsimmons S., Flanagan D., Instructional design as knowledge management: A knowledge-in-practice approach to choosing instructional methods. *Journal of Management Education*, 2016, 40.1.

Mertins K., Kohl I., Orth R., Ein Referenzmodell für Wissensmanagement, [in:] *Wissensmanagement im Mittelstand*, K. Mertins, I. Kohl, R. Orth (eds.), Springer, Berlin, Heidelberg, 2016.

Milosevic I., Bass A.F., Combs G.M., The paradox of knowledge creation in a high-reliability organization: A case study. *Journal of Management*, 2018, 44.3.

Mongardini C.R., *Merton and Contemporary Sociology*, Routledge, 2018.

Muche C., Diversity-Management als grenzüberschreitender Prozess in Organisationen? [in:] *Grenzüberschreitungen im Kompetenzmanagement*, Springer, Berlin, Heidelberg, 2020.

Münzberg Ch. et al., Fortschritt durch aktive Kollaboration in offenen Organisationen, [in:] *Vernetztes Kompetenzmanagement*, Springer, Berlin, Heidelberg, 2018.

Myers M.D., *Qualitative Research in Business and Management*, Sage Publications Limited, Thousand Oaks, 2019.

Nerdinger F.W., Organisationsklima und Organisationskultur, [in:] *Arbeits- und Organisationspsychologie*, Springer, Berlin, Heidelberg, 2019.

Nguyen H.N., Mohamed S., Leadership behaviors, organizational culture and knowledge management practices: An empirical investigation. *Journal of Management Development*, 2011, 30.2.

Nica E., Organizational culture in the public sector. *Economics, Management and Financial Markets*, 2013, 8.2.

Nisar T.M., Prabhakar G., Strakova L., Social media information benefits, knowledge management and smart organizations. *Journal of Business Research*, 2019, 94.

Nonaka I., Toyama R., The knowledge-creating theory revisited: Knowledge creation as a synthesizing process, [in:] *The Essentials of Knowledge Management*, Palgrave Macmillan, London, 2015.

Nörr M., Unternehmenskultur: Eine unternehmerisch denkende Organisation schaffen, [in:] *Key Learnings aus dem Serial Entrepreneurship*, M. Nörr (ed.), Springer Fachmedien, Wiesbaden, 2016.

North K., *Wissensorientierte Unternehmensführung: Wissensmanagement gestalten*, Springer-Verlag, 2016.

North K., Brandner A., Steininger T., Benötigtes Wissen bestimmen, [in:] *Wissensmanagement für Qualitätsmanager*, Springer Gabler, Wiesbaden, 2016a.

North K., Brandner A., Steininger T., Die Wissenstreppe: Information–Wissen–Kompetenz, [in:] *Wissensmanagement für Qualitätsmanager*, Springer Gabler, Wiesbaden, 2016b.

North K., Maier R., Wissen 4.0–Wissensmanagement im digitalen Wandel. *HMD Praxis der Wirtschaftsinformatik*, 2018, 55.4.

Nowakowska–Grunt J., Kabus J., Zarządzanie różnorodnością na uczelniach wyższych na przykładzie Politechniki Częstochowskiej, Zeszyty Naukowe Politechniki Częstochowskiej 2014, Zarządzanie Nr 14.

Osterhold G., *Veränderungsmanagement: Visionen und Wege zu einer neuen Unternehmenskultur*, Springer Verlag, Berlin, Heidelberg, 2013.

Pachura P., Kot S., Podejście integrujące odpowiedzią na wyzwania współczesności? *Prace Naukowe Instytutu Organizacji i Zarządzania Politechniki Wrocławskiej, Studia i Materiały*, 2005, 76.18/2.

Patrick M., *Derrida, Responsibility and Politics*, Routledge, London, 2018.

Petry T., Erfolgreiches Führen im digitalen Zeitalter, [in:] *Crowds, Movements & Communities?!* Nomos Verlagsgesellschaft mbH & Co. KG, 2018.

Pietruszka-Ortyl A., et al. Transfer wiedzy w warunkach nierówności na współczesnym rynku pracy. *Bezpieczeństwo Pracy. Nauka i Praktyka*, 2019, 569.2.

Pipus S., *Führungsstile im Vergleich. Kritische Betrachtung der Auswirkungen auf die Mitarbeitermotivation*, Disserta Verlag, Hamburg, 2015.

Prajogo D.I., Mcdermott Ch.M., The relationship between multidimensional organizational culture and performance. *International Journal of Operations & Production Management*, 2011, 31.7.

Punt A.E., et al. The effect of marine closures on a feedback control management strategy used in a spatially aggregated stock assessment: A case study based on pink ling in Australia. *Canadian Journal of Fisheries and Aquatic Sciences*, 2016, 74.11.

Radojevic M., Breunig Ch., Beyer D., Punctuated equilibrium theory, [in:] *The Routledge Handbook of European Public Policy*, N. Zahariadis, L. Buonanno (eds.), Routledge, London, 2017.

Rai R.K., Knowledge management and organizational culture: A theoretical integrative framework. *Journal of Knowledge Management*, 2011, 15.5.

Raupp J., Strategische Wissenschaftskommunikation, [in:] *Forschungsfeld Wissenschaftskommunikation*, Springer VS, Wiesbaden, 2017.

Reinhardt K., Kompetenzmanagement als strategisches Führungsinstrument im Zeitalter von Organisation 2.0, [in:] *Eigenschaften und kompetenzen von führungspersönlichkeiten*, Springer, Wiesbaden, 2017.

Rhein S., Stakeholder – Dialoge fur unternehmerische Nachhaltigkeit: Eine qualitativempirische Studie zum Diskursverhalten von Unternehmen, Springer–Verlag, Berlin, Heidelberg, 2016.

Riasi A., Asadzadeh N., The relationship between principals' reward power and their conflict management styles based on Thomas–Kilmann conflict mode instrument. *Management Science Letters*, 2015, 5.6.

Robin J., Burchell M., *No Excuses: How You Can Turn Any Workplace into a Great One*, John Wiley & Sons, 2013.

Rockstuhl T., Ng, Kok-Yee, The effects of cultural intelligence on interpersonal trust in multicultural teams, [in:] *Handbook of Cultural Intelligence*, S. Ang, L. Van Dyne (eds.), Routledge, New York, 2015.

Romani L., Mahadevan J., Primecz H., Critical cross-cultural management: Outline and emerging contributions. *International Studies of Management & Organization*, 2018, 48.4.

Romanowska M., Determinanty innowacyjności polskich przedsiębiorstw. *Przegląd Organizacji*, 2016, 2.

Ryan G., Introduction to positivism, interpretivism and critical theory. *Nurse Researcher*, 2018, 25.4.

Sackmann S., Wann ist eine bewusste Auseinandersetzung mit der Unternehmenskultur besonders wichtig? [in:] *Unternehmenskultur: Erkennen–Entwickeln–Verändern*, Springer Gabler, Wiesbaden, 2017a.

Sackmann S. A., Erfolgsfaktoren für neue Arbeitswelten–Unternehmenskultur und Führung, [in:] *CSR und neue Arbeitswelten*, Springer Gabler, Berlin, Heidelberg, 2017b.

Salunke S., Weerawardena J., Mccoll-Kennedy J.R., The central role of knowledge integration capability in service innovation-based competitive strategy. *Industrial Marketing Management*, 2019, 76.

Sandberg J., Tsoukas H., Making sense of the sensemaking perspective: Its constituents, limitations, and opportunities for further development. *Journal of Organizational Behaviour*, 2015, 36.S1.

Santoro G., et al. The Internet of Things: Building a knowledge management system for open innovation and knowledge management capacity. *Technological Forecasting and Social Change*, 2018, 136.

Sanz–Valle R. et al., Linking organizational learning with technical innovation and organizational culture. *Journal of Knowledge Management*, 2011, 15.6.

Sauter W., Scholz Ch., Kompetenzorientiertes Wissensmanagement: Gesteigerte Performance mit dem Erfahrungswissen aller Mitarbeiter, Springer Verlag, Berlin, Heidelberg, 2015.

Schein E.H., *Organizational culture and leadership*, John Wiley & Sons, 2010.

Schein E.H., Schein P., *Cultura d'azienda e leadership*, Raffaello Cortina, 2018.

Schmid C.H., *Planung von Unternehmenskultur*, Springer Verlag, Berlin, Heidelberg, 2013.

Schmidt S.J., Unternehmenskultur als Programm der Unternehmenskommunikation, [in:] *Strategische Kommunikation*, U. Rottger, V. Gehrau, J. Preusse (eds.), Springer Fachmedien, Wiesbaden, 2013.

Schmitt R., Schröder J., Pfaller L., Von der Theorie zur Methode, [in:] *Systematische Metaphernanalyse*, Springer VS, Wiesbaden, 2018.

Schneeweiß H., *Entscheidungskriterien bei Risiko*, Springer Verlag, Berlin, Heidelberg, 2013.

Schoeneborn D., Kuhn T.R., Kärreman D., The communicative constitution of organization, organizing, and organizationality. *Organization Studies*, 2019, 40.4.

Schönborn G., *Unternehmenskultur als Erfolgsfaktor der Corporate Identity: die Bedeutung der Unternehmenskultur für den ökonomischen Erfolg von Unternehmen*, Springer Verlag, Berlin, Heidelberg, 2014.

Schreyögg G., Organisationskultur. *Grundlagen der Organisation*, 2012.

Schröer H., Interkulturelle Öffnung und diversity management, [in:] *Soziale Arbeit in der Migrationsgesellschaft*, Springer VS, Wiesbaden, 2018.

Scott W.R., Davis G.F., *Organizations and Organizing: Rational, Natural and Open Systems Perspectives*, Routledge, 2015.

Senge P., Hamilton H., Kania J., The dawn of system leadership. *Stanford Social Innovation Review*, 2015.

Serafin K., Kultura organizacyjna jako element wspierający realizację strategii przedsiębiorstwa. *Studia Ekonomiczne*, 2015, 222.

Serrat O., Building a learning organization, [in:] *Knowledge Solutions*, Springer, Singapore, 2017.

Seufert S., et al. *Go Global: Herausforderungen für das internationale Bildungsmanagement. Herausforderungen, Spannungsfelder und explorative Fallstudien*, IWP-HSG, 2016.

Shujahat M., et al. Translating the impact of knowledge management processes into knowledge-based innovation: The neglected and mediating role of knowl(lge-worker productivity. *Journal of Business Research*, 2019, 94.

Simon H., Wandel durch Innovationen, [in:] *Der digitale Kulturbetrieb*, Springer Gabler, Wiesbaden, 2019.

Soukup Ch., *Wissensmanagement: Wissen zwischen Steuerung und Selbstorganisation*, Springer Verlag, Berlin, Heidelberg, 2013.

Sparrow P.R., Hiltrop J.M., Redefining the field of European human resource management: A battle between national mindsets and forces of business transition? *Human Resource Management: Published in Cooperation with the School of Business Administration, The University of Michigan and in alliance with the Society of Human Resources Management*, 1997, 36.2.

Stehr N., Knowledge societies, [in:] *Society and Knowledge*, Routledge, 2017.

Steinle C., *Organisation und Wandel: Konzepte-Mehr-Ebenen-Analyse (MEA)-Anwendungen*, Walter de Gruyter GmbH & Co KG, 2019.

Sułkowski Ł., Strategic management as the ideology of power. *Journal of Intercultural Management*, 2013, 5.3.

Szymańska K., Kryzys gospodarczy receptą na otwartą kulturę organizacyjną przedsiębiorstw. *Marketing i Rynek*, 2015, 5 (CD).

Taylor C.A., Harris-Evans J., Reconceptualising transition to higher education with Deleuze and Guattari. *Studies in Higher Education*, 2018, 43.7.

Thommen J.P., Grösser S.N., *Organization and Change Management*, Versus Verlag, Zurich, 2017.

Truong H.M., Integrating learning styles and adaptive e-learning system: Current developments, problems and opportunities. *Computers in Human Behavior*, 2016, 55.

Tseng S.M., The correlation between organizational culture and knowledge conversion on corporate performance. *Journal of Knowledge Management*, 2010, 14.2.

Turner J.H., Functionalism, [in:] *The Wiley-Blackwell Encyclopedia of Social Theory*, 2017.

Urbach N., Ahlemann F., Der Wissensarbeitsplatz der Zukunft: Trends, Herausforderungen und Implikationen für das strategische IT-Management. *HMD Praxis der Wirtschaftsinformatik*, 2016, 53.1.

Urbanowska-Sojkin E., Orientacja na ryzyko w procesie podejmowania decyzji strategicznych, *Zeszyty Naukowe Uniwersytetu Szczecińskiego, Studia i Prace Wydziału Nauk Ekonomicznych i Zarządzania*, 2015a, 39, T. 4, Zarządzanie.

Urbanowska-Sojkin E., Prewencja kryzysu przez zintegrowane zarządzanie ryzykiem strategicznym. *Marketing i Rynek*, 2015b, nr 5 (CD): 146–160.

Van Marrewijk M., Werre M., Multiple levels of corporate sustainability. *Journal of Business Ethics*, 2003, 44.2–3.

Voigt S., Wissensmanagement-Lösungen auswählen, [in:] *Wissensmanagement im Mittelstand*, H. Kohl, K. Mertins, H. Seidel (eds.), Springer, Berlin, Heidelberg, 2016.

Voigt V., *Interkulturelles Mentoring made in Germany: Zum Cultural Diversity Management in multinationalen Unternehmen*, Springer Fachmedien, Wiesbaden, 2013.

Von Au, C., *Führung im Zeitalter von Veränderung und Diversity*, Springer Fachmedien Wiesbaden GmbH, Oberursel, 2017.

Von Hehn S., Cornelissen N.I., Braun C., Der Einfluss der Kultur auf den Organisationserfolg, [in:] *Kulturwandel in Organisationen*, S. von Hehn, N.I. Cornelissen, C. Braun (eds.), Springer, Berlin, Heidelberg, 2016.

Von Rosenstiel L., Von Hornstein E., Augustin S. (eds.), *Change Management Praxisfälle: Veränderungsschwerpunkte Organisation, Team, Individuum*, Springer Verlag, Berlin, Heidelberg, 2013.

Waddell D., et al. *Organisational Change: Development and Transformation*, Cengage AU, 2019.

Wagner A.S., Lose Zugehörigkeiten von globalen Identitäten (Glopats) in internationalen Unternehmen–Konflikte zwischen Nationalkulturen und Hyperkultur. *Gruppe. Interaktion. Organisation. Zeitschrift für Angewandte Organisationspsychologie (GIO)*, 2018, 49.4.

Warnecke H.J., *Revolution der Unternehmenskultur: das fraktale Unternehmen*, Springer Verlag, Berlin, Heidelberg, 2013.

Weber J., Change funktioniert nur, wenn man die Menschen am Prozess beteiligt. *Controlling & Management Review*, 2017, 61.5.

Weber S.M., et al. Organisation und Netzwerke: Eine Einleitung, [in:] *Organisation und Netzwerke*, Springer VS, Wiesbaden, 2019.

Weber W., Kabst R., Baum M., Internationale Unternehmenstätigkeit, [in:] *Einführung in die Betriebswirtschaftslehre*, Springer Gabler, Wiesbaden, 2018.

Welge M.K., Al-Laham A., Eulerich M., Die empirische Strategy-Process-Forschung im Überblick, [in:] *Strategisches Management*, Springer Gabler, Wiesbaden, 2017.

Werner L., *Entscheidungsunterstützungssysteme: ein problem -und benutzerorientiertes Management-Instrument*, Springer Verlag, Berlin, Heidelberg, 2013.

Westwood R.I., Jack G., Manifesto for a post-colonial international business and management studies: A provocation. *Critical Perspectives on International Business*, 2007, 3.3.

Wicharz R., *Strategie: Ausrichtung von Unternehmen auf die Erfolgslogik ihrer Industrie: Unternehmensstrategie–Geschäftsfeldstrategie–Konzernstrategie*, Springer Verlag, Berlin, Heidelberg, 2015.

Wickert Ch., Schaefer S.M., Towards a progressive understanding of performativity in critical management studies. *Human Relations*, 2015, 68.1.

Wiedmann K.P., Corporate Identity als strategisches Orientierungskonzept der Kommunikation, [in:] *Handbuch Strategische Kommunikation*, Springer Gabler, Wiesbaden, 2016.

Wien A., N. Franzke, *Unternehmenskultur: zielorientierte Unternehmensethik als entscheidender Erfolgsfaktor*, Springer Verlag, Berlin, Heidelberg, 2014.

Wiener M., Förderliche Organisationskultur für Open Foresight, [in:] *Open Foresight und Unternehmenskultur*, Springer Gabler, Wiesbaden, 2018.

Winkel O., Brauchen wir einen konzeptionellen Neuaufbruch im Wissensmanagement? *VM Verwaltung & Management*, 2019, 25.3.

Wöhrle A., *Change Management: Organisationen zwischen Hamsterlaufrad und Kulturwan del*, Walhalla Fachverlag, Regensburg, 2016.

Wright E.W., et al. A new scorecard for strategic planning. *Journal of Business Strategy*, 2019, 40.2.

Wutti D., Hayden M., Zur Sichtbarkeit von erbrachten Leistungen: Die Darstellung von Wissenstransfer in den Geistes-, Sozial-und Kulturwissenschaften, [in:] *Colloquium: New Philologies*, 2019.

Yanow D., Schwartz-Shea P., *Interpretation and Method: Empirical Research Methods and the Interpretive Turn*, Routledge, 2015.

Yee Y.M., Tan C.L., Thurasamy R., Back to basics: Building a knowledge management system. *Strategic Direction*, 2019, 35.2.

Zaim H., Muhammed S., Tarim M., Relationship between knowledge management processes and performance: Critical role of knowledge utilization in organizations. *Knowledge Management Research & Practice*, 2019, 17.1.

Zamorano M.M., Reframing cultural diplomacy: The instrumentalization of culture under the soft power theory. *Culture Unbound: Journal of Current Cultural Research*, 2016, 8.2.

Zelle A., *Wissensmanagement: Schritte zum intelligenten Unternehmen*, Springer Verlag, Berlin, Heidelberg, 2013.

Zheng W., Yang B., Mclean G.N., Linking organizational culture, structure, strategy, and organizational effectiveness: Mediating role of knowledge management. *Journal of Business Research*, 2010, 63. 7.

Ziek P., Anderson J.D., Communication, dialogue and project management. *International Journal of Managing Projects in Business*, 2015, 8.4.

Ziółkowska B., Wiedza jako strategiczny zasób współczesnego przedsiębiorstwa. *Zagadnienia Techniczno-Ekonomiczne*, 2003, 48.2.

Index